Praise for Priscilla Buckley
and
String of Pearls
On the News Beat in New York and Paris

"Priscilla Buckley is known for her adventurous spirit; nowhere has that spirit been better evidenced than in her willingness to be at the center for almost thirty years of the whirlwind at 150 East 35th Street. That she has come through all this with a reputation unchallenged for journalistic skill and professionalism, as well as the sweetest disposition on the Eastern Seaboard, is testimony to her work and to her life. Priscilla, America and its President and all of us honor you and thank you."

PRESIDENT RONALD REAGAN

—

"Probably the nicest woman ever to edit a magazine, and definitely one of the best wordsmiths around. She humored me and encouraged me nonstop, and I shall always be indebted to her."

TAKI

—

"A great conservative woman ."

TOWN HALL

—

"Buckley . . . brings to [*String of Pearls*] a lovely, ladylike, wry touch. . . . This endearing . . . peep at her early life will delight."

WALL STREET JOURNAL

"[*String of Pearls* is] a real gem."

—

"Conveys the frenetic pace and hard-boiled culture of radio reporting."

—

"Recommended."

—

"Charming, delightful. . . . Buckley weaves together episodes from both the newsroom and her personal life into a rich mosaic. From funny landlords and apartments, to practical jokes on the newsroom floor, *String of Pearls* is a heartwarming read."

—

"You should treat yourself to *String of Pearls*."

LIVING IT UP

LIVING
IT UP

with National Review

A Memoir

PRISCILLA L. BUCKLEY

foreword by William F. Buckley Jr.

SPENCE PUBLISHING COMPANY • DALLAS

2005

Published in the United States by
Spence Publishing Company
111 Cole Street
Dallas, Texas 75207

Library of Congress Control Number
for the hardcover edition: 2005926623
ISBN 1-890626-59-7
978-1-890626-59-4

Printed in the United States of America

To Tasa
for putting up with Reid
and
the Spanish Armada

Contents

Foreword

William F. Buckley Jr.

P RISCILLA BUCKLEY, WHEN I WAS A BOY, would walk with me
to the drug store to buy candies, and walk back to the house
where I ate them, under the shade of a maple tree, knowing
great contentment. I felt under her special protection, because she
was senior to me and, at age thirteen, had already evolved as a quiet
benevolence, ready to give protective attention to a kid brother as,
later, she would give protective attention to elderly Nobel Prize win-
ners, lost college sophomores, tribal editorial warriors, despairing
French intellectuals, and, never putting aside her first obligation, to
the same kid brother she protected at the candy store.

I had founded *National Review* and reached out for an experienced editorial hand, dragging Priscilla from an exotic life as a reporter
and editor in Paris, into the indigent billet of a struggling-to-be-born
venture in opinion journalism.

What happened is widely documented by the hundreds of men
and women who came to us to be published, or whom she sought
out for editorial contributions. She helped them all, and made things
cheerful for them. There had been a single demurral, when I proposed

that she abandon her career in Paris and give us her full time. It was that in lieu of a salary that corresponded with her skills (we could not afford the salary, and deeply needed her skills), she would take six weeks every year away from the office, pursuing snow and ice, lions and tigers, forlorn islands and fractious winds and tides, to maintain her career as amateur adventurer and sportsman.

Yet even with six weeks away, she was the abiding central figure in the office, year after year, decade after decade, and when she left, we knew the meaning of desolation, so central was she not only to editorial operations, but to the good humor of office life.

In this book we have a color portrait of a woman who engaged life at every level, as an editor and writer, a golfer and balloonist, a midwife of manuscripts and newborn babies, specialist in the art of friendship. I say with great sincerity that I envy the exhilaration that will come to everyone who picks up this book, and discovers how, when left utterly alone, sometimes nature can really overdo it in creating a unique creature.

LIVING IT UP

Home Again

I T'S ALL TOO FAMILIAR, that painting with the two hunters wearing worn, loose Dukbak jackets moving in on the point. The pointer, in the lead, stands rigid, his nose down in the broom straw. Behind him, to the left is a setter honoring the point. You can almost see them quivering in the excitement of the moment. If you look closely you can discern the covey of quail huddling close, uncertain whether to run or fly. One bird has made the break, and now he's tumbling out of the sky. A wisp of smoke curls from the muzzle of the Purdy of the hunter on the right. The golden broom straw waves in the light breeze, and speckles of sunlight break through the heavy pines to rest like yellow diamonds on a bed of pine needles. In a second, the covey will explode into a dozen brown specks darting for cover through the longleaf pines, headed for the branch—and safety.

Well, I'm here to tell you that's not the way it usually happens. When those magnificently bred hunting dogs with their fine noses skid to a stop rather than run into that covey, you are not as close at hand as are the hunters in the painting. You are more apt to be two hundred yards away separated from the point by a muddy corn field, its ridges uneven and slippery. You head, at the best gait you can manage, toward the dogs. "Hold it, Boomer," you shout to the pointer. "Careful. Careful." "Whoa, there, Silver." Boomer is moving, a cautious half-step at a time, and then, when you are still fifty yards out, the covey explodes. It's a big one, by damn. Must be twelve or fifteen birds. And they're gone for sure, deep into the branch, snuggled in a briar patch in which they can move faster than any bird dog and a whole lot faster than any hunter.

It's 9:15 in the morning and my brother Reid and I have yet to get what our guide R.D. Pate calls "the skunk." R.D. Pate farms in the summer and guides quail hunters in the winter. Father had once entered into a farming venture with Mr. Pate, raising hogs. Father put up the money, and R.D. did the raising. They would split the profits. But that only lasted one season because, whenever one of the piglets died, Mr. Pate would call father and announce the dismal fact, adding parenthetically, "It's a shame, Mr. Buckley, but that little fellow that died was one of yours." But as a bird hunter R.D. is great. He is also a little fellow, with a brown pinched face and a large, beakish nose. He looks, in fact, rather like a quail as does his cousin and partner Roland McCoy.

Roland makes any quail hunt a lot easier because he stays with the old pickup truck, and after the dogs have pointed half a mile away and we have chased the birds through fields of brambles into deep branches and through spiny thickets, he comes chugging along, saving us the half-mile walk back to the pickup. Roland McCoy's favorite hunting garb is an antique black pin-stripped suit, wildly inappropriate for the terrain we are hunting and perilous—to Roland McCoy—inasmuch as he tends to fade into the background.

A few moments later, we walk up a single, and Reid nails it. "You got us the skunk," cries R.D. "Now let's get on with this hunt." I grin at Reid, and he grins back, and suddenly I wonder whether any of my

Paris newspaper friends, with whom I parted less than a month ago would recognize me now in my worn canvas-fronted hunting pants, muddy boots, khaki hunting jacket with its large, as yet empty game bag, hair and face sweaty from the recent encounter with the corn field, a speck of blood on the back of my hand where a stray bramble caught me. I do not look like *Mademoiselle Buckley de la United Presse, 2 rue des Italiens, première arrondissement.*

I had returned from Paris early in February of 1956 to work on my brother Bill's brand new weekly magazine, *National Review*. But first I thought I'd take a month or so off and spend some time here in Camden, South Carolina, where my parents winter and where I had enjoyed numbers of college Christmas and Easter vacations. I would be doing what I loved best, quail hunting in the mornings, golfing in the afternoons, and partying with good and old friends at night.

Last night mother had given me a coming home cocktail party, and I recounted to Reid what had happened when I had asked Leslie, the assistant bartender hired for the evening, for a sherry. Leslie had picked up a minuscule fluted glass, to the consternation of Jeff Boykin, our longtime butler. Jeff had removed the sherry bottle from Leslie's hand, picked up an old-fashioned glass, and, as he filled it, commented: "Leslie, Miss Priscilla, she likes her drinks in them Paris-style glasses." And he had given me a companionable grin.

It was so good to be home, with family, and friends, and with Jeff Boykin and Ella Boswell, the waitress, and Josephine the cook, and to wake in my big sunny third-storey bedroom to the sound of Walter Allen, the gardener, driving the old mule up and down the graveled driveway, flattening out its surface. This he did three or four times a week, mostly to fill in the holes resulting from our dear mother's erratic driving habits. It was mother's established belief that if she sounded the horn loudly coming out of her drive, that gave her the right of way over anyone intrepid enough to use Kirwood Lane when

Mrs. Buckley was at the wheel of her red Chevy. Residents of the Lane had long ago learned to approach the driveway of Kamschatka, which was what our house was called, with the greatest caution. Fortunately, Mother's approach came with a warning clatter as the little red Chevy bucketed down the drive, spitting Walter's carefully raked gravel left and right. But since everyone loved Mother, no one ever reported her driving eccentricities to the local constabulary, which also loved her and was too kind to notice her occasional u-turns and botched attempts at parking.

In the back of my mind during this idyllic interlude was the understanding that I was about to make a major career change, that I was entering a new world professionally. For most of the past decade since I had graduated from Smith College in 1943 I had been engaged in daily journalism, what the folk at the big news agencies liked to call "deadline every minute" journalism. Right out of college I had landed a job on the radio desk at United Press in New York where for four or five years I was what they call a rewrite man: turning the incoming news on the regular news wires into peppy, five- and fifteen-minute news summaries that disc jockeys around the nation would tear off the teletype machine, interrupting the almost nonstop flow of Big Band music with short interludes of news. Radio news writing was different from regular news writing: it had to have a certain rhythm or beat, be to the point, unfolding fast to fit into the abbreviated time allotted it. In all of this speed was of essence.

A year or so later I was again working for United Press, this time in Paris as a general correspondent on the Paris bureau. Here, I was a reporter as well as a rewrite man. In the Paris bureau, seven Americans, working around the clock, gathered incoming news from the entire French empire which extended to Africa, North and sub-Saharan, the Middle East, particularly Syria and Lebanon, the Far East, Indochina, Polynesia, and the Caribbean. The news arrived at our bureau in various guises, from other UP correspondents and stringers, from the Agence France Presse news wire, and the local press in French. It was our job to rewrite it in English and send it on a leased cable line first to London, then to New York for distribution to the world. Here, too, time was of essence. At any minute of the day or night some client newspaper somewhere in the world would be putting together its front page, and we wanted to be there, ahead of AP, INS, and Reuters, with the most up-to-date rendition of whatever was the major story of the day, hence the "deadline every minute" urgency.

That kind of news coverage and emphasis on speed I would leave behind when I went to work for a magazine with a weekly deadline. I would still be dealing with news but in a far different way. I wasn't sure how satisfactory this would be, but it would be a new adventure, a chance to see if my skills were transferable.

Back in New York

FINDING AN APARTMENT IN NEW YORK turned out to be easy. When I left United Press Radio News in New York, in 1949, I spent the winter as news editor of WACA in Camden and in the summer, at the urging of my friend Letitia Baldridge, who would later be Jacqueline Kennedy's social secretary, I went to work for the Central Intelligence Agency in Washington. My old friend and fellow spook, Sally Garfield, who had shared my office at the CIA and who had lived right across P Street from me in Georgetown, was now living and working in New York and looking for a roommate.

Sally had rented a spacious fourth-floor walk-up apartment from a doctor's widow, Mrs. Hamilton, at 52 East 66th Street. Mrs. Hamilton, after her husband's death, had rented to a young couple the basement quarters which he had used as an office. She had kept the first and second floors for her own use and leased two large bedrooms and the bathroom on the third floor to young businessmen who occasionally, when working late, had to spend the night in town. The fourth floor she rented to Sally for a reasonable fee, both because it was a walk-up and because it had no front door of its own. You reached it simply by walking up that last flight of stairs. Sally had moved into the single bedroom with the connecting bathroom. I ended up in the larger double bedroom with a basin and a shower across the hall. The large, airy living room ran across the whole front of the building, with a tiny kitchen at the end tucked into what had I'm sure originally been the bathroom to my bedroom.

The furnishings were comfortable, but haphazard: chairs and sofas and lamps that had seen better days fitted in nicely with our slipshod housekeeping style. The place would have been a mess but for Mrs. Hamilton's foresight. One condition of the lease was that we were required to use Mrs. Hamilton's cleaning woman, Hazel, for at least four hours once a week, the prior tenants having left the quarters in hideous shape. Hazel, whose middle name was not energy, complained that the four flights of steps—she included in her count the steps up the stoop to the front door—were exceedingly painful to her chronic water-on-the-knee condition. This she told us that first day, when she also informed us of her many other ailments and of what she would and would not do for us, rounding off the peroration with the observation that on the whole she preferred water in her scotch. It saddened Hazel that both Sally and I preferred bourbon to scotch, but that didn't entirely spare the liquor closet from periodic incursions when Hazel felt the need to fortify herself for the long descent to Mrs. Hamilton's quarters.

Bill was anxious for me to see the *National Review* offices, so he called me that first night to invite me for a quick lunch the next day with him and my sister Maureen. It would have to be quick, he explained, because they went to press on Wednesday, which was the day of our rendezvous.

Maureen was the next to youngest in the family, eight years younger than Bill and twelve years younger than I. She had graduated from Smith College a year earlier, the only Buckley of the ten to graduate *magna cum laude*, and after a very brief interlude landed a job with the Christophers working for Father Keller. She was very happy there and doing extremely well when Bill called one day to tell her that her services were urgently needed at the yet to be founded *National Review*. Bill has this wonderful feeling that his sisters can do absolutely anything, and do it competently, and at one time or another five of the six have worked for NR. The sixth, our oldest sister Aloïse, was a contributor to the first issue and to many another. Her Christmas stories became so famous that, forty-five years later, NR still reprints one every Yuletide. (Arlington House published a book of her essays, *Will Mrs. Major Go to Hell?*, posthumously.)

While Bill assured Maureen that she would really enjoy working at *National Review* much more than she had at the Christophers, he was afraid he couldn't match Father Keller's far from lavish salary. But her position would be unique, he assured her: she would be NR's *only* editorial assistant. He did not mention that that would make her answerable to every other person on the editorial staff. And so Maureen said a sad farewell to Father Keller (who continued such a good friend that he would officiate some five or six years later at her wedding to Gerald Ambrose O'Reilly) and became NR's Girl Friday. But the senior staff soon learned that Bill Buckley's kid sister, a blondie with long, slim legs, an easily curled lip, and a highly developed sense of the ridiculous, was not to be trifled with. There was a set to her shoulders, when displeased, that was unmistakable, and after a very little while it was understood that to mess with Maureen could be a perilous business.

Some of her retaliations were glorious. When one senior editor bugged her once too often, hovering over her as she opened the morning's mail demanding to know if anyone had commented—favorably, it went without saying—on his last column, she spent the following weekend concocting a suitable revenge. She borrowed stationery and typewriters from half a dozen friends and wrote a series of sarcastic and just short of vicious comments on Mr. Big Shot's work. The following Wednesday, when the pest set about his pestering, she let him have it, opening one critical letter after the next. It was only after the fifth or sixth that he caught on, and, incidentally, stopped badgering her. Maureen tamed not only NR writers; she cut readers off at the knees. To an irascible subscriber who canceled her subscription every time the editors wrote a single word she disapproved of, Maureen finally gave an ultimatum. One more CMS (cancel my subscription), and she was out for good. The lady did not take the warning seriously, and, after her next CMS, it took her three months of increasingly humble and contrite notes to get back in. Her final letter started: "I surrender, dear. Maureen, please, please resubscribe me. I promise to be good." And so Esther Dunlop was reinstated, and while she continued to complain at what she considered our editorial infractions of conservative tenets, as understood by Esther Dunlop, she never again canceled out.

National Review's first offices were on east 37th street, cheek by jowl with the exit from the Midtown Tunnel, about as un-chic a business address as it was possible to have. The rent was dirt cheap. *National Review* started life in November 1955 impoverished and remained impoverished for many a year, its circulation and advertising revenues always falling short of its expenses. Under the circumstances, every penny had to be watched. Those first offices were Spartan. A tiny reception area opened up into a big bullpen of a room, with a scattering of desks, typewriter tables, and wastepaper baskets. The ancient, rebuilt Royals and Underwoods were rumored to have cost five dollars each. Maureen sat at one of the desks, and the others accommodated visiting editors who would come in on Tuesdays and Wednesdays to write the final eight-thousand-word editorial section.

Around the perimeter of the main room was a series of small cubicles for the senior editors. (I would inhabit one of those cubicles.) At the back of the big room were four larger, more conventional offices for Bill and Willi Schlamm, second in command, who served as book editor, and, with Bill, associate articles editor, and wrote a brilliant and witty weekly cultural column, called "Arts & Manners." Suzanne La

Follette, the managing editor (a cousin of Fighting Bob, the Progressive Labor Party senator from Wisconsin), occupied the third office, and a fellow called Ted Driscoll, the business manager, occupied the fourth. Driscoll soon faded from the scene. It was Willmoore Kendall's contention that when Mr. Driscoll left in the spring of 1956, he still thought NR was in the business of manufacturing shoes.

It was Driscoll who had found the five-dollar typewriters and had also brought in Miss Fairclough as bookkeeper. Miss Fairclough was a sight to behold. She teetered around the office in three-inch heeled sandals and wore, at all times, a tiny hat perched on the top of a bun of mousy brown hair. It was to be discovered later, some months later, that Miss Fairclough was a very strange bookkeeper indeed. For one thing, she kept no record of the checks she wrote. But when anyone asked her how we were doing financially, she was cheerfulness itself. "Don't worry," she would say, "Mr. Buckley will find the money."

It was only months later, when Bill persuaded William A. Rusher, a young conservative lawyer working in Washington for the Internal Security subcommittee, to abandon that career and become publisher of *National Review*, that Miss Fairclough was replaced by the young and very capable Rose Flynn. That was when Miss Fairclough's bizarre accounting practices came to light, or, to be more accurate, failed to come to light, for Rose found few records of most of NR's earliest financial transactions. This is a situation that would send the average accountant to a shrink, but it struck Rose's funny bone, even as it outraged her every professional instinct, and she set about repairing the damage as best she could. A certain sanity prevailed from that day onward in NR's financial affairs, under the watchful and efficient management of Bill Rusher, Rose Flynn, and the inspired promotional genius of Jim McFadden, but some of us old timers missed Miss Fairclough's serene confidence in Mr. Buckley's ability to find the money to placate our accommodating, but also deeply stressed printer and numerous other creditors.

⚏ 3 ⚏

I Sign On

A COUPLE OF NIGHTS LATER, Bill invited me to dinner at l'Armorique, a small French bistro on east 54th Street, whose owner, and chef, produced delicious meals that included his specialty, a *soufflé de laitue* (lettuce souffle), which may not sound it, but was superb. It was a wonderful evening. We drank quite a bit of wine, caught up on family affairs, and then plunged into the subject of the moment, *National Review*, its personnel and its problems, and what Bill thought my role in the enterprise should be. I would help write the weekly editorials, take over whatever reportorial tasks needed to be handled, and edit a column of Washington news briefs that had proved less than satisfactory. We sat at the table late into the evening over our espressi—and the Calvados to which I introduced Bill that evening—discussing whatever came to mind, everything, in fact, but my salary. Somehow it seemed inappropriate to bring in such a mundane consideration on such a joyous evening. The result was that I was paid nothing at all in my first few months at *National Review*. It was only when the efficient Rose noted this omission and asked Bill about it that I went on the payroll, at the 1956 equivalent of the initial $18.50 a week I took in during my old United Press Radio days a dozen years back.

Two or three weeks after I reported for work, the receptionist called Bill. There was a young fellow in the outer office who wanted to see Bill about a job. Bill asked her to send him in. In walked a dark-haired young man, with a pleasant unmistakably Irish face, a cocky, jaunty air about him. He was immediately likeable. His name, he told Bill, was Jim McFadden, James P. McFadden to be exact. He was an ex-newspaperman from Ohio, more recently an Army NCO who had just been discharged after two years' service in an intelligence unit in Germany. He had arrived in New York that morning aboard a troop transport and had headed directly for the *National Review* office.

Although NR was then just about six months old, McFadden was familiar with it. He had read every single issue since first running across a copy in a USO canteen several months earlier. He had been stunned and delighted by the contents, both as a conservative and a Catholic, and he had decided then and there that when he got out of the Army, into which he had been drafted, he would enlist as a foot soldier in the conservative cause as a *National Review* employee. He'd like to be a writer or editor, he told Bill, "but if those jobs are filled I'll do any job you give me, Mr. Buckley, and I'll do it well."

Bill hired him on the spot.

For James P. McFadden there was no such word as "impossible." Looking the operation over he spotted a flaw that the editors with their super IQs had totally overlooked. The subscription operation was a shambles. It took considerable perseverance for a would-be reader to surmount the barricades NR's circulation people had erected against him, apparently under the impression that they had been hired to keep the general public at bay. The genial young man who was running circulation was eased out and replaced by Maureen's intelligent, well-organized, and quite stunning looking roommate,

Rosamond "Reggie" Horton. Between them, she and Mac, as we called Jim McFadden, reorganized the circulation operation until it fairly hummed.

With circulation in good hands, Mac turned his attention to the problem of attracting readers to this newest entry into the journal-of-opinion field. It would be years, perhaps never, before *National Review* could depend on advertising to sustain it, so circulation revenues would have to provide the bulk of its cash. This was immediately evident to Mac. At first he hired professionals to write promotional material, but they didn't really understand what NR was all about, and their direct mail solicitations bombed. So Mac sat himself down at the old Royal, pipe hanging out the side of his mouth, pounding out copy that not only sang but also enticed readers to try this new, intellectually abrasive product, a conservative journal of opinion, if you please. And the subscriptions rolled in. He had innovative ideas about what mailing lists might just work for NR, tried them out scientifically, and hit hard with lists that proved they could produce more NR readers.

But once you got them in you had to keep them satisfied, and keep them renewing their subscriptions. The content—what the editors had to say and how they said it—was of great importance, said Mac, but so also was the way the product looked. To sell the magazine it should look better, more with-it, more contemporary, Mac thought, and before you knew it another bright young man, James P. O'Bryan, the art director of the *New York Mirror*—who was also Catholic and conservative—was dropping in after work to help streamline the product. Soon Jimmy O'Bryan was designing more galvanizing covers, producing attractive looking mail solicitations, designing ads, and enlisting talented young artists to help out. Eventually, he was persuaded to quit the *Mirror*. He and Jim McFadden set up their own commercial art shop, Ultra Arts they called it, with an inward chuckle, which gave O'Bryan, who was married and had two children, the kind of financial security NR was unable to provide. Ultra Arts' artists moonlighted for NR in their spare time.

And so in March 1956, I entered *National Review*'s vineyard and found some of its winemasters—how shall we put it?—difficult. The start-up group of editors included Willi Schlamm, who had originated the idea of a new and more political conservative journal of opinion. He had come to NR from *The Freeman*—a conservative journal that concentrated more and more on economic matters, and was thus less and less relevant in the political battles ahead—along with Suzanne La Follette, who would be the managing editor, Mabel Wood Naft, the production editor, and John Chamberlain, who would write the lead book review every week.

Also on tap was Willmoore Kendall, the brilliant and erratic Yale political scientist who had done much to shape the political thinking of his Yale students, Bill Buckley, and Bill's brother-in-law L. Brent Bozell. Willmoore would be very briefly in charge of the book section. He would ride the train in from New Haven every Tuesday and Wednesday to write editorials. He also wrote a column, "The Liberal Line." To fill the economic slot, there was Jonathan Mitchell, tall, shy, rather sad looking, gentle, and kind. But Jon was soon gone. He had developed a terminal writer's block and sat in agony week after week in front of his typewriter unable to produce copy on time to meet the intractable deadline. His pain was deeply felt by his colleagues who came to the conclusion that Mitchell must have suffered a series of small strokes that rendered concentration on the work at hand well nigh impossible.

James Burnham, the political philosopher and author of such widely acclaimed books as *The Managerial Revolution* and *The Machiavellians*, took the train in from Kent, Connecticut, every week to write the strategic editorials. His weekly column was called "The Third World War." Brent Bozell, a lawyer who was married to our sister Patricia and lived in Washington, handled the Washington political and judicial scene in a weekly column.

This brilliant, but also highly combustible group, soon erupted in flames as various elements and combinations of editors sought to become dominant in *National Review*'s affairs. John Chamberlain's wife, who feared with reason that his association with NR might ruin his career as a major book critic and economic analyst, was reluctant for him to appear on NR's masthead, so he more or less freelanced with the magazine. But he remained a close and loving supporter of NR, and his contributions brightened its pages.

Willi Schlamm lasted a tumultuous two years. He had felt that he could manipulate the twenty-nine-year-old Bill Buckley and, in fact, run the operation. But it didn't work out that way, and after a number of eruptions of increasing unpleasantness, he too was gone. Willmoore Kendall, another combustible personality, stuck around for a while, but he kept taking leaves of absence from Yale, where he was a tenured professor, to visit Europe, or teach at Stanford, so matters never reached a boil. So long as the staff had to deal with his copy, rather than cope with his personal quirks, all went well—at least in the short run.

Kendall was a brilliant political philosopher, but he had a cantankerous streak that in the end destroyed friendships, even friendships he cherished. The quarrels, and there were many, were all of his making. One by one, he stopped speaking to his colleagues, to Bill Buckley, and then to Brent Bozell. He cut off all relations with Frank Meyer, who tried his hardest to keep their relationship going, and finally turned his back on Jeff Hart when Jeff refused to leave Dartmouth for the brand new Catholic University of Dallas, where Willmoore eventually settled after Yale bought out his tenure for $45,000, a hefty sum at the time. It was a tragedy all around. Willmoore was a great theoretician, but his private devils kept him from producing the body of serious work he was capable of.

However, Willmoore did leave a concrete mark of sorts. Somewhere in *National Review*'s current, bright, modern, and efficient new offices at 215 Lexington Avenue, sits a broken-down brown leather sofa which is known to old-timers as the Willmoore Kendall—or alternatively, as the Suzanne La Follette—Memorial Couch. It was named in remembrance of that stormy morning many years ago, when Suzanne arrived in the office early to take care of pressing editorial matters, only to find Willmoore and the assistant copy editor engaged in business of quite another sort on *her couch*. Bill had no sooner arrived and settled himself at his typewriter than the door to his office was flung open and Suzie stormed in, thundering in that deep, resonant, and unmistakable basso profundo: "There will be no fornication in my office!"

The assistant copy editor was fired.

Suzie didn't win all the La Follette–Kendall encounters. When Suzanne approached Willmoore once, dictionary in hand, to rebuke him for producing a dangling adverb (in an editorial paragraph he wrote which started, "The weekend conference at Arden House, which by the way, why doesn't someone burn it down ..."), Willmoore told her, "Suzanne, don't you realize that when people get around to writing dictionaries they come to people like me to advise them."

But when the smoke had cleared, the people at the helm of our blue-bordered ship were Bill Buckley and Jim Burnham, in the New York office. Onetime Communist functionary Frank S. Meyer served as book and cultural editor, operating from his secluded home in Woodstock, New York. When Bill Buckley was out of town, which occurred with increasing frequency in those early years, either as a favorite on the lecture circuit or filming his TV program *Firing Line*, Jim Burnham ran the editorial section and made any other major decisions that called for instant action. In time, Jeffrey Hart, an English professor at Dartmouth, who had studied with the Trillings at Columbia, started to come in weekly to write mostly cultural editorials.

He ran the all-important editorial section that we called "The Week," if both Bill and Jim were away. Three years later, when Suzanne La Follette, then in her middle seventies, decided to call it quits, Bill asked me to become managing editor, and the team that would run *National Review* for the next score years was complete: Bill Buckley, Jim Burnham, Jeff Hart, Frank Meyer, Priscilla Buckley, and on the business end, Bill Rusher, Jim McFadden, and Rose Flynn. But of equal importance to the smooth running of the operation were two remarkable women at the center of the web, Bill's secretaries, first the redoubtable Gertrude Vogt, and following her, the equally redoubtable Frances Bronson, Great Britain's gift to American conservatism.

National Review was, from the start, a shoestring kind of operation which, because of its (at the time) revolutionary politics, attracted talented young people, among them such future literati as John Leonard, Joan Didion, Arlene Croce, and Garry Wills, and such inspired political analysts as George Will, Richard Brookhiser, Paul Gigot, David Brooks, and Mona Charen. But it also attracted other valiant and energetic right-wingers, some of whom, however, bordered on kookery. It became my job as resident reporter to investigate some of the conservative horror stories generated in these circles and try to sort out the truth from the fantasy.

A major preoccupation of the moment was the debate over fluoridation. Was fluoridation a sound theory? If it was, how best to see that every American child was treated with it? Most importantly, was the optimum way of dealing with the problem to inject fluorides into municipal waterworks? Those were the basic questions, but among conservatives fearful of ever greater government intrusions into their daily lives, they were soon enveloped in a miasma of misunderstood scientific findings and horror scenarios.

While the point was not indisputably proved, all signs indicated that fluoride could prevent tooth cavities if very young children with baby teeth were treated with it. But it was also true that fluorides might stain a child's teeth and that people with certain ailments might have to use bottled water when fluorides were inserted in the waterworks. These were reasonable arguments, but they were accompanied in too many cases by unrealistic fears about the safety of the nation's, states', or cities' water supplies.

One splendid argument against fluoridating whole water supplies was insufficiently argued in my opinion, perhaps because it was insufficiently exciting. And it was that children don't drink water. They drink orange juice, they drink milk, they drink more soda pop than they should, but have you ever seen a five-year-old pour himself a glass of water? So why wouldn't a better method be to add fluorides to the milk children drank with their school lunches? That moderate argument, which I came up with, aroused deep suspicions in the embattled anti-fluoridationists among NR's readers.

The suspicions of many of them were confirmed when I was asked to look into a vile government program which, in mimeographed scare sheets that seemed to come in every day's mail, went under the ominous name "Siberia U.S.A." This, according to these releases, was a nefarious plot on the part of the federal government to get rid of political dissenters and critics on the right, particularly those who favored the Bricker Amendment, by deporting them to Alaska. You see, what the government was planning to do was to set up a concentration camp in Alaska, a huge affair encompassing one million acres. Anyone who got out of line politically could be first judged insane, then shipped off to this brand new asylum in Alaska, which—a knowing leer indicated by three underlinings—was only "a skip and a jump" away from Siberia. All of this would be done under the pretense of building a mental asylum in Alaska, but all that good sounding talk didn't fool us because *we* knew what *they* were up to.

I took the train to Washington, contacted the House committee that was writing the bill, and talked to its legislative assistant. He was delighted to be able to explain to someone who would listen what the legislation was all about.

He told me that there had never been an insane asylum—that's what they were still called at that time—in Alaska when it was a territory, before statehood. If anyone became violently insane in Alaska the only recourse the community had was to get a judge to issue an order for the person's arrest. He would be taken into custody and held in jail until arrangements could be made to send him to Washington state, where mental asylums were available. It was a high-handed procedure but the only way to prevent the poor madman from harming other people or himself.

Once statehood was achieved, Alaska placed a high priority on building its own mental facility to handle these violent cases. But how was this new facility to be funded? Alaska itself had very few resources since the federal government owned nearly 98 percent of its land. A good way, it was decided, was to handle the situation by a land grant. Historically, land grants had been made to many new states to enable them to finance the building of state colleges and universities. The government would deed over to the new state of Alaska—it achieved statehood in 1959—one million acres of land (the size of the concentration camp in the fevered rhetoric of the pamphlets). Alaska could then sell that land and with the revenue accrued from the sales build itself a modern hospital to which mental patients could be sent for treatment by doctors and psychiatrists rather than by judges and sheriffs.

I emphasized these points in my story, pointing out a few of the mental elipses that had set off the rocket, but most of NR's readers who believed they knew the truth about "Siberia U.S.A." were not convinced. One letter writer, more in sorrow than in anger, suggested that perhaps "Miss Buckley had remained in France too long, and acquired socialistic notions."

It was at about this point in my career at *National Review* that Suzie quit—as eruptions had gone at NR this was a small one—and Bill asked me to take on the job of managing editor. (It wasn't until years later, when Bill published his book of correspondence with Whittaker Chambers, *Odyssey of a Friend*, that I learned that Whit had been very impressed by a profile I had written of Pierre Mendès-France a year or so earlier and suggested then that I be appointed managing editor.)

I was of two minds about accepting. To start with, my grammatical grounding, while adequate, was simply not on a par with Suzanne's. Under my guidance a solipsism or two was bound to slip into the magazine, but more important, it would mean a much more rigid routine. Up to this point, I had taken part in the editorial conferences on Tuesday mornings, at which the editorials for the week's issue were assigned, and had handled those assignments. I had pretty much taken over the brisk news column at the front of the book called "For the Record." I had written numbers of articles and book and theater reviews, and had handled whatever translation needed to be done from French. But I hadn't done any copy reading or copy editing, nor had I dealt with printers, the advertising department, artists, cartoonists, and the like, or directed an editorial staff. As I thought it over, I realized that in my professional career, going back to the mid 1940s, at United Press, Central Intelligence, and now at *National Review*, I had been singularly free of managerial responsibilities. I realized, too, that in the back of my mind, the possibility of a return to Paris was, simply, there.

If I agreed to become managing editor it would be for the long term: a career at *National Review*, a great deal of responsibility, and very little money. This last was not of paramount importance since I had a private income, but still, my college contemporaries were now entering the big time financially. What would make the mix palatable, I decided, was plenty of time off to take the kind of vacations, many of them offbeat, that I greatly enjoyed. So I told Bill I would take the job providing it was understood that I have six weeks off a year to disport myself in whatever fashion I liked, and, by the way, I was planning a week in South Carolina in September for the dove season.

The Great Dove War

MY FRIEND FRANNY GRIGGS, now on her fourth husband, has just bought a small house in Boykin, South Carolina, about eight miles from Camden, and she's on the phone. "You must come down, there's just no question about it, Pitts, you must come down. It is going to be the best dove season ever, ever, ever!" Franny is an enthusiast. "You just can't afford to miss it. Just think of the fun we will have."

Since it has never been known in the history of man that anyone has been able to turn down Franny Weeks-Ryan-Betner-Griggs when she wants something, I find myself on the plane to Columbia, South Carolina, a week later, where an ebullient Franny picks me up. She is full of terrible stories about the sneaky, mean-spirited way the wardens have taken to behaving in recent years while I was in Paris and missing out on Carolina dove shoots.

On the whole, a dove hunter is happier when a warden doesn't show up. But on steaming South Carolina September afternoons in the years before The Great Dove War, the appearance of a neat, khaki-clad figure with badge and a polite "Afternoon, ma'am, could

I please see your license?" was generally little more than a colloquy that might get in the way of a dove determined to fly down your gun barrel. Mostly, if he was questioning a woman, the warden didn't even bother to count the bag. And after the shoot, more often that not, he would be invited to partake in a cold beer and help finish off the fried chicken left from lunch.

But from opening day this year things had been different in Kershaw County. The wardens had gone mad, *mad*, bee-serk. They were dotting the ɪ's and crossing the ᴛ's of every regulation in the book as they'd never been dotted and crossed before.

I ran into old C.C. Whittaker when I went downtown to pick up my hunting license at Burns' Hardware the next morning, and he had a story to tell about opening day. Would I join him in a Coke? We repaired to the City Drug, and he brought the Cokes, poured over shaved ice in tall wax paper cups, to the ricketty, marble-topped table in the soda fountain section, under the ceiling fan.

"D'ya hear about Henry's shoot, Priscilla?" I hadn't. "Well, sir, if a whole pack of wardens didn't just about surround the field and didn't they fine every man, woman, and child toting a gun *twenty-five dollars*. Should have seen old Dwight's face." (Dwight's notorious tightness is a town joke.) "Course Henry had kinda sweetened up the field, a bit of wheat 'n corn. You know. But it wasn't as if anyone had been shooting over the limit, and all the guns were plugged, except maybe old Buddy's—no one can control Buddy."

C.C. was outraged, and he wasn't the only one. Must have been that new fella from Sumter who was causing the trouble, everyone reasoned, the warden no one knew. Old Dick Jones, the local man, wouldn't do such a thing. Why, Dick liked to shoot a fast-flying dove just as well as the next man. And Mamie's dove pie was famous. Something was up.

And it was. Day after day, as the temperature hit the high 90s, the dust rose in clouds from the sun-parched fields, and the hot winds did nothing to dry the sweat on camouflage shirts and under waist bands, the wardens took their toll. It got so that when Anc, or Caleb, or Whit, or Bolivar invited you to a shoot, they'd warn you: "Be sure to bring twenty-five dollars. No telling what those crazy wardens'll do next."

No longer did rattletrap pickups meet at the Dusty Bend Esso station and head for the field, twenty or thirty miles down the road, in easily spotted caravans. Dove hunters doubled up in fewer cars, drove to the dove field by circuitous routes, and parked off the road, back of the trees, hiding their cars so carefully not even a dove could see them. "You got nothing to worry about this afternoon," a confident Anc or Caleb of Whit or Bolivar would assure his guests as they drove up, sure that this time the wardens would be caught off guard. But they seldom were. Franny Griggs got so spooked she began to wear her running shoes to shoots instead of her boots, snakes be dammed. She urged me to do the same, but I prefer wardens to rattlers.

By late September, only a handful of dove hunters still wore the red-white-and-blue pom-pom of the Order of the Nimble Nimrod, a decoration worn only by those sports who had not in the course of the season been caught and fined by a game warden. The unrelenting crackdown by the wardens on any shoot over a field that showed any sign of having been baited was getting more than aggravating. It was getting downright serious. Folks were actually talking of putting up their guns. They'd wait till the bird season in November, or the duck season later on. "Ain't no point in paying twenty-five dollars for a passel of doves." And running from wardens across a plowed field or into a swamp or down a ditchbank, with a gun and a dove seat and two or three boxes of shells was—well, some folks were just too old for that kind of nonsense.

But not Icky. Icky Guy was made of sterner stuff. Edwin P. Guy Jr. had picked up his nickname from Ichabod Crane, so long of neck and angular of frame had he been as a youth. Also deeply ingrained in him was the steely determination of his Yankee forebears. Icky owned Bluelands, a vast acreage of fields and swamp, and every year, almost as far back as anyone could remember, the last Saturday of the season was the day they shot Bluelands. You could get sixty, seventy guns in that field and never crump up too close to another stand. Icky's shoot was the *meringue glacé* of the fall season.

Icky let it be known, discreetly, that his shoot was still on even though the hot rumor of the hour was that federal wardens were moving in, and the Feds, as is well known to the hunting confraternity, can be trouble with a capital T. The Feds could take your gun, or your car—just take it, grab it, confiscate it, right then and there—for the smallest, littlest kind of no-count offense. But Icky wasn't scared of the Feds or anyone else. Icky had it all figured out.

There were only two ways to get into the swamp, everyone knew that: one road over a narrow dam, another winding through the cotton and soy fields and dipping down through a marshy area to a gate that was kept padlocked most of the time. The way Icky had it figured, he'd get the guns in earlier than the wardens expected. They'd rendezvous behind the old abandoned church in Boykin, park their cars out of sight in the back, and be trucked into the field in bunches of ten or twelve. When the last hunter had reached his stand, Icky would station a couple of men at the choke points, with hunting horns. It may be strange to see a man carrying a hunting horn in September, but it sure isn't illegal. If the wardens arrived, Icky's sentinels would blow three times—three long blasts—and everyone in the field was to drop everything but his gun and head into the swamp as fast and as hard as he could run. There were places in the swamp no warden would ever find.

By the time the wardens reached the field it would be deserted, and when the law had departed, suitably chastened, the All Clear would be sounded—two blasts of the horn. The hunters could then emerge and proceed with the shoot or, if it was too late in the day, repair to Icky's cabin for a victory celebration. Icky guaranteed he wouldn't leave the swamp until every last hunter had been accounted for and retrieved.

Saturday dawned clear and cool. By 11:30 every hunter was at his stand and the sentries posted. The temperature was in the low 80s, and the breeze cool for a change. About 1:30 the doves commenced to come in. They swooped low over the pines across the field from my stand and would be rising fast to clear the trees behind me as they skittered out, diving, swooping, a dove's version of broken field running. Guns were barking deep in the swamp, boom, boom, boomboomboom—that must be Buddy, up on the hillside by the abandoned cabin, and over where the Wootens had their stands by the telephone pole near the ditchbank. Bang, bang, boom, bark went the guns. "Mark," "Low over the field," "High over the pines," "Coming at you out of the sun," yelled the hunters.

But also coming at us out of the sun were fast-striding figures— no, not wardens, but messengers dispatched by Icky with the latest word. If a light, single-engine plane flew over low, dusting the field with pesticide, the word was to head for cover, because the wardens were coming. Seems someone had spotted a helicopter chugging this way, and the suspicion was that Feds were aboard, armed with binoculars to spot every last hunter. But trust old Icky. He'd gotten on his CB, called old Rusty Hawks down at the airfield, and hired him to play sentry from his crop-dusting plane. If old Rusty spotted the helicopter headed toward Bluelands, he was to fly low over the field and dust it three times.

And so the afternoon progressed, the doves coming in driblets and drablets, and then in droves. Hunters moved off their stands as they got their limits to give others a chance. And wheeling high above them, the sun highlighting the bright blue wings of the little plane, flew Edwin P. Guy Jr.'s counter-air patrol keeping watch.

It was kind of an anticlimax that the Feds never did show up in their chopper and that Rusty never had occasion to dust up his first field of dove hunters. But there was no argument that this had been the finest, most enjoyable shoot of this or any season. Bottles were broached, ice dumped into plastic glasses, and tall tales were a-telling, when there came a single shot from the swamp.

"Who the hell could that be?" asked Icky. All eyes turned in the direction of the shot, and tension turned to laughter. Out of the woods trudged a bedraggled Franny Griggs, white sneakers plastered with mud, her daddy's heavy 12-gauge over her shoulder, hauling a dove seat still sagging from the weight of unshot shells. (Franny has been known to bring six boxes of 12's to a shoot.)

Young McKee—those Boykin boys have the best manners—ran over and relieved Franny of her gun and gear, while Whit assembled a monster Bullshot, Franny's favorite drink. Old Franny had gotten her signals mixed and, at the first sight of Rusty's plane, had fled so deep into the swamp that it had taken her all this time to find her way back. No one's laughter in the contemplation of this mishap was louder or more genuine than Franny's.

Everyone agreed that the age of chivalry had not died when old C.C. unpinned the Order of the Nimble Nimrod—the very last one left in all of Kershaw County—from his own shoulder and ceremoniously affixed it to Franny's, then bussed her on either cheek, twice, French-style.

$$\sim 5 \sim$$

Managing Editor

I<small>T WAS ARRANGED</small> that I would start my new career as managing editor the first week in October 1959. Suzanne had started up that particular issue and carried it through the first preparatory week. (We had been a fortnightly for about a year, having had to move back from weekly publication for financial reasons.) And I handled the closing week with the able help of Mabel Wood, the experienced production editor who tripled as advertising manager and copy editor. Mabel was in her late fifties or early sixties, a stout lady with once-red hair that was now reddish, compliments of a bottle. She was business-like, rather silent as a rule, but you could tell there was a bit of that red-haired temper quietly smoldering, somewhere, and every instinct told you that you never want to see Mabel erupting. She had had a hard life. Her husband, Stephan Naft, was a Hungarian anarchist in his youth, an unsuccessful publicist who went blind fairly early on in their marriage. Mabel nursed him and supported him until his death many years later. She loved him dearly.

She told me an amusing story once about Stephan's experience as a young man around the turn of the century. He was on every international list of potential political trouble makers and happened to be in Gibraltar when the newly crowned King Edward VII, Queen Victoria's son, was scheduled to make a visit to the Rock on a naval tour of various imperial outposts. Fearful of a possible assassination attempt, or even of an unmannerly demonstration, British authorities on the Rock had simply rounded up the usual suspects, of whom Stephan Naft was one, and tossed them all in the clink for four or five days, the duration of the royal visit. They were handsomely fed and generally well treated, and when the royal yacht set sail, each of the detainees was handed a ten pound note to compensate for any inconvenience the incarceration might have caused and let loose. Mabel was still amused by Stephan's continued irritation over the episode. She pointed out to me that while Naft was himself an anarchist, and believed in no rules, it outraged him when legally constituted authority acted anarchistically. It was just *not* right.

My position at the moment was a bit anomalous. My brother Bill, his public reputation notwithstanding, can't bear to hurt anyone's feelings. He just can't bring himself to do it, and sometimes this failing leads to complicated situations. Sometime earlier in NR's story, he had brought in Maureen's roommate, Reggie Horton, to replace the ineffective Don Lipsett as circulation manager, but failed to inform Don of his change in status because it might hurt his feelings.

This time he had decided that Suzanne, who had been around editorial shops since Albert Jay Nock's original *Freeman* in the 1920s, would be insulted to be replaced by someone of my limited experience in magazine work, not to say by someone so very much younger than she was. So Bill decided not to make any changes in the masthead, other than to excise Suzie, dropping her into the Contributing Editors category where my name rested. He would postpone my elevation in the masthead until some future date when he would slip it in without fanfare, in the hope that enough time would have passed for Suzie not to notice. After four years of close association with Suzie, Bill had not learned a most basic fact about her which was that no one could slip anything over on Suzanne La Follette.

Despite this contretemps in the making—one which in fact never occurred—Suzanne and I continued as good friends. She lived in the rundown but prestigious Hotel Chelsea on 23rd Street, just west of Fifth Avenue where numbers of artists, writers, poets, and other luminaries resided. Suzanne's brother Chester was one of them. Chester was as easygoing as Suzie was tempestuous, a small man with a gentle manner and smile, and a hint of sadness about him. He had had a daughter who died young and tragically. It was Helen Tremaine, our editorial secretary, I think, who told me she had committed suicide when still in her twenties.

Chester was both a portrait painter and a musician. In addition to their apartments, he and Suzie shared a large room in one of the top floors of the Chelsea which he used as a studio and in which he gave his piano and violin lessons; her office was at the opposite end. At about the time that I first met Chester, the United States Senate decided to have portraits painted of seven senators with particularly distinguished records, one of whom was Chester and Suzanne's cousin Bob. Chester entered the contest for portraitist under an assumed name—he didn't think it fair to the other contestants to enter under his own name—and, in the spirit of fun sent in a sketch of Andrew Jackson under yet another name. To his astonishment, and Suzanne's great amusement, he won both commissions. But there was no greed in gentle Chester La Follette's heart. He confessed to his true identity and suggested the jury pick one of the other contestants to do the Jackson portrait. His interest was in the opportunity to immortalize the cousin he had so admired.

On Sunday night, just back from the dove shoot in South Carolina, I got a call from Mabel's nephew, a commercial pilot who lived in Kingston, New York. Mabel had been rushed to the hospital with acute appendicitis. The appendix had burst and there was no telling how long Mabel would be hospitalized, but certainly ten days or so before she would be back at work. He sent me, by messenger, a sheet from a yellow lined pad on which Mabel—ever the trooper and awaiting the anesthetist—had scratched out the outline of the current issue: what articles would be running, which columns were in house, which needed work, which editors I should phone to remind them of their deadlines, what art work was still at the engraver's, anything she thought I should know. I had not the slightest idea what most of this meant.

Up to this moment, I had been pretty much a voyeur at *National Review*, writing my column, contributing to the editorial section, researching and writing articles and book reviews, and reviewing plays, particularly musical comedies. But I didn't know beans about how a magazine was actually produced: how many words there were in a one-page article, for instance, what typeface we used for the body type, how to indicate what fonts we wanted on the headline of which article or column, or even how wide to make each column of type. What in fact was a font? A pica? A 1-*n*-dash? Or the difference between a 1-*n*-dash and a 1-*m*-dash? None of this had mattered because Mabel was there, and Mabel knew everything. Mabel would take me through this learning process step by step. Inasmuch as Mabel had deeply and mostly, but not always silently, resented Suzanne's bossiness in the dozen years they had worked together on *The Freeman* and NR, Mabel was pleased by the change. She looked forward to the prospect of teaching me to do things her way which was in every way, she sniffed, preferable to Suzanne's way. But just for the moment, Mabel wasn't there.

The phone rang. It was Jim Burnham, from Kent. He had just come back from a most interesting motor trip across the country, which he was writing about in his current column, and he realized that he needed more space. "How is the holdover situation?" he asked. He might as well have asked if I understood the theory of relativity. I had never heard of "holdovers" and told him so. He explained, kindly. There was usually, he told me, a page at the back of the magazine with a couple of small ads in it, that carried any copy that wouldn't fit into its designated space in the front of the book. What he needed to know was whether that holdover space had been filled, and if it hadn't could he use at least twenty lines of it?

"Jim, I'll just have to call you back," I said, and went into Mabel's office.

And I stood there, not knowing what I was looking for. Mabel's desk was clear, not a paper on it. Hung from a large corkboard at the back of her desk were long galleys, each numbered in ink, the number slashing across the copy. On the desk were a large pair of shears, long enough to cut through a galley at one stroke and a large ashtray full of straight pins. Where would I find the holdover page, if there was one? At about this point, Helen Tremaine, the editorial typist who had worked with Mabel for many years and shared her tight little office in our new quarters at 150 East 35th Street, walked in the door. I told her my predicament and she pulled out the top drawer of a file cabinet in which Mabel kept the pages she was currently working on. We found the holdover page. There were, indeed, about forty lines yet to be filled, and I called Jim Burnham back with the good news. But already I was learning caution. "Jim that's forty lines minus two lines for the 'continued on' and 'continued from' page notices."

I returned to my office and considered the situation and the available staff. The available staff was slender: Maureen and our brand new, untested nineteen-year-old editorial assistant, John Leonard. John had been in his first year at Harvard when his parents got divorced and the tuition dollars dried up. But while ever so briefly there he had written an article for a short-lived college magazine called *Ivy* which Bill had come across in a doctor's waiting room. The piece charmed Bill. He called the magazine, got John's address, called him, and, hearing of his situation, offered him a job. John Leonard was a natural born writer—we had very little to teach him in that department—but we also failed dismally in converting him to conservatism. Nonetheless, we had a rollicking year or so together and remain dear friends. (After leaving NR John returned to California to finish up his undergraduate studies and took a job at a Pacifica radio station, which is about as far left as you can get this side of the Communist Party. Subsequently, he became editor of the *New York Times Sunday Book Review*, and remains a columnist for *New York* magazine and *Vanity Fair*, and appears regularly in the *New York Review of Books* and other bigdome magazines.)

But here were two bodies at my disposal. Maureen, as editor of the "To the Editor" column, had done quite a bit of copyreading in the last three years, so I assigned her to Mabel's copy editor duties. I informed John that for at least the next ten days he was *National Review*'s production editor, and delivered him to Helen.

She dug out Brent Bozell's column from the copy that had arrived back at 150 East 35th Street from the printer that morning. Then Helen opened a copy of the last magazine to Brent's "National Trends" page. This, she pointed out to John (and, incidentally, to me), was set in three columns, each of them 13½-picas wide. (A "pica" is a printer's measurement for width.) Each of the first two columns on the page, in which the logo, the column's title, and the author's name would fit was nine lines shorter at the top of the page than the third column, which was sixty-three lines long.

Helen, who typed every single word that appeared in the magazine every week, explained to John (and, incidentally, to me) that approximately thirty-six characters would fit in a 13½-pica column, so that when, for instance, she typed Brent's copy she set her margins to a comfortable seventy-two characters, "that's twice thirty-six," she explained, making sure that we understood, "and so we count each line of type on the 13½-pica pages as two lines."

On the editorial "The Week" pages, as we were to learn the next day, there were only two columns to a page, and the type was larger (10/12 Textype, as opposed to 9/11 Textype) and the columns 20½ picas (or fifty-two characters) wide. She set her margins at fifty-two characters when typing the editorials, and hence each line counted as one.

John looked lost, and so did I. But Helen persevered. She placed a galley, numbered thiry-eight, on the table, and counted down fifty-four lines. She instructed John to cut the galley at that point and to pin that portion on a master sheet. They then counted a second fifty-four lines, John cut it off, and pinned it in the second column of the master. There were still a few lines on the galley he had been working on, but the article was concluded on the next galley, which was numbered thirty-nine. Now there was a problem. There were sixty-three lines left to complete the page, but there were seventy-one lines left of type.

"You don't cut those eight lines," Helen told John sternly. "You must ask the copy editor, Maureen, to cut them. Carving up or correcting copy is her job. Carving up galleys is yours." For Helen, who was ordinarily a loveable milquetoast, this was very stern language, so we pay attention.

We got through the next day with a huge assist from Helen. The last editorial paragraph was written and entrusted to the printer's messenger, who picked up his packet every evening at 5:30 and took the train out of Grand Central to New Haven, where the printers pounded it out on their old hot-lead linotype machines on the overnight shift. Helen warned me that I must write at the top of every single piece of copy that went out instructions as to type, font size, and pica width—9/11 Textype, 13½ picas, or 10/12 Textype 20½ picas— because in a single shift a printer may be working on two or more magazines and it is essential that he know what type to use.

The veteran printers at Wilson & Lee, the plant just outside New Haven that we used, were astonished to see the emissaries *National Review* sent them Thursday morning to correct the final galleys and lay them out. John, nineteen, and Maureen, twenty-four, struck them as a mite young and inexperienced, but they were kindness indeed in helping them out when they got stuck. The Kreuttner cartoon, which was so funny that we gave up a whole page to set it off properly and make Kreuttner's long and always convoluted captions readable, came back to John at a distinct kilter. But maybe that was the way Kreuttner wanted it, he figured, and approved the page. Our cartoonist was not pleased with the result, but John and I thought it looked rather dashing, tilted sharply to the right as it was.

When Kreuttner was not pleased he tended to let one know, as in the note I received from him a couple of years later, when I should no longer have been making such mistakes and the printer was no longer so accommodating in correcting them: "Dear Priscilla. Apropos the fate of my cartoon. I've been studying El Greco. I understand that when he painted his view of Toledo, he sent it to NR and they reduced it to one column. He was so dismayed that from then on he painted all his popes and saints 8 feet tall and 3½ inches wide. Love. J. Kreuttner."

~ 6 ~

Here She Comes

THIS IS PROVING TO BE A TUMULTUOUS YEAR. I get a fascinating new job. My roommate, Sally Garfield, gets married to Peter Smith and moves to Guatemala where Peter is in charge of the W.R. Grace operation, and my brother Jim and I take over the apartment mother and father had bought at 60 Sutton Place South shortly before father's death.

This is late January 1960, and I have given a small cocktail party earlier this evening to which I have invited my new, practically next door, neighbors, my sister Maureen and her husband Gerry O'Reilly. They have moved into an apartment less than a block away with two bedrooms, in order to accommodate Maureen's second child, due in about a month. The party having ended, I've cleaned my place up, put the dishes into the dishwasher, emptied the ashtrays, opened the door to the terrace to let in some fresh air, and taken a bath. I'm in bed reading when the phone rings. It's Gerry O'Reilly. "How about coming over for a Cointreau or something?" he asks. "Are you mad?" I replied, "It's almost one o'clock." Gerry stalls a bit, tells me how much they enjoyed the party, and finally comes to the point.

"Actually, Rhoda [his pet name for Maureen] isn't feeling too well." Maureen's baby isn't expected for another five or six weeks, but she's having contractions. They've called Dr. Hawks, her obstetrician, and he has told them to go right to the hospital, that he would meet them there. But there is a residual problem. Would I come over and babysit eleven-month-old Patricia? Of course I will. But it's not without trepidation. I have never changed a diaper, or fed or dressed an infant. I get dressed, put pyjamas, bathrobe, slippers, a toothbrush and comb, and Alan Drury's *Advise and Consent* into a flight bag and rush out. They live just around the corner, at 411 East 53rd Street. The night is clear and very cold.

When I arrive Maureen is lying on top of the covers in the red wool dress with gold buttons she is particularly attached to that year. She smiles politely. "Hi, Pitts," and then adds, almost apologetically, "I don't know whether I can make it to the hospital." "Ho, ho, ho," say Gerry and I, in concert, "don't be silly, of course, you can get to the hospital."

Maureen lies back on the bed for a couple of moments, then announces that she is feeling better and can probably make it. She darts into the bathroom to powder her nose and put on lipstick. Gerry says he'll go down to the street and flag a cab. I'm to watch out the window, and when he has one, I'll bring Maureen on down. The Lying-In hospital is at 70th street and the East River, not more than seventeen blocks away. It never, not for a moment, crosses our minds that we are in for an *accouchement*, let alone that we will be *les accoucheurs*. As Gerry is putting on his coat, Maureen calls out, peremptorily, "The baby is coming *right now*." I yell at Gerry not to leave, and rush into the bathroom. Gerry calls the police and they promise to send an ambulance immediately.

How long the actual birth takes, I don't know. It can't be more than ten or fifteen minutes. I do know that when I grasp the baby gingerly by its tiny shoulders and pull it free, Gerry is saying: "Yes, this is Mr.

O'Reilly and I did just phone from 411 East 53rd street, Apartment
11-H." (The police always double check emergency calls.)

It's my big moment. I know that you hold up newborn children
by the heels and swat them on the back to make them breathe (after
all, I have seen *Gone with the Wind* five times), but I am upstaged by
the baby who emerges from the womb bawling. "My God," I hear
Gerry tell the police, "my wife has had the baby!" I reach up and jerk
a towel from the rack and wrap the baby in it. I ask Maureen if she
can hold it for a moment, and I go into her bedroom to gather pillows
and blankets and try to make her more comfortable. She is shivering. Gerry meanwhile is now on the phone to Dr. Milt Singer, the
pediatrician—who happened also to have attended my party earlier
that evening—getting instructions on what to do next. Milt asks if
it's a boy or a girl. I don't know. I hadn't looked. I unwrap the child
and inform Gerry that it is another girl.

"Do you think we should clean her up?" I ask Maureen. The child
is kind of grey and sticky. Maureen doesn't know, but the question
strikes her as funny, and she starts to giggle. The shivering is dimin-
ishing, which relieves me.

Gerry is now transmitting instructions from Milt Singer. We are
to put a pair of scissors and some string into boiling water. When
that is done we are to tie off the umbilical cord, once about an inch
from the mother, once about an inch from the baby, and then cut it.
"What's this 'we' stuff?" I ask Gerry, knowing who it is who will boil
the water and do the snipping. We find the scissors, but Maureen
doesn't know that she has any string. We finally find some; it is the
elasticized gold cord that Lord & Taylor uses to wrap its Christmas
packages. I balk at the idea of delivering mother and child to the
hospital so bedecked.

"Ask Milton how soon this has to be done," I tell Gerry. Anytime
in the first twelve hours, is the response, and with New York's Finest
about to arrive, I shelve that project.

There's a ring at the door and enter: two large Polish policemen, an intern, an orderly, and an ambulance driver. "Where's the linen closet," one of the officers asks Gerry as the doctor goes in to see Maureen and the orderly takes over the baby. "Linen closet?" Gerry hasn't the slightest idea, so the policemen rummage around until they find it and carry great handfuls of towels to the bedroom. They then help the other men carry Maureen to the bed and cover her up. The doctor thinks it best for her to stay put for the afterbirth. And to pass the time the ambulance driver tells us happy little stories such as what happened last night when this bozo either jumped or fell under a subway train, and "you'll never believe it, but when I jumped down onto the tracks there was that fellow's head sitting on his chest, just looking at me."

He is also in charge of the records.

"What's your name?"

"Gerald O'Reilly."

"The father?"

"Yes."

"What's her name?" motioning to the bedroom.

"Maureen O'Reilly."

"The mother?"

"Yes."

A thoughtful silence, and then:

"Married?"

"Yes," says Gerry, ever so patiently, and winks at me.

They carry Maureen out on a stretcher about forty-five minutes later. The orderly follows, baby in arms, then the two policemen, the driver, and Gerry. The elderly Irish overnight doorman sweeps off his cap: "Congratulations, Mrs. O'Reilly."

Gerry rides up to the hospital in the squad car, though it is pointed out that this is not standard operating procedure. An exception is being made because "your wife is one hell of a wonderful broad."

And there I am at 2:30 in the morning, all alone in the apartment, and now I have the shakes. I have to tell someone, so I call my poor long-suffering mother to inform her that she is once again a grandmother, and I blurt out the circumstances of the baby's arrival. Mother's first remark is typical. "Dear, I do hope you washed your hands."

"Washed my hands! I hardly had time to take off my coat!"

The child is called Priscilla.

❧ 7 ❧

For the Record

B Y SPRING, I've conquered the mechanics of the job. I can tell Garamond Bold from Bodoni, from Times Roman, from Textype. I know the difference between a 1-*n*-dash and a 1-*m*-dash, and under Mabel's supervision have become expert at correcting typeset copy by inserting exactly the same number of characters into the correction as the offending words I am taking out, so that the printer will have to change only one line of type. In the old hot lead operations which have dominated printing roughly from the days of Gutenberg to the present—which is to say 1960—when a printer makes a correction he has to remove the line or lines from the form, which is a dangerous business since he may replace them in a different order. This is why, when checking out a correction, the copy reader checks three or four lines above and below the revised copy to make sure the lines are in proper order when the form is locked in. Tricks of the trade, and learnable. I've also mastered *National Review*'s style sheet and know when to capitalize Federal and when to lower case it, when to spell out numerals and when to use arabic numerals,

43

all the stylistic rules that provide consistency in capitalization and punctuation throughout the book, or magazine.

But I'm having trouble finding the time, given constant interruptions by people who need a decision on this or that, immediately—How does this spot look here? Don't forget the plug we promised Stan [Evans] for his journalism school. Have you seen the latest Kreuttner, it's hilarious? But why can't I have another page? I absolutely need the room to make my point.—to do the basic research for the news column I write, called "For the Record."

"For the Record" is a great favorite with our readers. It has been moved from the back of the book to the front. It is the first thing after the "Table of Contents" that the readers see. It was started by our original Washington editor Sam Jones, continued by Lyle Munson, a conservative who ran ads for his mail order book business, The Bookman, in every issue of the magazine. But both had done a relatively lazy job of it. The column was of secondary interest to them, and I had gradually taken it over. I liked it because this was news and I had been trained in news gathering and disseminating at United Press.

What I didn't want was to have anything in "For the Record" that a reader could get from perusing the front page of the *New York Times* or the *Washington Post*. I wanted the tidbit that they would glean only elsewhere, something that would alert them to hidden agendas. So in time I found myself reading—well, not exactly reading, but skimming—the daily *New York Times*, *Washington Post*, *Wall Street Journal*, and *Christian Science Monitor*. We subscribed to, and I read, Kevin Phillips's and the Evans & Novak newsletters, and the Washington-based weekly *Human Events*, which was the conservative watchdog of liberal shenanigans on the Hill and a splendid source of inside the Beltway information. I also read a then weekly international publication which carried the best of the intellectual left, which is to say excerpts from the *Guardian* (Britain), *Le Monde* (France), and the *Washington Post* (U.S.). To find out what the bad guys were up to I also subscribed to, and cast a critical and often amused, but more often, bored eye on the Communist *Daily World*, and the various Trotskyist, New Left, and socialist organs such as *The Militant*, *The Guardian*, *Ramparts*, and whatever other subversive literature I could put my hands on.

Reading the *Daily World* was particularly onerous. The first dozen times one came across "running dogs of imperialism," it was kind of fun, but the fortieth or fiftieth time, less so. But I persevered because of pearls such as Philip Bonosky's touching description of the death of the Communist Chilean poet Pablo Neruda: "As he lay dying the greatest poet of our age rose from his bed of pain and delivered a curse on the betrayers of his country that will yet scare their corrupted bones. 'Voracious hyenas,' 'hellish predators,' 'rodents gnawing,' 'satraps who have sold out a hundred times.' Then he cursed them. And he named them: Nixon, Frei [former Chilean president], Pinochet. He pronounced anathema on them. He indicted them: 'Prostituted vendors of the North American way of life,' 'pimps of the whorish bosses.' He hurled his contempt for them with his last breath."

In time, I had informants around the country who would call and give me tidbits from the local press that were frequently titillating.

It amused me that in addressing far left audiences, including not only the political leftists but also the gay and lesbian groups, the Black Panthers, and such, radical chic intellectuals could be so incautious, sure that the outrageous statements they made to please those crowds would not be reported in politer political circles. Ramsey Clark, the former attorney general, gone intellectually gaga, was particularly vulnerable in this respect. I set up a file which I called "Quotable Quotes" and would visit from time to time to make an editorial point. It was great fun, but time consuming.

Eventually I found a solution to the problem, and took to driving out to Sharon on Thursday nights of what we called around the shop "Magazine Week." (On the alternate week, "Bulletin Week," we put out an eight-page conservative news sheet for which I provided two shorter columns, called "People" and "Briefs.") We would have finished work on the current magazine on Thursday and Frank Meyer's book section for the next issue would, ideally, be in the office Friday and ready to start its journey back and forth to the printer. This Mabel could handle, so I would bundle in my briefcase most of my column reading and any manuscript that needed editing and head for the Connecticut hills. My two brothers, Jim and John, had a little office in an old carriage house at Great Elm, our family home in Connecticut, where they worked on Mondays and Fridays and they offered me a room on the second floor which I used on Friday and often on Saturday as well. With the bulk of my column reading done over the weekend, the Wednesday morning go-to-press crush was eased.

I sometimes mused that if I should ever have an accident en route home Thursday evening the police would not be guilty of profiling if they notified the FBI, given the contents of my briefcase.

~ 8 ~

150 East 35th Street

A COUPLE OF YEARS AFTER OUR START-UP, *National Review* outgrew its original quarters and moved two blocks south and one block east to a large eight-storey building in the more fashionable Murray Hill district. The landlord, a Mr. Scholem, was engaged in turning what had been an apartment building into a building for small commercial firms, which paid better than the tenants he had had in his badly rundown establishment. How Mr. Scholem got around Murray Hill zoning requirements we did not ask since the rent was cheap and he was anxious for NR's custom.

There was, as you came in from the street, a rather classy illuminated stained glass sign indicating that Gabrielle de France did business on the premises. Gabrielle herself had long since departed, but she didn't take her sign with her, and Mr. Scholem left it in place since it seemed to add a much-needed *je ne sais quoi* to the joint.

We moved into four of the old residential apartments. Each of our offices had an unusual appurtenance, an old-fashioned claw-foot bathtub, which Mr. Scholem had not bothered to remove when he renovated, and which on the editorial floor held extra toilet paper,

47

paper towels, a dysfunctional coffee machine, and various other odd-
ments, including seldom used cleaning materials.

The editorial department, which included the copy and production desks, various offices, and cubbyholes for writers and editorial
assistants, had three bright and sunny (but never very clean) offices
across the front of the building on the second floor. Jim Burnham and
I shared the corner office. The middle office, which housed the Suzanne La Follette Memorial Couch, was occupied first by the assistant
to Frank Meyer and later by Frank's successor, Chilton Williamson.
Slowly in the course of weeks, this office filled up with books sent in
by publishers for review. They were piled on the Memorial Couch,
on the windowsills, around the file cabinets, in every free space.
Hundreds more books arrived than could be reviewed and one of the
perks of the book editor was that he was permitted to dispose of the
surplus, through sales to the huge Strand second-hand bookstore,
and pocket the proceeds. The man from the Strand, a giant with a
reddish beard, would arrive about every six weeks with a trolley and
a handful of flattened cardboard boxes into which he would load the
books, and wheel them away. Pitiful were his protestations on those
days, which could not be counted on the fingers of one hand, when
the elevator did not work.

The third front office was occupied by Maureen and whatever
other editorial assistant we had at the moment, and it had a couple
of desks for the visiting editors who arrived every Tuesday to write
the final editorials. Helen Tremaine and the second editorial typist
occupied a small, dark office by the bathroom, overlooking a dingy
inner courtyard filled with debris. When Whittaker Chambers agreed
briefly to join the editorial writing team in New York, until his heart
condition made the trip impossible, he was given an office on the third
floor overlooking the same courtyard. He was startled and amused
one afternoon when a tenant, vacating an eighth floor apartment,
disposed of his old bedsprings by pitching them out the window.

We had a bookcase built in on the long corridor that led from my office to Maureen's and Helen's. It contained much of our reference materials: dictionaries, thesaurus, *Bartlett's*, complete Shakespeare, the Bible (KJV), the indispensable *Facts on File*, *World Alamanac*, *Who's Who*, and an accumulating army of red NR Bound Volumes. On several shelves under the bookcase were our newspaper files: *New York Times*, *Washington Post*, *Christian Science Monitor*, *Wall Street Journal*, *New York Daily News*, and *New York Post*.

In those early days, we had no research library, and the editorial floor was filled with writers asking, querulously, "Has anyone seen the February 8 *Times*? I can't write my editorial without it." If it was a cardinal sin to clip anything from the office copy of any newspaper, and it was, let it be known that we were a sinful lot. All this bickering came to an end with the arrival of the efficient Miss Agatha Schmidt who, within a matter of weeks, had put together such an efficient library that when they returned from the Tuesday editorial lunch, each editor found on his desk a folder with the relevant clippings for each editorial he had been assigned. Aggie was the daughter of Godfrey Schmidt, a New York lawyer who did much to bring together movement activists in New York through his Cocktails for Conservatives parties.

On the third floor, in the front of the building, directly above the editorial department, were the managerial offices: Bill Buckley occupied the large office right above my room. Bill's secretary Gertrude Vogt, the indispensable Jim McFadden, and Rose Flynn, the treasurer, were dispersed in various adjacent rooms, and Bill Rusher, the publisher, and his secretary—correction—secretaries, had a small suite across the mail hall.

The irreverent junior staff organized an office pool on how many secretaries Bill Rusher (known as WAR) would hire and fire in any given year. WAR, who was punctilious, meticulous to the extreme, in an office of unreconstructed individualists, took a deal of good-natured ribbing in those early, rather frantic days, when he tried to inject orderliness into an only too often chaotic operation. But when the going got tough, really tough, the junior editors would turn respectful and admit that they'd better bring in "the WAR department." Rusher could and did adjudicate disputes that might have gotten heated in other, less competent hands. There were seldom any ruffled feathers in any of the conferences WAR called to adjudicate disputes. But he did have trouble hanging on to his secretaries, with the exception of two or three—over the thirty-odd years he was publisher—who figured out what the job required, and adored him.

At first there was a great deal of scurrying up and down stairs on Tuesdays and Wednesdays as the writers, most of whom were on the second floor, attacked the editorials they had been assigned and rushed them to the third floor for Bill to edit. But this up-and-downsville only lasted a few weeks. Bill can be wonderfully practical. The situation could be solved, he figured, by a very simple household device which is, however, rare in business offices. Bill soon persuaded a reluctant Mr. Scholem to put in a dumbwaiter between his, Bill's, office and mine. This meant that the writers could bring their edits to my desk. I would ring a bell—it was a small turtle my sister Aloïse had brought me from Toledo, Spain, which could be rung by pressing either its head or its tail. Then I'd pull up the dumbwaiter. Bill would signal that he had received the consignment by ringing his bell, and when he had finished editing the pieces would put them in the little tray and run them down so energetically that they would clang to a stop in front of my desk. No bell needed on the return trip. I'd pick them up, and return them to the writer if they needed further work, but if not, I'd take them to the editorial typists who would retype them, fifty-two characters to the line. Back to my desk they'd come for copyediting and instructions to the printer (10/12 Textype, 20½ picas). I'd check out the count, add four lines to accommodate the editorial title, and put them in the editorial folder.

Later on Wednesday afternoon, Bill and I and a couple of editors would meet around the big table in Bill's office. "What's the line count?" Bill would ask. "782 lines," might be the reply. I would have subtracted from the total number of lines available for the "The Week" section—say, 832 lines—the space occupied by two cartoons, and Bill von Dreele's verse. We'd spread the material out over every possible surface and start picking those editorials that must run, and get a count. We'd subtract that from the total and then turn to the editorial paragraphs, those short one-paragraph edits, that became a *National Review* trademark. It was heart-breaking work because we routinely wrote about a third again as much material as we had space for. A young writer, just breaking in, might find that nothing he had written had made the cut. Despair. Frustration. Misery.

In addition, there was considerable competition among the young fry to write the most amusing, the sharpest, the spiffiest, the most smart-ass, if you will, paragraph of the week—the one Bill would pick to lead off the editorial section, or to end it with. Many were, we thought, amusing.

A few samples:

Foreign

- Mao-Tse-tung, proclaims a *New York Times* headline, still "turns a neat furrow," The better to plow us under, my dear.

- Having looked and looked and looked for the New Frontier, we finally spotted it last week when the negotiators foregathered in Geneva to seal the fate of Laos. It's 500 miles closer to us than the Old Frontier.

- Disarmament talks recessed at Geneva after seven months of fruitless negotiations. Disarmament months recessed in fruitless after seven talks of Geneva negotiations. Negotiations disarmed to talk less and seven fruits were recessed in Geneva. And everybody renewed his lease for January.

Domestic

- Most delightful caption of the week, under a photograph of Goldwater in the British news magazine *Time & Tide.* "'Senator Goldwater, his first name is not really 'Stop.'"

- The AMA has reported an outbreak of Spiro Angina among Democratic politicians. The ailment is a mild cardiac strain brought on by overuse of the lower metaphor, "only a heartbeat away."

Just plain silly

- Available at the Government Printing Office: pamphlet entitled "Tea Drinking in 18th Century America. Its Etiquette and Equipage." Will you have cream and sugar in your harbour?

- The American Academy of Dermatology and Syphilology has dropped the last two words of the title. Perhaps the members think skinicism is only sin deep.

And a particular favorite of mine after the Mt. St. Helens eruption in 1980

- I'm sorry I made an ash of myself. Lava, come back to me. Love. Helens.

This last was by that all-time master of the paragraph mode, be it political or smart-ass, Timothy J. Wheeler.

$\backsim$ 9 $\backsim$

Sailing

ANYONE WHO HAS EVER COME within Bill Buckley's orbit has, sooner or later, found himself aboard a sailboat, with one notable exception, the aforementioned WAR department. Bill Buckley and Bill Rusher were friends and close associates for over thirty years, and in all those thirty years Bill Rusher managed never to set a foot aboard any sailboat that Bill Buckley was skippering. He didn't like sailing, he said, and therefore he would not sail with anyone, let alone with Bill Buckley. The nearest thing to retribution for this singular failing that Bill Buckley could effect was to book a fancy dinner cruise ship for Rusher's farewell party when he retired as publisher of *National Review* in 1988, a sail around Manhattan. This at one fell stroke violated two of Rusher's most cherished taboos: (1) sailing and (2) crossing Sixth Avenue in a westerly direction.

But others were less strong-willed. As children, Bill's siblings—mostly those his age and younger—were pressed in the late 1930s into acting as crew on his seventeen-foot sailboat which, as a supporter of the America First movement, he called *Sweet Isolation*, in the summer Lakeville Lake regattas near our home in Connecticut.

As a sister, colleague, and buddy, I have sailed with Bill in the Caribbean, on Long Island Sound, up the New England coast (Newport, Nantucket, Hyannisport, Bar Harbor). We once sailed from Atlantic City, the night the Democrats nominated Lyndon Johnson and Hubert Humphrey in 1964, to Halifax, Nova Scotia, and the enchanting Canadian Bras d'Ors lakes. I've sailed with Bill on strings of islands in the Pacific, the Atlantic, and the Aegean.

Our last big sail together, a New Year's cruise to celebrate Bill's seventieth birthday in 1995, was so catastrophic that I will mention it only *en passant*. One afternoon, full of good cheer, we boarded at Antigua the sleek sixty-seven-foot yawl *Seabreeze*, which had just crossed the Atlantic with a crack three-man crew. Three days later, we abandoned ship—a ship that was now engineless, rudderless, and outboard-motorless, a pathetic crunkled-keel wreck of a vessel—in St. Maartens about eight tropical islands short of our original plan. It would be too painful to recount the hour-to-hour disasters that befell us, but they amounted to this:

Day One: Motor suffers terminal illness.

Day Two: Dinghy which we are towing flips over, and the outboard motor sinks full many fathoms deep.

Day Two-and-a-half: A kindly mariner pulling us into St. Maartens' harbor runs us over a coral reef where we stay, rock-crunch, rock-crunch, rock-crunch, for some hours.

Day Two-and-three-quarters: It takes twelve dinghys to get us off the reef. Our bottom is badly bruised. Autopsy report: The *Seabreeze* will have to be towed to its next port of call and undergo lengthy repairs before she can be chartered again.

Day (almost) Three: We insist on going ashore for a lovely, peaceful French meal on St. Maartens, where the wine is both good and plentiful. We return to the dock to find that the tide has gone out. The captain, in his whites, gives me a hand. I step way down—my legs are short—to the side of the dinghy he has borrowed. My foot slips and I plunge into the harbor bringing the captain with me. He is not altogether happy at going swimming with a septuagenarian. Later that evening, after we have dried off, we toast the New Year—by candle-light. The generator has gone on a sympathy strike. But the caviar and the champagne that Bill's wife, the provident Pat, has brought from New York are plentiful and bracing.

Day Four: We fly home five days ahead of schedule.

But most sails with Bill are great.

I. AEGEAN INTERLUDE

It has been a startling day. As we pull into the port of Linaria, on Skyros, we find a bus waiting for us, summoned by some genie. Our captain tells us to board it, and we do, headed we know not where. It twists and swaggers its way, king of the cowpath, up a narrow winding road to a headland at Tris Boukes, where the driver, who thinks he speaks English, points with pride at a monument that is passing strange: a statue of a naked Greek athlete of Homeric di-mensions, topped by the incongruously twentieth-century head of a British aesthete. Here, under the baking summer skies of Greece, overlooking a blue-green bay, "in some corner of a foreign field that is forever England," lies the English poet Rupert Brooke, killed by a fever contracted in the Dardanelles campaign in 1916. One suspects it was the Greek equivalent of the WPA that devised his grave.

Over dinner tonight, a splendid dinner of fresh-caught lobster (crayfish, really), Greek salad, fruit, cheese, and wine aboard the yacht *Sirocoi*, we discuss our plans for the days to come. There are ten of us in the group, sailing the Aegean for eleven days in two yachts: the

Sirocoi is chartered, a comfortable, broad-beamed motor sailor with a crew of four; the *Bushido*, a swift, sleek racing sloop, has been lent to us by Bill and Van Galbraith's friend, Taki.

The plan had been to tour the northern Sporades islands, historically less interesting and consequently less tourist-ridden than the better-known Dodecanese and Cyclades. We are having second thoughts. If we are to change our plans it must be now. The men take over happily, with weighty wagging of heads, and rumps, as they crouch over the chart table mapping alternative courses.

Finally, they have it. It will be a long sail, they tell us, but—they consult with the captain—the wind will be out of the southeast (or is it southwest?), which is good. This means to the men that the *Bushido* will fly like Icarus in the morning, and to the women that with a friendly wind behind them they won't be tossed about too badly in the often tempestuous Aegean waters. A couple of long sails—eight to ten hours—will bring us to the Dodecanese in two days.

And so it's off in the morning, on a southeasterly course for Psara. Life—even such life as there is on remote Aegean islands—has passed Psara by, and so do we after a brief overnight stay, to head for Fourni, an island the tourists have ignored and Fodor and the *Guide Bleu* have yet to discover. It is a delight.

Samos, 4,700 high, comes into view in the early afternoon, a grey haze, a rosy outline, a looming presence. We are close enough to pick out the spunky stone walls that march up over the hill and out of sight and crisscross the flanks of every island we pass, separating, to our untutored eyes, nothing from nothing, so rocky and barren is the terrain. We pick out an occasional lighthouse on a point, a blue-domed church on a crest. Then, outlined against the blue of the sky, we spot four crumbling windmills, their sails forever stilled, on the right arm of the harbor, with a fifth windmill on the left. We tack in toward the town, passing under a hillside church, stunningly, blazingly white in its frame of ochre-green hills.

The town is jiving. Our captain's wife rushes ashore to see if she can pick up lobster for dinner; the mate and the steward disappear into town and come back with fresh lettuce, delicious tender peaches and apricots, ripe red watermelons, cherries, and big perfect fresh tomatoes which we will have for lunch tomorrow, stuffed with rice and spiced ground meat.

Small boys climb from fishing boat to fishing boat, yelled at by fishermen who are trying to unload their catch, diving overboard in shrieking, laughing droves, only to climb back when the sailors aren't watching. The little girls take no part in such rough sport. They gather on the pier in clean pastel cotton dresses—and stare. A shepherd drives a herd of goats, their bells ringing clear above the portside clamor, into the town. They are diapered. Fourni is a clean town. Its broad stone-paved main street, with the ancient plane trees providing shade, is spotless. On the white-washed trunk of every other tree is tacked a small plastic trash basket.

Fourni is a fishing village, untouched by history, unspoiled; Patmos is a Christian shrine of great antiquity. Looming over it like a Crusader's castle is the immense Monastery of Hagian Yoannis Theologos, which houses, among other Byzantine treasures, the five-foot-long deed on parchment by which the Byzantine Emperor Alexander II gave Patmos to St. Christodoulas. The monastery is as grand as the sacred grotto of St. John the Evangelist is simple. Exiled to Patmos by the Emperor Domitian in 95 AD, the Beloved Apostle lived for a year or two in a rock chamber, a cave. The rock on which he rested his head at night is still there, outlined by silver paint, as is the shoulder-level outcropping of rock which his disciple Prochorus used as a desk to take down the sacred revelations St. John dictated to him, which we know as the Apocalypse: "I, John, saw another angel come up from the east holding the seal of the living God . . ."

Our visit is rushed. It is nearly 7 o'clock and the guide is anxious to lock up. In truth there isn't much to see—the stone pillow, the desk—

though much to ponder. Earlier in the day, someone had formed a Greek cross of gardenias on the desk. They are brown-rimmed and wilted now, slightly askew, but the aroma lingers, as does St. John's witness.

Mykonos is tourist heaven. A large, well-protected port, lined by waterside tavernas and shops. Its white-washed houses with their blue and green painted doors and window sills, carved wooden balconies, and flowers stretch back, away from the harbor; the streets are dotted with discotheques, craft shops, boutiques, jewelry stores, you name it, and always, churches, blue-domed, orange-domed, pink-domed. It is loud, brassy, a hippy haven, and still it should not be missed. What the gentlemen in our party did miss—the *Bushido* is generally an hour or so behind us—was the cocktail party on the motor yacht next to ours to which the men wore bathing trunks, which the French call *le minimum* and the women wore, on top, *le rien du tout.*

Delos, the Sacred Island. Poseidon caused it to be anchored in the sea to give shelter to Leto, fleeing from the wrath of Hera, that quintessential spurned wife. Here Leto gave birth, a year apart, to the twins Apollo and Artemis (that's mythology for you).

Once, forty thousand people lived on Delos. The Treasury of the Delian League was lodged here; pilgrims and merchants came from afar to worship and do business. Now there are fewer than two hundred people on the island, and most are connected in some way with the ruins: row upon row of broken columns, headless statues, marble and granite debris. We stand among the ruins, guidebooks in hand, bickering. We don't know where we are.

A heavy-set fellow comes to the door of a shack and asks if he can help. "Are you a guide?" we ask. No, a watchman. In poor, but adequate English, he tells us where we will find the extraordinary Naxian lions—guardians of the island, crude, powerful figures from the seventh century BC—and where the famed mosaics are located. We start out in three different directions. He sighs, slips his feet into laceless, cracked black pumps, and shows us everything—the lions; the forums of the ancient, classical, and Roman cities; the huge theater cradled in rock; the shops and houses of the rich merchants. Our watchman-guide's enthusiasm, faltering English notwithstanding, is infectious. It is he who tells us that in the Golden Age of Athens no executions were carried out until the Sacred Vessel had returned from its annual trip to Delos. Socrates waited for that return to drink the hemlock.

We climb aboard the *Sirocoi*, dripping with perspiration and thirsty. Our captain sails around the island to a quiet inlet. We swim and laze the long afternoon away and think of that day when the ships of King Mithridates landed on these same quiet beaches. By nightfall, twenty thousand Delians were dead.

We spend our last night in a sheltered cove in Pouros, just a couple of hours' sail from Piraeus, the port of Athens. The water we swim is aquamarine blue and speckled with reflected gold as the setting sun catches the quiet ripples.

What does one bring back from it all? Memories of long sails and bleak, stark, rocky islands; comradeship and laughter; a row of lions at Delos that have withstood the hot suns of 2,700 years; teasing small boys in Fourni harbor; and the lingering, heady smell of gardenias in a cave in Patmos.

II. DANKLY IN BORA BORA

God knows it's a good try. It's 4:00 AM at FAAA airport in Papeete, Tahiti. As my brother Bill and I, bone-weary from an eight-hour flight from Los Angeles, pass through passport control, a gentleman in a Harry Truman shirt, khaki shorts, and a wilted headband of white flowers places a bloom behind the ear of each arriving passenger. A three-piece string band strikes up in melancholy fashion. Welcome to Dorothy Lamourland. We find our bags on the carousel, including the spinnaker that Bill has felt we simply cannot do without on our projected final sail from Bora Bora back to Tahiti—we will never use it—and are greeted by a sprightly Marta from the tourist office, who flings leis around our necks and drives us to the Hotel Tahara'a, perched on a hillside overlooking Matavia Bay. That's where Captain Cook first dropped anchor in these waters more than two hundred years ago. We walk across an open-sided gallery to the elevator. The all-weather carpeting is wet. We take the elevator down to our rooms. In the Tahara'a, a splendid hotel run by splendid people, the reception area is at roof level, and each bedroom so placed that it looks out over the bay from its own terrace; from your room you see no other. But it rains hard that night and we don't breakfast on the terrace. It's swamped.

Next morning I find Bill engaged in conversation with the manager, a genial young Australian, who explains that a depression has formed in the east, or wherever it is the prevailing winds come from, and has remained obdurately in place for ten days. Disappointing news. But Marta is here to take us on a morning's tour of Tahiti, the largest island of the three clusters that make up French Polynesia, so we hurry on.

Marta takes us first to Point Venus where in April 1769 James Cook and his astronomers charted the transit of Venus, one of the major goals of this, his first great voyage of discovery. A tall white lighthouse stands on the point and behind it the monument to the discoverers: Cook, who arrived in Tahiti a year after his countryman, Samuel Wallis, and a year before the French admiral, Louis Bougainville, after whom the flower is named.

Tahiti is marvelously fertile, the trees pregnant with great bunches of fruits: mangos, bananas, avocados, the breadfruit that Captain Bligh hoped to take back to the Caribbean on the HMS *Bounty*, and everywhere coconuts, great plantations of coconut trees.

Tahiti is shaped like a pingpong paddle with the head of the paddle, which includes Papeete, joined by a narrow isthmus to the smaller, rounded handle. Each part is formed from a volcanic cone, the larger of which rises over seven thousand feet above sea level, but all the living is done on the coastal plain. Heavy waterfalls cascade down its green flanks on this western coastal stretch of the island. Here the fresh water pouring into the sea prevents coral reefs from forming, and consequently the Pacific roars in unbroken to the delight of surfers, of whom at the moment there are few. You see, it's drizzling. We pass the isthmus and a couple of miles farther on come upon the Gauguin Museum situated in a lovely tropical garden just about as far from the capital as you can get. The museum is a delight, laid out in a series of small thatched-roofed buildings with displays that tell much about Gauguin's life and work and travels, but it lacks one thing: a painting by Gauguin. Tahiti can't afford one.

We fly off to Bora Bora that afternoon where the yacht *Sealestial*, on which Bill sailed the Atlantic several years ago, awaits us. On board are Christopher Little, the photographer who made the Atlantic crossing with Bill, and his wife Betsey. They arrived five days ago and have yet to see the sun. That may be why they are so very happy to see us. It is they who inform us that this is the rainy season in the South Pacific, something no one had thought to tell us and we had not thought to ask about before embarking at Christmastide on a seven-thousand-mile flight from New York.

Bora Bora, we are told, is untouched and beautiful—one of the loveliest islands in the world—but we will have to take the guidebook's word for it; the windshield wiper on the car we rented for our tour of the island works only when turned by hand. We see very little between the gusting sheets of water. But at the yacht club there is a touch of romance: small palm-thatched house boats for rent. Pick a spot in the lagoon, and your house boat is towed out and anchored there. Maid and room service are provided by launch.

Captain Cook called these islands—there are eleven of them stretching over 180 miles from Bora Bora to Tahiti—the Society

Islands, because they are so closely clustered in the vast expanses of the South Seas. The French call them *les îles sous le vent*. Some are of volcanic origin, with soaring peaks and waterfalls, the others are atolls, islands formed from coral reefs. We will sail from Bora Bora on a southeasterly course toward Tahiti, passing by or stopping in Tahaa, Raiatea, Huahine, and Moorea.

We sail through the pass in the reef that surrounds Bora Bora in mid-afternoon accompanied by a pair of frisky dolphins that skim and slide along our bow. On the far side of the reef the waters are dark, a cobalt blue as you look down into them, but a black-gray at any distance. In no time at all we are cruising through another pass and into the aqua-emerald lagoon that Tahaa shares with Raiatea. The crystalline waters foam milky white as they hit the reef. Tahaa is your dream of a Polynesian island. We cruise along its shores noting the *pandanu*-roofed huts—that's the native word for the pale thatching we have seen everywhere—tiny marinas, a road that runs a few miles along the shore and peters out. Keith, our British captain, decides to moor here for the night and sends Martin, the mate, and Christopher forward to watch for coral heads. The depthometer tells us we have fifty-five feet of water under the hull but nonetheless we scrape a coral head.

Captain Fred Boehme's *Cruising Guide to French-Polynesia*, without which Keith and Bill agree no one should ever attempt to cruise these islands, urges mariners to drop the hook by 3:30 PM, when it is still light enough for the lookout on the bow to spot the sudden color changes in the water that mean coral-danger. Boehme's book, however, while indispensable, is also unprocurable: it is not to be found in the hotels, tourist shops, marinas, bookstores, or yacht clubs. To procure a copy you must first find Boehme himself—as Keith was lucky enough to do a fortnight ago. Boehme lives aboard a yacht and his yacht happened on that particular day to be in Papeete.

We drop anchor a few minutes and two rain squalls later. Chris, Betsey, and Martin take the zodiac to do a little snorkling and to take pictures. Chris, a well-known photographer, is very conscious of his editor back in frigid New York eagerly awaiting his return with twenty rolls of tantalizing photographs of sunny, sunny Polynesia, its beautiful *vahines* (babes), handsome bronze fishermen, and waving palms. (No problem with the waving palms.) But Expedition Snorkel returns in very short order routed by a combination of no-see-ums, a local biting mite, and see-um-plenty-good mosquitoes. In the distance we watch black clouds forming and breaking over Bora Bora's soaring Mount Faia, but the weather clears by dinnertime, and we sup on deck.

New Year's Eve turns out not to be the best day in the year to visit Huanine, "and its village on stilts in the waters of Maeve Lake." This, and much else on Huanine, we don't see. One car rental office is closed, the second has no car. The island's taxi is at the airport. So we take a walk, and it is very pleasant, not one drop of rain. A gaggle of four- and five-year-olds, two of them in the altogether, are leaping off a low wall into the water, laughing, giggling, splashing each other. We pick up a couple of loaves of French bread for Caroline, *Sealestial*'s wonderful cook, and suntan oil (some people never say die).

The next morning we set out on the longest leg of our trip, an eighty-five-mile sail from Huanine to Moorea. We are beating into the wind under motor, but the seas are calm and the sun shines intermittently. Still, it is half past dusk when we sight the ragged cone of the volcano that signals Moorea ahead, and nearly 9:00 PM when we slide into Cook's Bay—probably the most beautiful bay I have ever seen, a completely sheltered half-moon of a harbor rimmed right and left by green-topped volcanic craters, with clusters of *pandura*-thatched huts here and there, waving palms, and no disfiguring modern touches.

The next day is our final day, our final leg, the twenty-mile passage from Moorea to Tahiti. We are motoring along, with the wind on the nose (as usual—Remember that tropical depression? Well, it still hasn't moved), the helmsman in his sou'wester against the frequent rail squalls, when Caroline notices a red light on the instrument panel, never a good sign. The gents are galvanized. Martin and Keith disappear into the engine room. Bill cuts the engine and changes course to get some wind in the sails. And pretty soon we are spinning along at eight, nine, sometimes, ten knots. The skies clear. This is the sail we've been waiting for. Keith reports back that the seacock that lets the water in to cool the engine is clogged—probably with seaweed. In due course, he and Martin emerge from the engine room hot but no longer bothered. They have rigged another line to bring in the cooling waters. We could now point back into the wind and set a direct course for Papeete. But we are so enjoying our sail that we hold on the tack for another hour or so and then tack again, and eventually sail into Papeete where, for the moment, it has rained itself out. Obviously, it is time to go home.

✑ 10 ✑

The Young Fry

THEY'VE COME AND GONE OVER THE YEARS, dozens and dozens
of them. Some stay for a summer, some for a year or two: NR's
editorial assistants. They open the editorial mail and answer
much of it. They give incoming manuscripts a first reading, sort
them out, and send them on their way, either back to the author or
up the editorial chain of command. (One article, with the contemp-
tuous comment, "utaly rediculas"—a hilarious piece on "Rioting as
an Olympic Sport"—we published.) They field phone calls, answer
requests, deal with the cranks. (The gentleman known as "The Whisperer"—he whispers because men from outer space are monitoring
his conversations—was solemnly instructed by a desperate young
assistant after the twenty-second call to carry aluminum foil at all
times in order to jam the Martian listening devices. We never heard
from The Whisperer again.) They console aspiring young writers
whose work has been rejected, tell Mrs. Cadwallader firmly—the
Mrs. Cadwalladers take firm handling—that much as they'd like to
oblige, they are not empowered to produce Bill Buckley for Jennifer's
junior high school graduation picnic, June 2 next. They learn—in very

short order—how to deal with CCs (Constant Correspondents) and CMSS (cancel my subscriptions).

They mark up copy for the printer (heads, type faces, size of type, width of column), learn the rudiments of proofreading and copyediting, enlist enthusiastically under the banner of the pro-hyphen and anti-hyphen factions among the editors, familiarize themselves with the basics of editorial production and paste-up. They take turns going to the plant in Connecticut on closing day to handle last-minute production and editorial chores. They do their share of the writing for the editorial section of the magazine. They brighten the lives of the senior staff, inform the editor-in-chief—"Peerless Leader," as he is irreverently called—why everyone is talking about Hank Aaron this season and what The Who are. They are a delight and, very occasionally, a despair. One of them, Shermayne Billingsley—yes, you guessed it, the daughter of Sherman Billingsley of Stork Club fame—will marry another of them, our beloved Tim Wheeler, forty-two years later.

Occasionally even their parents get into the act. When Jim Burnham walks in to our office one Tuesday morning from Kent I'm on the phone with a worried mother. Seeing that I am busy, he waves his hello.

"No," I'm saying, "you really have nothing to worry about, Mrs. Ritchie. Dan will be perfectly safe. We are in a very safe part of Manhattan and there's a police station halfway down the block." I listen for a moment, and ask: "Where will he be staying? Upper East Side? In the high 70's? No problem." I listen some more. "Actually the subways are safe, but Dan won't have to use them. He can take either the 2nd or the Lexington Avenue buses, or probably hoof it." Eventually I hang up.

"What was that all about?" Jim is curious. I laugh. "A nervous mother," I say. "Young Dan Ritchie, who has just turned seventeen, will be our editorial assistant this summer. He's never been in New

York, and his mother, hearing all those stories about violence in our fair city, is worried. I have been reassuring her."

At supper that night—Bill and Jim and I cut out at about 7:30 and go to our favorite small French restaurant, Le Moal—and over drinks Jim recounts the one-sided conversation, as he overheard it, to Bill. "Bill, you and I think we are putting out a magazine but what we actually have is Miss Buckley's finishing school for young ladies and gentleman of conservative persuasion."

We all laugh, and I add in an extra two bits.

"On top of everything else," I said, "Mrs. Ritchie is worried because poor Dan won't be able to practice his piano. He'll be staying with friends whose apartment is so cramped they don't have one."

In due course young Ritchie arrives, a serious, blonde boy with freckles and a round open face on which honesty and decency are written large. He is overwhelmed at being at *National Review* and is stunned at the editorial conference the day after his arrival when, as we are breaking up, Bill says:

"Dan, could I see you for a moment?"

The rest of us troop out. Bill welcomes Dan and tells him he has heard that Dan is a pianist. Dan mumbles that he's not much good, and can't believe it when Bill gives him a key to his apartment and invites him to drop in after work any day and practice on his Bössendorfer. (Mrs. Ritchie was the only parent of a summer editorial assistant ever to write me a thank-you note at summer's end. I thought it charming.)

A lot has been written about the men who were the heart and soul of *National Review* in its initial formative years—Bill Buckley and Bill Rusher, James Burnham and Frank Meyer, Willmoore Kendall and Brent Bozell—but very little of the youngsters who passed through NR's portals at the start of their careers. We hired one or two editorial assistants, usually college sophomores or juniors, every summer. After the first year or so we would hire one and occasionally two college graduates who worked at NR for a year or two before moving on. Some remained journalists, others became lawyers, bankers, PR men, ministers, stockbrokers, engineers. Some in turn became famous, notably Paul Gigot of the *Wall Street Journal*; David Brooks, late of *The Weekly Standard* and now of the *New York Times*; Mona Charen, the syndicated columnist; Arlene Croce, for many years ballet critic of the *New Yorker*; Ross Mackenzie, who followed James Jackson Kilpatrick as editorial page editor of the *Richmond News-Leader*; Tony Dolan, who won a Pulitzer Prize in journalism and went on to become Ronald Reagan's chief speechwriter.

But the others also made their mark—even if sometimes negatively—and kept us, the older editors, young and on our toes. It was Andy Gollan who instructed us in street talk, who first enlightened us that the fuzz were the police, and that we were honkies. Unfortunately, he wasn't around when we designed a cover that read, "The Jig is Up for Adam Clayton Powell Jr.," to tell us that "jig" had a racist pejorative meaning. So help us we didn't know it, but no one really believed our protestations.

Poor Craig Chawkins, with his unruly head of hair, had not a single editorial talent, but there was a distinctive flair there—deep down there somewhere—that we were simply not able to tap. But you'll have to agree there was a touch of the mad genius about Craig's prose. When asked to write a report to the editors on the incoming mail—what our readers liked, what they hated, what made them mad—Craig once produced the following:

My fellow Americans. We have received even more letters on the "Israel Overkill?" editorial than on the Ayn Rand thing. Stacks of them. Boxes of them. Roomsfull. Houses aplenty with an Island of letters. A nation-full. A world of words and a galaxy of outrage. Not one, no siree—not ONE (not even one-half) has been laudatory. On the other hand, WFB's column on "Isreal Should Be Responsible" has received a most hearty and welcome response from some of the same people who were appalled by the editorial. Listen, dollink, I wouldn't even bother to quote from them because, well, does it make any difference, Sylvia? In the end we are all gonna die.

Poor Kenneth Shorey was the victim of a *huge* failure in communications. He arrived from Canada one morning and announced that he was our new theater critic. Hum! Who the hell was he? I didn't have a clue, nor did Gertrude Vogt, the all-knowing. When the story was unscrambled it turned out that Russell Kirk had told Bill Buckley that young Shorey was the most brilliant theatrical critic of our generation. We must pick him up before anyone else realized his potential, Russell insisted. Bill, who was just about to emplane for Switzerland, where he spent six weeks every year during which he wrote a book, phoned Ken, hired him sight unseen, and boarded his plane to Geneva singing a happy tune.

What Bill omitted was to inform Frank Meyer, who ran not only the book section but also the "Arts & Manners" section. He never even gave a thought to the fact that Frank might already have commissioned a number of theatrical reviews for the upcoming Broadway season. The airwaves between Woodstock and Gstaad were blue for a couple of days as Frank berated Bill and Bill apologized abjectly, but there in the office on East 35th Street was Kenneth, in person. It was we, Jim Burnham and I, who had to find him a desk and things to do. Ken, it turned out, was a better than competent but less than brilliant theater critic, and, alas, a lousy writer of editorials. There's a knack to editorial writing, some have it, others simply don't. Eventually, Russell Kirk came to the rescue and hired young Shorey as his personal assistant. Thereafter, Russell's fortnightly column, "From the Academy," would arrive from Mecosta, Michigan, neatly typed by Ken, the covering note invariably signed: "Your Obedient Servant's obedient servant, Kenneth Shorey." Nice fellow.

One young fry—let's call him George—a graduate of a posh Eastern prep school and a sophomore at a posh Ivy League college, came into my office indignantly of a Wednesday morning. "The typists refuse to type my copy," he says throwing two scribbled over sheets of yellow manila bond on my desk. I explained, kindly, that we reserve the typists for the copy that Bill has already edited, to be typed for the press to the correct line length. (In all my years as managing editor I never was able to persuade anyone—not even Jim Burnham—to type their editorials fifty-two characters to the line.) I pointed out to George that both Jim Burnham and Jeff Hart write out their work in longhand and then type it up before showing it to Bill, and told him to do the same.

"But you don't understand," he said. "I don't type."

"George," I said, somewhat less kindly, "you have eyes to see keys with, and fingers to peck with. You are now a typist."

And for the rest of the summer, for the good of his soul, George spent the first hour and a half each morning in the typing pool, honing his "seek and ye shall find" version of typing.

When my niece Priscilla, my brother Jim's daughter, graduated from Williams, she got a job at *Vogue*, but she flunked her typing test. She could come to work, they told her, just as soon as she passed it, so for three or four weeks she came to *National Review* every morning and, under the care of Evelyne Kanter—our irascible, but not so to Priscilla, French secretary—got her typing up to speed and went on to a distinguished career in freelance journalism.

David Condit was a large, booming young man without a single inhibition, a joy to have around because you always knew where you stood with David. On the day that Bill found he had two extra tickets for an impossible-to-get Beatles concert, he called down to me and asked if there was anyone in the editorial department who would like them. David was the only youngster around, and when I offered them to him, the sonic boom he emitted could have been heard all the way to Madison Square Garden where the Beatles were rehearsing.

When David graduated from college he went to England for a couple of years to study at Cambridge and was elected president of the Cambridge Union, a singular distinction. The Union president customarily provided the subject of the final debate of the year, and David's was "Resolved: That to be born an American is to be a winner in God's lottery." Against all odds, the Affirmative won.

Angkor Wat

I AM NOW LIVING in a spacious two-bedroom apartment on Sutton Place with a splendid view of the East River. It's a tripartite affair. Mother spends three weeks in New York in December in the interval between closing the house in Sharon, Connecticut, after the Thanksgiving weekend, and taking the train to Camden, South Carolina, where she spends the winter. In the spring, she reverses the procedure, spending another three weeks in New York before moving back to Great Elm for the summer. She sleeps in the other bed in my room.

My brother Jim and his wife Ann occupy the back bedroom. Jim, a lawyer, is working for Catawba, the family oil company, and spends very little time in New York. A while back he was investigating oil leases in Libya, Greece, and Israel, but in the last year or so he has become point man for Catawba in the Philippines. Between trips he stays in the apartment at 60 Sutton Place South.

One night, over supper at Billy's steakhouse, a neighborhood landmark, Jim and I discover that we are both fascinated by what we have read of the ruins of Angkor Wat, in Cambodia, and have a burning desire to visit them. The next day we consult our calendars and come up with a plan.

Jim and Ann and mother, if they can persuade her to join them, will fly to the Philippines in late January 1962 where Jim has about a week's business. I'll fly to Taiwan and visit my old United Press boss, Arnold Dibble, and his wife Louise, and we will rendezvous in Bangkok early in February and proceed to Cambodia. Cambodia was at the time a sleepy, backwoods little country where very little happened. I had covered the end of the French war in Indochina while working for United Press in France and had dubbed Geneviève de Gallard Terraube, the French nurse who had been stranded in Dien Bien Phu, the "angel of Dien Bien Phu." America's active involvement in the Vietnamese civil war that would spill over into Cambodia was still a couple of years ahead.

And so, a couple of months later, I found myself at the Air France counter in Bangkok.

"*En principe*," said the young lady behind the desk, "it is not possible to go to Angkor Wat from here." And she explained that there has been a temporary closing of the Thai-Cambodian border over a disputed temple. This particular temple—one of thousands—is important enough to the Cambodians to take retaliatory steps against Thailand, which has seized it. The major result is to discommode tourists who are not allowed to fly into Cambodia from Thailand, although they may arrive from anywhere else in the world.

Was I crushed? No. Anyone who has lived in France quickly learns that *en principe* nothing is possible. It's all part of an intricate game, the rules of which you learn only through playing it.

It was during my years in France, 1953-1956, that I had first succumbed to the lure of Angkor Wat. Our news editor at United Press in Paris, Ken Miller, liked to sit well above his typewriter, the better to plunge into it when pounding out the night lead on the French Indochina war that we, in the Paris bureau, monitored. To achieve the proper elevation, Ken sat on three thick volumes, *Jane's Fighting Ships*, *Who's Who in America, 1937*, and a lush and marvelously illustrated 1910 stroll through Indochina by a French colonial with an eye for beauty, a gift for description, and a full-blown orotund prose style. My friend Nick King and I had gotten in the habit of consulting the old guidebook for details of the terrain the French and Vietminh were fighting over to lend verisimilitude to our front-line stories, but also, in part, because removing the guide from Ken's posterior had become an office joke.

The guide devoted nearly thirty pages of excited prose to the discovery of the lost cities (thoms) and temples (wats) of the Khmer Empire by the French botanist Henri Mouhot in 1860, and their subsequent reclamation from the jungle. Mouhot was to write later that coming upon the ruins of Angkor in the Cambodian jungle was to be "transported from barbarism to civilization, from profound darkness to light."

The capital city of Angkor (great) Thom was abandoned in the mid-fifteenth century—just about the time the Ottoman Arabs over-ran Constantinople—after having suffered several sieges and sacks by invading Thais, themselves under pressure from Mongol hordes moving in from the north. A Khmer king, so wrote our colonial spinner of tales, had moved his court south from Angkor Thom to Phnom Penh (the present capital) after the sack of 1434, and with the departure of the court, the elaborate grid of canals, lakes, irrigation ditches, and rivers that had made the land around Angkor a fertile rice and fruit bowl, started to silt up.

Over the years the peasants too moved away and the jungle took over, swallowing the temples, uprooting the statues, intertwining its tough vines with the elaborate railings of the seven-headed Nagas (serpents) that guarded the esplanades that led to the pyramidal temples. As the physical evidence of the Khmer Empire was engulfed, so did the memory of its history fade.

"*En principe*," continued the Air France representative, "you should fly from Bangkok to Saigon, then in Saigon book passage back to Phnom Penh."

"That won't do," I said, with unaccustomed firmness. And that was when it developed that the Bangkok-Saigon flight did put down in Phnom Penh. If we didn't mind being somewhat out of order, the Air France representative said, we might, upon arrival in Phnom Penh make ourselves inconspicuous and not reboard the flight when it was called. Cambodian customs people, she told us, were notoriously inefficient and probably would not notice. She would arrange to have an Air France representative contact us and put us on the twenty-minute flight to Siem Reap (we would have to carry only such luggage as we could take aboard the plane with us). Air France even agreed to book two double rooms at the Grand Hotel Siem Reap, the only French hotel in the sleepy village whose major industry was the preservation and digging out of the ruins.

It all went off as planned until we arrived at the Grand Hotel where *monsieur le patron* told us kindly, but firmly, that no rooms had been booked in our names. He had two rooms but was holding them for passengers on a later flight. However, he said, given the quality of Air France booking agents these days, the later passengers might well not arrive, and he suggested we stick around.

Were there other accommodations in town? I asked, my French having catapulted me into the role of tour director. He mentioned another, smaller, non-French-run hotel and obligingly reserved two rooms for us there. How good a hotel was it? He shrugged. "*Potable, madame, potable,*" which word when applied to water means it is drinkable, but when applied to wine and the other good things of life means it ain't necessarily so.

Two hours later the manager informed us that the rooms were ours. We would, he told rather than asked us, be demi-pension, *of course*. And we were escorted upstairs to large, airy, high-ceilinged rooms: cool tile floors, big brass beds, lazy ceiling fans, bathroom fixtures circa 1920s, but the water ran hot, and you could lose yourself in the bath towel.

Downstairs for an aperitif and the no-choice *menu maison*: a bottle of ice-cold Meursault, followed by quail on fried toast thinly spread with paté, salad, cheese, and for those still strong enough, an apricot tart. Coffee was served in the sparsely furnished grand lounge.

Revivified Jim, Ann, and I took a short taxi ride to Angkor Wat. Mother had a bad cold and thought she would sit this one out. The air that February evening was balmy, a light breeze, a clear sky, and a half moon just making its appearance. Our first sight of Angkor was of the soaring central tower and its four flanking softly rounded pyramids as we walked toward them along the broad esplanade that carries you over half a mile of moat to the temple proper. A hundred yards or so in front of the temple proper two dozen folding chairs had been set up in neat rows. We surrendered our tickets and took our seats. A floodlight illuminated the terrace and a Khmer Corps de Ballet came dancing on. The girls might have danced off the friezes of the temples—they were only slightly less stylized, slightly more flexible than the bands of Asparas (heavenly dancers) frozen for hundred of years in the stone of Khmer monuments. (An Aspara, writes Angkor scholar Malcolm MacDonald, "is a heavenly figure with no parents, born in the flying spray of ocean waves.") The music was mournful and repetitive, the finer nuances lost to our untutored ears. The slow, sinuous movements and the play of light against the massive backdrop of Angkor accentuated both the temporary—the dancing girls—and the permanent—this gargantuan sandstone edifice erected about the time Notre Dame and Chartres were being built. The dances went on and on, and presently we slipped away.

On the advice of the *patron* we hired a guide for our three-day stay. He would save us time, said the *patron*, and he did. But much of the history of the ancient Khmer Empire itself we acquired from material we had brought along, from our own observations, from later reading, and from our old friend the colonial chronicler of Indochinese tales. Our young guide, affable, courteous, and energetic, had at the tip of his tongue the height of every tower, the length and width of the moats, and the names and dates of what must be the most unpronounceable of dynasts: Jayavarman, Yasuvarman, Suryavarman, Udahadityavarman, and more. But if we asked him a question for which he hadn't been prepared—why was Angkor Thom deserted, for instance, or what happened to the people who had lived there?—he was stumped.

Still, he showed us marvelous things, wondrous to behold, breathtaking. Angkor Wat with its moat a mile long on each side; its huge grass-green enclosures, its platforms, libraries, galleries, staircases, and towers, towers so tall that if you stood too close to them and looked straight up, the sight was dizzying. And over all of this tremendous edifice—possibly the largest religious structure ever built—exquisite carvings: of battle scenes and Indian and Shintu legends, of demons and evil spirits, and of dancing girls, monkeys, lions, and serpents, in bas- and high-relief. Some are barely discernible where wind and sun have taken their toll, other parts, in the shade of protective galleries, as sharp as from the sculptor's knife. This alone would be worth a trip half way around the world, but Angkor Wat is only one of the hundreds of temples the Khmer left behind. Like Mayan ruins, also lost in a sea of vegetation, many have yet to be excavated, perhaps even discovered.

It's not much of a trip from Angkor Wat to Angkor Thom, the remains of the capital city of the Khmer that once covered an area, we are told, greater than that of ancient Rome. The entrance gateways over the five causeways that crossed the moat surrounding Angkor Thom were at one time high enough to permit the passage of elephants. Today these have disappeared, but not the long balustrades of Naga serpents, held in the arms of giants and demons along either side of the causeway. Here you mount the Royal Terrace with its bas-reliefs of elephants, lions, and other birds and beasts, and come to the Terrace of the Leper King. Along its walls are carvings of the princes and princesses of the royal houses of ancient Cambodia—a royal rogue's gallery—and, sitting apart, a statue of the "Leper King." Our guide tells us that this pitted figure, with its enigmatic smile ("*le visage un peu triste*") is, it is now believed, neither a leper nor a king, but that's all he knows. The carving is cruder, rougher, but somehow more appealing than the stiffly royal figures that surround it in this the greatest architectural achievement of the greatest of the Khmer kings, Jayavarman VII (1181-1220), the city of Angkor Thom.

At its heart stands the Bayan, a temple both enchanting and preposterous. Here Jayavarman's megalomania took over. The Bayan hasn't one or two or five towers, it has fifty, and on every side of each of the fifty there is carved a large Buddha-like face, each and every one in the image of Jayavarman VII.

En route back to the hotel we stop by an elephant standing by a tall stepladder. If we wish to see Bakheng, our guide suggests we use this method of locomotion, the temple being situated halfway up a steep hill overlooking Angkor Wat. Mother bails out, but Jim, Ann, and I clump up the ladder and take our places on the howdah. We ramble two or three hundred yards past Angkor Wat, turn left into the jungle following a narrow, one-car-at-best dirt track. Within minutes we are engulfed in foliage.

At Bakheng, which is in truth a rather simple temple, its carvings badly eroded, but with a magnificent view of the nearer ruins and of West Baray Lake in the distance, we get off—on the second storey. This is the appropriate landing place for elephant promenaders.

On our final day, our guide produces a Land Rover to take us to the temple of Banteai Srei, some twenty miles from Angkor Wat, passing through fields and widely spaced native villages, many with thatched-roof houses on stilts, the men and women working half naked in the fields, protected from the sun by airy, wide-brimmed straw hats. It's a bone-crunching, rib-jarring, fascinating drive but we are happy to reach our destination, which is something else again.

Banteai Srei is a tiny temple, three-quarter size. No soaring terraces and pyramids here, it is built on a single level of a very soft rose-grey sandstone. Where the other temples are bleached ochre-white by day and gold in the evening, this temple stands out musky-rose. The carving is exquisite and different, more imaginative, lighter, often playful, the color of the stone itself softening the lines. The doors do not soar above you. No elephant could enter here; a man on a donkey might not clear them. Our guide points out the legends of Vishnu recaptured in light and graceful bas-relief. How and when this was built, we ask, and why is it so different? He does not know.

Later, we learn that Banteai Srei was one of the earliest temples erected by the Khmers, in the tenth century, marking the culmination of an earlier generation of builders. It was from Banteai Srei that later architects and sculptors took their departure.

We picnic from a box lunch put up by the hotel—a necessary precaution. We are the only tourists on the scene. There are no gates to this temple, no admission tickets to be bought, no postcards, no cold drink kiosks, no custodians. Today Banteai Srei is ours.

En route home the Land Rover stops at the small-scale temple and sanctuary of Banteai Kdei, a minor gem meticulously restored. We spend only a few minutes here, however, and understand why when we pull up again a couple of miles down the road at another temple of about the same dimensions which, like Banteai Kdei, was built by Jayavarman VII. It is Ta Promh.

Here the undergrowth has been cut back so that you can walk through it and certain minimal structural repairs made to halt further erosion of the buildings. But nothing else. Ta Promh is today pretty much the way it was when Henri Mouhot arrived on the scene, left this way so that visitors can more readily understand the immensity of the job that faced French archaeologists when they set about the restoration of Angkor. The light flickers through the canopy of encompassing trees in speckles of yellow and green. It is like walking into a green twilight, a cool towering, swaying—and very noisy—cathedral of vegetation. Monkeys chatter in the branches above and bright-feathered parrots and parakeets dart down and around, screeching. We're thirty feet from the road and deep in a tropical jungle. A huge tree grows out of the entrance gateway, its roots lunging down either side of the gate in search of the sustaining soil. Demons and lions stand a dilapidated guard over broken sections of the Naga balustrade. Thick vines—thick as an elephant's trunk—squeeze huge chunks of masonry off kilter, tilting them at impossible angles where they remain, held improbably in place against the forces of gravity by a scaffolding of vines. You find yourself speaking in whispers as you climb about. The friezes, the dancing Aspara, the musing Buddhas are hard to make out in the freckled light that slithers through the green arch above. Ta Promh is like one of those fascinating Catherwood etchings of the overgrown Mayan ruins he and John Stephens discovered in their travels in the Yucatan in the 1830s. That Ta Promh has managed to survive eight hundred years of wind, rain, jungle, and neglect is a tribute to the architects who designed it and the workmen who built it.

In the 1970s a new brand of Khmers, Pol Pot's Khmer Rouge, supported by the North Vietnamese, overran Siem Reap and the Angkor ruins. Five years later, on April 17, 1975, darkness fell over all of Cambodia. It was rumored that the Khmer Rouge, in their mad lust to destroy every vestige of previous civilizations in Cambodia, had dynamited Angkor Wat. That did not happen. But in the ensuing years, segments of temple friezes, heads of Aspara, busts of Buddahs and guardian demons, lions, and monkeys, turned up in antiquarian shops in Bangkok and other Asian cities. They could only have come from Angkor.

In April 1981, the new North Vietnamese-controlled government of Khmer permitted Christian Hoche, a reporter for *L'Express*, to visit a very few of the temples under military escort. The world awaited his report, breathlessly. He found tremendous damage, whole friezes hacked off walls and removed. One tower of the Bayan had toppled to the ground, the heads of many of the statues holding up the balustrades at the entrance of Angkor Thom had disappeared. Ten years earlier, nine hundred trained men worked at the Angkor ruins under French direction. By 1981 only five of them were known to be alive. The painstaking records of eighty years of clearing, reconstruction, dike-building, and restoration—blueprints, charts, files, water control systems, irrigation plans, work schedules—all had been wantonly destroyed.

On the Royal Terrace, the Leper King sits, smiling sadly, his neck half sawn through. Was the thief frightened off, or did he discover halfway through the beheading that the original statue was one of the few that had been removed for safekeeping before death and isolation fell over modern Khmer? No one knows.

A Study in Contrasts

N O TWO MEMBERS of the *National Review* staff could have been more different than Daniel P. Oliver and John S. Coyne, who arrived within months of each other in the very late 1960s. Dan Oliver, a classmate of young Jim Burnham, was a junior member of a well-known New England family, had just graduated from law school, and was reluctant to go directly to work with the family law firm. He was a great fan of *National Review* and thought a year or two working for the magazine, where he could hone his writing skills, would be useful in his future career and, in the meanwhile, great fun. He applied for a job at a time when Bill Buckley was piling on himself one chore after another, writing a syndicated column three times a week, originating his TV talk show, *Firing Line*, lecturing on college campuses all over the country, appearing on network TV, writing numerous articles and book reviews, plus, of course, editing *National Review*. He needed a right-hand man to handle much of the detail work, so Danny signed on as a combination associate editor and personal assistant to Bill.

The combination worked out beautifully for all concerned. Dan was slim, very good looking, blond, and always well turned out. He would catch a commuter train early every morning in Greenwich where he lived with his wife, Louise, and growing family, neatly shaved and wearing a dark business suit with a button-down shirt, conservative tie, and highly polished shoes. The only thing that distinguished him from the usual early morning commuter was that in addition to a briefcase he invariably carried a dark green laundry bag slung over his shoulder. This was Daniel P. Oliver's personal Grand Central Emergency Kit.

In those days, the Grand Central commuting line was in a state of high disrepair, its cars dirty and badly ventilated, and its schedule a shambles, but it would not catch Mr. Daniel P. Oliver short. He was prepared for any and every contingency. His Emergency Kit held: (1) a three-legged folding stool lest there be no seats for the fifty-minute (with great good luck) ride from Grand Central Station to Greenwich; (2) a miner's helmet with a light to read by should the power go off in a stalled train; (3) a minimum of four hours' worth of reading material; (4) an 8-ounce can of whiskey sour mix; (5) a can opener to open it with, and (6) a straw through which to sip it.

Dan was spit and polish. John Coyne, on the other hand, was a rough and ready sort of chap. He was a few years older than Dan and had been a friend and drinking companion of Jack Kerouac, the beatnik author of *On the Road*, while an undergraduate at Columbia. A bohemian at heart, John had moved west to finish his graduate studies at Berkeley, where he very soon had his fill of both the flower children and the lefty rowdies who were turning Berkeley into a dope-filled people's republik. Outraged, he wrote a stunning article on the Berkeley scene, "Crime on the Campus," and sent it to *National Review* over the transom some time in 1968. It was just what we were looking for, filled with good solid reporting and a sparse but devastating writing style, punchy with no excess verbiage. It was ideal for us since we were (correctly) perceived to be too New York-East Coast oriented. We urged John to do a follow-up piece a few months later, and some time in the following year John either applied for a job at *National Review* or Bill sought him out, I don't remember which. At any rate, he drove East with his wife and several children arriving in the outskirts of New York smack in the middle of the devastating St. Valentine's day blizzard of 1969.

It took the Coynes a couple of days to dig out from the motel in which they had found shelter during the storm, so we were not surprised when John reported for work that first day wearing his old Marine Corps boots, green fatigue pants, an oversized grey sweatshirt, and a genial, lopsided grin. This, however, turned out to be John Coyne's go-to-work uniform. But NR was an informal organization, and it didn't much matter what one wore to work.

John proved to be a great addition to the staff. When you asked him to do something he didn't tell you how difficult it would be, or that he was engaged in another project, or that it wasn't the kind of thing he did, he would simply say, OK, sure, and the next thing you knew it would be done and on your desk. His first article as a staff writer was titled (deliciously): "Is John Lindsay Ungovernable?" He was a stylistic writer and a first-rate reporter.

A couple of NR alumni were at this point working as senior editors for Neil McCaffrey's brand new conservative publishing company, Arlington House, and one of them, David Franke, or it might have been Tim Wheeler, asked John to write a book about the Berkeley scene. John wrote a devastating critique of Berkeley called *The Kumquat Statement*. A few weeks after its publication he was delighted to receive a fan letter from Vice President Spiro Agnew not only in praise of the book but also demonstrating a familiarity with John's work in *National Review*. It was very flattering for a young author.

It was probably six or eight months later that Bill Rusher and NR's advertising department staged one of their occasional lunches at Bill

Buckley's Park Avenue duplex for prominent businessmen who might be persuaded to advertise in *National Review*. Bill always insisted on inviting someone prominent in the conservative movement to give a short talk at the luncheon in order to make the whole operation seem less crassly commercial. The guest of honor on this occasion would be Spiro Agnew, then a rising star within the conservative community.

But there was a hitch. The very morning of the luncheon, Agnew's office called Bill Rusher and said the vice president would very much like to have John Coyne participate in the affair. He was looking forward particularly to meeting him while at Bill's. Bill Rusher came down to the second floor where the editorial staff hung out, and gasped in dismay when he caught sight of John in his usual attire. That would never do. Then he caught sight of Dan Oliver in his usual attire. Dan and John were about the same size, both slender and medium tall. The WAR department swept them both upstairs to his office and they emerged transformed, John looking stiffly proper in Dan's navy pin-stripped suit, button-down shirt, dark school tie, and polished brogans. But the sight that convulsed us all was Dapper Dan Oliver looking distinctly uncomfortable in John Coyne's messy fatigues. It was a sight to be savored, and savor it we did, vocally.

It turned out to be a momentous day for the magazine. Agnew was so taken with John Coyne that he offered him a job on his speech-writing team, and within the month John Coyne was gone to Washington, leaving a great big hole in our office life. But he didn't forget his pals on East 35th Street. A year or so later when Agnew was forced to resign as vice president, his resignation speech was scheduled for a Thursday morning of magazine week. John, remembering that the printer's messenger left NR's office at 5:30 Wednesday night with the final batch of editorial copy for the plant, sneaked out to a pay phone that afternoon and dictated Agnew's resignation statement to me so that we could include it in the issue that was just then going to press. The one stipulation he made, for John is an honorable man, was that NR's production editor carry the editorial we wrote on the resignation to the plant Thursday morning rather than putting it in the bag with the regular copy on Wednesday. This would ensure that it would be set in type at about the time Agnew spoke, so there would be no advance leak of its contents in the press.

In the aftermath of the Agnew-Nixon debacle, John Coyne claimed a record of sorts. In the course of one eighteen-month period he served as speechwriter for two presidents and two vice presidents of the United States: Vice President Spiro Agnew, President Richard Nixon, Vice President Gerald Ford, and President Gerald Ford.

John Coyne and I had, and have, a little joke. Whenever it fell to him to inform the readers about the contents of a given issue in which I had written a piece, he would identify me as "the nation's prettiest managing editor." I would then amend it to read, "the prettiest managing editor on East 35th Street," which seemed relatively safe since there probably was no other managing editor on East 35th Street. Last Christmas the card I got from John, thirty-five years later, wanted to know whether I was still the nation's prettiest managing editor.

Dan Oliver served a couple of years in the family law firm but found the work unsatisfying. He put in another year or so at NR, this time as executive editor, and then moved on to other jobs, all within the growing conservative mainstream. He never lost his appetite for politics, and served a term as chairman of the Federal Trade Commission in the Reagan administration.

~ 13 ~

The Seine

I'VE BEEN YEARNING TO VISIT FRANCE AGAIN. It has been too long, and here it is late spring and I have only taken two weeks of my allotted six weeks vacation. But what shall it be: a motor trip? A stay in Paris? Or something new for my sister Jane and me? We have heard that a French cruise line, anxious to move in on the burgeoning hotel barge business, has put into service two river boats that cruise the Rhone and Saone rivers in Burgundy and the Seine from Paris to Honfleur, the picturesque Normandy port. I'd frequently visited, and grown to love, Normandy while working for United Press in Paris a few years back. So we made inquiries and booked passage on the *M/S Normandie.*

It was a blistering hot June evening when Jane and I boarded the *Normandie* at the Quai de Grenelle in Paris, just west of the Eiffel Tower. The *Normandie* is a spic-and-span white two-decker, with fifty small but comfortable double cabins, each with its own bathroom. The public rooms include a large, tastefully decorated and comfortable lounge, a good-sized, dining room and an upper sundeck, half covered, half open, with a roof that slides down to permit the *Normandie* to squeeze under the low bridges of Paris and its delighted passengers to view the City of Light lit up on the opening evening's cruise past the Ile St. Louis and the Ile de la Cité.

We spent the first lazy morning of the six-day sail from Paris to Honfleur, watching the river traffic along the Seine—mostly working barges, *péniches* they are called. We are moving along at about nine knots and tie up not too far from Monet's home, at the town of Vernon. After dinner, on a walk through its ancient streets, we are drawn to the Flamboyant Gothic Eglise de Nôtre Dame by a choir singing. We enter the church just behind the high altar on which sits, jauntily, a shiny black motorcycle helmet. The choir, a motley group in civvies, stands under a bright light above the altar. The choirmaster brings out the best they have, which is very good indeed, and clips off the last note with precision. We listen to a second offering, the Gloria, then slip out unnoticed, uplifted.

By 9:30 next morning, a small group of us is let into Claude Monet's Japanese garden at Giverny ahead of the morning crowd of tourists. We saunter through the gardens and lily ponds, over the Japanese bridge, explore small paths, and generally luxuriate in the rich smells and sights and sounds of a scene any one who loves Monet's painting knows so well. A cuckoo obligingly coo-coos for us.

We walk up through a far more conventional French garden to the Clos Normand, Monet's spacious manor-house home, explore the house and the bright and roomy studio he built at the end of the yard to accommodate his final huge paintings of the water lilies.

When Richard the Lion-Heart built the huge Chateau Gaillard on a promontory above the Seine near les Andelys, he vowed that he could defend it "if its walls were made of butter." After his death Philippe Auguste took it (by guile) and a couple of centuries later Henry IV had its battlements dismantled. But even in ruins it is formidable, dominating a long stretch of the Seine as it winds and twists below. The day is misty and the landscape beyond the castle looks for all the world like an Impressionist painting.

After a ride through the Fôret de Lyons, the hunting grounds of the dukes of Normandy, and a walk around Lyons-la-Fôret's well-preserved half-timbered houses and covered market, we come to the Château Vascoeul, the kind of attraction you will certainly miss unless taken by hand, as we are, and shown it.

Vascoeul is a delight. Its owner, whose name never appears on the brochure, restored the small château but himself lives in a thatched-roof home he built on its grounds. The château, when we were there, housed an extraordinary exhibition by a master of trompe l'oeil, Jacques Poirier. One painting, the life of Helen of Troy, is provided by the artist with a brief history of the lady's complicated life and adventures, concluding that when she returned to Greece after the fall of Troy she was "*très âgée.*"

Throughout the manicured gardens and around a swift flowing stream and a beautiful dovecote, Mr. Nameless has scattered manic sculptures to make one chortle with delight: sculptures, among others, by Braque, Dali, and Leger. It is here that the rains that will dog us from now on first appear.

From Les Andelys to Rouen the scenery is lovely. Double rows of tall poplars outline country roads and lanes. The river twists and turns and doubles nearly back on itself. Small villages hug the hillsides, each with its church and steeple encased in green meadows and, it being Normandy, in apple orchards. A couple of turns later and we come upon a steep escarpment of rock on our left, its ragged peaks like the ghosts of ancient turrets. From time to time we glimpse an occasional stone château, sitting back from the river, almost hidden from view by its encompassing woods and protective iron grill gates. The sun is fighting to break through low, grey clouds, but it is a losing battle. As we approach the river port of Rouen the water turns lighter and clearer. The tidal flow, we are told, can be felt this far inland.

What is new and exciting (to us at least) in Rouen is l'Eglise St. Jeanne D'Arc. In the market square where Joan went to the stake in 1431, an exciting modern church has risen over the old market, the inspired vision of the architect Louis Arretche. The interior vault resembles the hull of a ship. The twisted roof-line reaches up toward the sky like an eager flame, reminding us of the manner of Joan's death. Inside, at eye level as you descend polished stone steps toward the altar, are preserved the sixteenth-century windows from St. Vincent's Church, destroyed during the Normandy landings: the light pouring in speckles the church in ruby and sapphire splinters, larded with vibrant yellows and greens.

The rains have now turned into what would, back home, be called a Nor'easter. And when we return the next afternoon to Caudebec-en-Caux after a moist visit to the ruined Benedictine monastery of Jumièges, we are told that waves are ten feet high at Honfleur and the *Normandie* will have to stay here at Caudebec.

And so it is by taxi and bus that we visit what is called the Peace Museum, near Caen, but which is in fact a museum about the Normandy landings: impressively reported with films and slides, one of which shows on one side of a huge screen the allied preparations, and the D-Day operation, while on the other it shows German forces building and manning their defensive positions. We could have spent hours there, but Bayeux—and Queen Mathilda's tapestry—calls. The tapestry—well preserved and imaginatively displayed—tells the story (from the victor's, the Norman, viewpoint) of Harold of England's broken oath and William the Bastard's consequent invasion of England, culminating in Harold's death at Hastings in 1066, an arrow through his eye. This set in motion events that will result in the burning at the stake in Rouen of a teenage French peasant girl 365 years later.

It is blowing hard. Sheets of rain get under umbrellas, down necklines. Our feet are drenched. But the little streets of this fishing village made famous by its own beauty and the works of the very early Impressionists, Boudin and his disciples, are charming, and the art galleries worth far more time to explore than we have. We duck into the simple fisherman's church near the market place, enticed by a full-throated organ. A bride and groom are plighting their troth on this vigil of the great Feast of Corpus Christi. We pause to light a candle in memory of missing friends, and hurry back to the *Normandie* and our farewell dinner.

⌒ 14 ⌒

Spring of 1968

THE SPRING OF 1968 was tragic for the nation, but it was also traumatic for this particular managing editor. March 31 was a Sunday, a beautiful sunny early spring day, so I had an early supper with Jane and her children in Sharon and didn't get back to my apartment in New York until well after ten. I took a quick bath, poured myself a glass of milk and turned on the TV to catch the 11 o'clock national news. Lyndon Johnson was droning on about something or another—I wasn't paying much attention—when he cleared his throat, started afresh, and announced that he would not be running for reelection in November.

A hemi-demi-semi-quaver of a second later the phone rang. It was Jim McFadden.

"Pitts. What are we going to do?"

Good question. What we had on the cover for the issue that would start rolling off the presses on the midnight shift on Thursday was a rather fanciful political analysis of discreet recent conversations that were said to have taken place between LBJ and Claude Kirk, the maverick Republican governor of Florida about whom we at *National Review* and a great many other good folk were worried. Our cover read:

The Plot Between Claude Kirk
and Lyndon Johnson
to Steal the Election

What to do, what to do?

Jim and I arranged to meet at the office at 8:00 the following morning. He would call Art Director Jimmy O'Bryan and get him in as well. Bill was off on a speaking tour, and Jim Burnham, who would run this week's editorial meeting, was still at his home in Kent, Connecticut. One thing was perfectly clear. We needed a new cover and a new cover story, but this was only Sunday so we had some wiggle room.

What we did have in house was a sound reportorial piece by Phil McCombs on the very recent Poor People's March on Washington. Phil, a former NR editorial assistant was now working as a reporter for the *Washington Post*. It had come in the previous Friday and it was scheduled as the cover story for the following issue. Jimmy O'Bryan devised an impressive black and white cover using a poster from the march. The only color on the cover was the blue border and the yellow streamer that appeared on every issue. We sent the new cover to the plant by special messenger, pulled the Claude Kirk-LBJ piece, and put Phil's article in its place.

Then, three days later, on Thursday morning while Production Editor Dorothy Rea and Copy Editor Pat Carr were at the plant putting the final editorial pages to bed, Martin Luther King Jr. was assassinated in Memphis.

What to do now? After a brief consultation with Jim Burnham, now back at his home in Kent, we splashed a new title in white letters over the poster picture of the masses of black marchers: "The End of Martin Luther King: The Beginning of What?" We phoned the plant and instructed Pat to kill the last two pages of editorials. We would substitute for them, at the beginning of the editorial section, an editorial on Martin Luther King that Jim Burnham was busily writing in Kent to go with our new cover title. He would dictate it, as soon as written, to Pat. It was a close call, too close for comfort, yet a far greater editorial trauma lay just ahead.

A month later, after a very pleasant dinner with Jim Burnham at our favorite Chinese restaurant, Uncle Thai's, on a go-to-press Tuesday evening, I walked home and flipped on the TV to check on the California Democratic primary. It revealed a jubilant Bobby Kennedy. He had pulled it off, won the California primary and was headed for probable nomination for the presidency. Then came the terrible shots, the stumble and fall, the blissful crowd stunned into silence. It couldn't be happening, not to another Kennedy! The nation tuned in, mesmerized by the ongoing tragedy, the horror, the waste.

The phone rang. It was Jim McFadden. It rang again. It was Burnham. Bill was again away, this time sailing somewhere in the Aegean and unreachable by us, although he called in most days. Another phone call, this one from James Jackson Kilpatrick, offering to fly in from Washington in the morning to help out. "Do come, Kilpo," I said. "We're in big trouble."

Our cover story, timed to appear the week of the Democratic primary in California featured a ten-page profile of Robert F. Kennedy by Kilpatrick, a slashing attack on the former attorney general and present U. S. senator, a skillful, a wonderfully achieved piece of political mayhem. The magazine's cover, over 100,000 copies of which had by now been printed, depicted Kennedy as a coiled cobra, ready to strike, venom dripping from his fangs.

We were all in the office by 7:30 the following morning, Jim McFadden, Jim O'Bryan, Jim Burnham, and I. Kilpo would arrive on the 9:00 AM shuttle from Washington. Burnham took charge.

"We can't run the piece if he dies. We can't run the piece if we still don't know whether the wound is mortal. We can't run the piece if he has been brain damaged. He was hit in the head." We all nodded in agreement.

"In short, it's dead. The piece is dead."

"Any ideas, Priscilla?"

I'd been pondering the question all night. We had to fill ten pages, we had to write the editorials that would fill out the seven page "The Week" section. And not unimportant so far as I was concerned was that I still had my own "For the Record" column to write.

I threw out a few suggestions, and we came up with a final plan. We would add three pages to the regular editorial section and Kilpo would write a running editorial on the events of the past night and an obituary recounting the story of Robert Kennedy's achievements in his tragically foreshortened life. By this time we knew that he was dead. We had in hand a splendid article by Arlene Croce who had covered the just concluded trial of the Harrisburg Nine for us. That would be our cover story with a stark simple black headline: "Meanwhile, in a Boston Courtroom. . . ." We also had, in house, a two-page article Jeff Hart had written some weeks earlier on the growing violence in America resulting both from the anti-Vietnam demonstrations and Black Panther agitation. We retitled it, "Violence in America, Before it Happened" and ran that in the streamer. Between them, these additions—the Kilpo obit, Arlene's and Jeff's pieces—sopped up nine of the ten pages that had to be replaced, and we slipped in a one-page column by Erik von Kuehnelt-Leddihn to fill it out.

I got Pat Carr, the copy editor, to read every line of copy that we had sent to the plant in the two weeks prior to today's deadline to see if there were any invidious mentions of Bobby. One turned up in the caption to a cartoon that we had inserted in Russell Kirk's "From the Academy," page which had run a few lines short. Not one of us could remember what the cartoon was about, it had gone to the plant a week earlier, but we instructed the printer to pull it and substituted another of exactly the same size.

At about 3:30, the phone rang. It was Bill from a Greek island, on a lousy connection that flickered in and out.

"Pitts, what can you do?"

I told him, briefly, that Kilpo had come in and had written the most beautiful obituary, but I said I had to hang up because I was just too busy to talk to him now. I suggested he call back after six when the printer's messenger had picked up our final copy.

I had copy-read the new material, and now I had to write my own piece. I hadn't wanted to do it before Kilpo finished his so that I wouldn't duplicate any of the material he was using. This was when my early training at United Press in New York and on the Paris desk came in handy. At UP, where there was a deadline every minute, speed was prized, and speed was what I needed now.

If we failed to get our copy into the messenger's hands tonight, the presses at Wilson and Lee would not be belching out 100,000 or more copies of *National Review* Thursday night on the overnight shift. Those machines were reserved for NR at those hours, and if we missed the deadline then we would have to stand in line behind the other magazines Wilson and Lee printed and might get into the mail two or three days late.

We made it, we just made it, and over the go-to-press drink that Wednesday afternoon we congratulated ourselves that we had missed nothing.

But, alas, we had. What none of us had thought about was the promotional card that was bound into each magazine. On the upper right-hand corner of the card was a tiny picture of the original cover—the one of a tousled-haired Bobby Kennedy, as a coiled cobra ready to strike.

❦ 15 ❦

Fun & Games

O N THE DOOR between Bill's office and Gertrude Vogt's was
pinned a large black-and-white photograph, its edges curl-
ing as the years progressed. At the center of the picture was
a small donkey with a sign around the neck indicating his name was
ADA (for Americans for Democratic Action). Standing to his right
were Suzanne La Follette, Bill, and me, and to his left, Jim Burnham
and Willmoore Kendall. The year was 1960, shortly after the Ken-
nedy-Nixon presidential elections, and the occasion was the awarding
of a booby prize.

We had run a contest to spot our truly sophisticated readers
that spring and summer, inviting their estimates on how the major
candidates would do in the primaries, and finally, in the Electoral
College. Since the contest required a number of entries over several
months we had announced that we would have not one, but *ten big
prizes*, the winner to be announced in a late November issue. What
filled us with unholy joy when the designated youngest editorial assistant finally came up with the results was that the contestant who
placed just out of the winner's circle, at number 11, was that prestigious

scholar and stalwart liberal Harvard professor Arthur Schlesinger Jr., soon to become a member of the victorious Kennedy brain trust. We hadn't known until this point that Professor Schlesinger was a subscriber to *National Review*, but for him to come in just short was too good to be true.

What, oh what, to get him as a prize. And that was when someone—probably Bill Rickenbacker—suggested that a live donkey, representing both the party of his choice, and his position in the contest, would be most appropriate. And so the smallest donkey we could find was bought, smuggled into the building at 150 East 35th Street when Mr. Scholem, the landlord, wasn't looking, and brought into Bill's office on a Wednesday afternoon when that particular issue went to bed. What a wonderful NR photo op! After we had toasted ADA, we dispatched him to Cambridge, where sad to say, his reception was cool.

Professor Schlesinger was not amused, and poor ADA came back by return mail. He presented less of a problem than one might have imagined because my brother Jim, who had several small children, had recently built a house on a farm the family owned near Sharon, which was equipped with barns and suitable pastures. There ADA ended up, to the great enjoyment of Peter, Jay, and little Priscilla Buckley.

The billboard in Bill's office over the years became the repository of salacious events in NR's history. There Bill would post infuriated letters from readers, particularly insulting newspaper comments on NR and its editors, a stray Committee to Save Katanga newspaper ad, plus numerous editorial paragraphs by Bill Rickenbacker which even in our most irresponsible moods we didn't dare publish. (Bill Rickenbacker was a blithe spirit who worked for *National Review* off and on for nearly thirty years. He was hired after he sent Bill Buckley a copy of a nineteen-page letter to the editor of the magazine *Modern Age*, commenting on one of its issues. Bill figured that any one with that much time on his hands might be most useful to *National Review*, and a deal was struck. Rickenbacker was the adopted son of the World War I ace, Captain Eddie Rickenbacker, and was immensely talented. He spoke a number of languages, was a first-rate pianist, a par golfer, an Air Force pilot who had fought in the Korean War, a perfectly splendid writer, and a great provider of merriment wherever he was, whatever he was doing.)

Also on the door was an ancient and tattered Shirley Temple fan someone had found at a tag sale. The fan was pinned to the door by a button for "The National Committee to Horsewhip Drew Pearson," a committee we created after Drew Pearson wrote something ugly about Shirley. Our Drew Pearson buttons were particularly popular with our readers and we sold hundreds of them before his death forced a cancellation of the campaign. We announced this in the magazine in an obituary which read: "The National Committee to Horsewhip Drew Pearson is dissolved, its subject having become the responsibility of a higher authority."

It was around the table in Bill's office, at the Wednesday evening cocktail hour, that we occasionally got into mischief. On this particular evening Bill Rusher had left early to pack since he was departing the following day for a lengthy trip to the Far East. We were expatiating on the orderliness of Bill Rusher's world when Bill Rickenbacker came up with a brilliant idea—RRR, he called it—for the Rearrangement of Rusher's Rooom.

Rusher, you have to understand, was everything that everyone else at NR was not, the epitome of order, of tidiness, of organization, of structure, and it got on our nerves. The only thing unstructured about the WAR department was his inability to hang on to a secretary, although at this particular moment he was the happy employer of Miss Ann Turner, an attractive and, needless to say, efficient young Brit whom we all adored. (Prior to hiring Ann, Bill had once told me that when looking for a secretary he felt "a little like the Roman impresario who calls a talent scout and tells him, 'One of my Christians just died. Do you know anyone who would like a big night in the Colosseum—one night only!'")

RRR was a splendid idea, we all thought, and we trooped into Rusher's office. The idea was to change everything in it, but just a little bit. We reversed the order of his stacked magazines so that January 1 was on top, and September 12 at the bottom. Bill Rickenbacker himself rethreaded Rusher's desk calendar so that when he would return on September 28 and turn the page, September 27 would come up, followed by September 26. The pile of manila folders that lived at the left of his desk was left there, but the order of the folders changed. Every picture on the wall was moved a notch to the right. The master stroke—this was the inspiration of Chris Simonds—was that the buzzer that summoned the people Rusher dealt with most frequently (Associate Publisher Jim McFadden, Treasurer Rose Flynn, and Ann Turner) to his office was tampered with, rearranged so that when Rusher rang for Mac, Rose would appear, and when he rang for Rose, Ann Turner would come in.

RRR proved more successful than in our wildest dreams. Unknown to us, Bill Rusher had arranged to have his apartment painted in his absence and his cleaning woman had promised to come in after the painters left and put everything back in order for his return. But something had gone wrong, so a tired Bill Rusher, after the long flight home from Taiwan, unlocked the door of his apartment to find a scene of desolation: most of it was under dust sheets. He gave a cry of dismay, dropped his bag, and rushed to the security of his office, where not only was everything out of whack, but we had persuaded Ann Turner at the last moment to leave a note on his desk: "Dear Mr. Rusher. I find I am a Democrat so I must resign. Sincerely, Ann Turner." Mortally wounded, the WAR department staggered out to the street, hailed a taxi, and ordered the driver to take him to the University Club, from which he phoned Ann Turner and told her to call him as soon as every single thing in his office had been restored to order, and not before.

Ann did her best, but she overlooked one small detail. On one wall Bill Rusher had hung a framed cartoon by John Kreuttner about the Senate subcommittee on subversive activities hearings, depicting a woman with hat pulled down low over her forehead, greatcoat buttoned to the collar, and arms hugging her sides, only her two furtive eyes visible. The caption read: "I am Amelia Thwarp, and I have nothing to conceal." We had persuaded a delighted John Kreuttner to replace this with the picture of a rosy-cheeked damsel, her arms outstretched in a gesture of welcome, whose caption read: "I am Amelia Thwarp, and I have everything to disclose." Amelia Thwarp missed Ann's sweep and hung on Bill's wall for a number of months to our secret delight. By the time this was discovered NR's publisher had regained his sunny good humor and he laughed along with the rest of us.

Rusher's rapid turnover of secretaries proved a treasure trove to the conservative community since it was universally agreed that anyone who had worked for Bill Rusher, however briefly, must be a crackerjack performer. Ann Turner left *National Review* to become secretary to Brent Bozell in Washington, where he and my sister Patricia were putting out a conservative Catholic magazine, *Triumph*, which they founded to counter the malign effects on Catholics of *Commonweal* and *America*, the left-leaning Catholic journals of the day. Liz Doyle quit Bill Rusher just in time to join my brother Jim's successful Senate campaign in 1970, and she ran his New York office during his six years in the Senate.

Mary Lynch, who lasted only a brief six weeks with the WAR department, did us the biggest favor of all. She called one spring to recommend to us her brother Kevin who had just graduated from college. Kevin arrived, was hired on the spot, and was, and is, a dreamboat. He worked like a top-of-the line very quiet vacuum cleaner. What Kevin gobbled up quietly and efficiently were jobs that were being handled haphazardly, or not at all. Within weeks of his arrival he had relieved the overburdened Mabel Wood of production chores for the fortnightly *National Review Bulletin*, an eight page newsletter that we published on alternate weeks. Soon he was operating as managing editor of the *Bulletin*, relieving me of dealings with recalcitrant and often dilatory columnists. Kevin was quiet, never made waves, and saw everything. He would alert me to awkward situations that were developing and help handle them. He was bright and witty, kind, soft-spoken, and efficient. He became articles editor and managed our most difficult contributors with both tact and firmness. Aleksandr Solzhenitsyn's wife, who handled all her husband's business arrangements, would deal with no one at NR but Kevin.

He was a joy to have around, and he stuck around for a good many years before he was made an offer by Voice of America that he simply couldn't refuse. It meant he could move his wife, Josephine Gallagher Lynch, Jim McFadden's longtime girl Friday, and their three small children from a cramped Riverdale apartment to a house in Arlington, Virginia, with a yard that would in due course include a bouncing Labrador puppy. Both Kevin and Jo were sorely missed.

Jokes beget jokes. It was at another of the Wednesday evening drink sessions that the Swiss edition of *National Review* was born. Bill Buckley had departed a fortnight earlier for his annual six weeks in Switzerland to write that year's book, *Four Reforms*. We missed the precision he demonstrated in editing our copy, and, in discussing his particular editorial likes and dislikes, my sister Carol, who was our editorial assistant that year, suggested that it would be fun to produce an entire page of editorial paragraphs, each carefully crafted to contain some element that would make Bill, the editor, curl up inside: a grammatical error, a stylistic aberration, too many exclamation points, a vulgarism, an overworked cliché, an inept foreign reference, a tinge of kookery, a mention of himself. What a splendid idea.

Elsie Meyer, who was now working at NR as copy editor following Frank's death, turned out a paragraph, one of the best, that managed to include three exclamation points !!! and the felicitous phrase, "before Britain, France and the U.S. saw the oil painting on the wall, as it were." There were mentions of Justice William O. Douglas's "motorized old ticker," of John-John's pondering that his uncle never "seemed to have swim trunks when he needed them." "*Quod licet Joves, non licent boves, as Bill Buckley likes to say*," was the final sentence of a paragraph about Bill ("let it grow") Proxmire. (Proxmire had recently undergone a hair transplant.) The bogus paragraphs, which were chosen from entries by every member of the editorial staff by the judges (Bill Rickenbacker, Elsie Meyer, and me), a montage of awfulness, were pasted into two copies of the issue of March 15, 1974, by Jimmy O'Bryan, and dispatched to Switzerland. It arrived there after I did on my annual vacation in Gstaad.

Back in New York the staff was on tenterhooks. What would be Peerless Leader's reaction—would he be taken in for even a moment? Or were our examples too crass to be believable? The reaction was: Nothing. Bill, it seems, had broken his Swiss vacation to tape various segments of *Firing Line*, his weekly TV show, in a number of African capitals. So it took his memo on the Swiss edition two weeks to reach New York. Frances Bronson, Bill's secretary, called me in a state of shock. Better brace yourself, she told me, a memorandum had come in from Bill like nothing she had ever seen. It was addressed to me and to Jim Burnham, who edited the editorial section in Bill's absence, but had not been informed of the Swiss edition substitution of editorial paragraphs lest he veto the idea.

It was a *cri de coeur.* "I was terribly distressed on reading the editorial paragraphs in the March 15 issue," Bill wrote:

> The paragraphs, or a lot of them, are truly appalling. . . . How coarse to refer to Proxmire's operation. The concluding sentence is a rhetorical disaster. . . . Why on earth make fun of Douglas's artificial heart?. . . . I have implored every one at NR not to use a Buckley joke or make a Buckley reference. . . . Is there a joke that escapes me in changing the nouns from dative to nominative?. . . . I wish I could destroy every copy of this issue. To bring Chappaquiddick into a comment on John's little boy excitement over a prize fight would I should think be blue-penciled in *American Opinion* [the John Birch magazine]. . . . How is one supposed to know his name not having been mentioned earlier, who is Yurii Arkadyevich Shikhanovich?. . . . And why, oh why "CFR-er David Rockefeller"? In a stroke we abolish the distinctions we have always made between us and the Dan Smoots [a right-wing demagogue] of this world. . . . The seizure of coyness in this section is quite impossible to understand . . .the parenthetical remark is on a level of "Governor Malcolm Wilson (no relative to Harold!)," and makes me weep. . . .Why the exclamation point? By the way, the cumulative count on this page is now 5. . . . "the oil painting on the wall, as it were!" Oh no. . . . Henry makes it 6. . . . I am very sad. We should see on those weeks when two of the senior editors are away [in this case WFB and PLB] if other arrangements can be made, like having the paragraphs completed by noon Tuesday, or, judging from this batch, noon Sunday.

We had succeeded beyond all expectations, but we were not altogether pleased with ourselves. The hurt had been too deep even though Bill was assured that he, and only he, had seen those particular paragraphs. But Bill himself was not above organizing a massive deception: *National Review*'s very own Pentagon Papers.

Richard Nixon didn't know it at the time, but his world started to unravel that day in 1971 when Daniel Ellsberg gave Neil Sheehan of the *New York Times* the Pentagon Papers, and the *Times* and *Washington Post* decided to publish them. Unwilling at any time to be outdone by the *New York Times*, *National Review* came up with its very own Pentagon Papers, *ex nihilo*, as the editor told a thoroughly outraged press corps a week or so later, after NR's phony papers had made front page news in America and been sent out over the air waves by Voice of America in "Armenian, Burmese, Korean, Lao, Portuguese, Russian, Spanish, Ukrainian, and Vietnamese."*

The day the story broke, WFB was in British Columbia, WAR in London, Jeff Hart in Austria, and James Burnham wandering about Rhode Island. Unable to reach any NR spokesman—I was hiding under my desk—the press checked with the VIPs mentioned as authors of NR's Papers. NR's phony papers had been so thoroughly crafted that Secretary of State Dean Rusk said he was not sure that he had written a particular note but that "it was quite possible that I did." Frank Trager and Douglas Pike couldn't deny they had penned a memorandum attributed to them, although Trager didn't specifically remember writing it. Young Jim Burnham, who had recently been discharged after two years in naval intelligence, had provided NR with information on how naval intelligence was transmitted, which tended to authenticate those documents. It fooled almost every expert except one coony former U.S. ambassador, who phoned NR, delighted by the prank, to ask what we would like him to say when the press got to him.

Harry Elmlark, Bill's irascible, lovable, and frequently puzzled syndicate agent, got through to me. I assured him that *National Review* had violated no security laws in that we had made up every single word of Our Pentagon Papers. "It's a hoax," I told him. "Harry, it's a

---

* *Washington Post*, July 24, 1971.

joke—j-o-k-e." There was silence at the other end of the phone, then a prolonged sputter. "Well, I don't think it's very funny to get every single editor in America mad at you. Now, Priscilla, admit it. That's not very funny." Nor did Bill Rusher, who arrived back from London that very day, think it funny. He was (1) horrified at the thought that his irresponsible colleagues might have committed treason in his absence by publishing classified government documents, and (2) far from mollified when he found that they had not.

Sometimes the joke was on us.

"Notes & Asides," November 17, 1975 carried the following notice: "The editors of *National Review* are bringing to New York to deliver a special lecture composed for the occasion [NR's 20th Anniversary], Professor Michael Oakeshott of the London School of Economics. He is, roughly speaking, the most eloquent man in the world. Don't—whatever you do—miss this one [Oakeshott's Hunter College lecture]. In the years to come, it would be as sinful as having missed a public lecture by Thoreau or Emerson."

Well, not quite.

The senior editors had been suitably impressed when Bill reported that he had actually secured the services of the brilliant philosopher of political history as a highlight to our twentieth anniversary festivities. Not only would Professor Oakeshott speak briefly at the anniversary dinner but he would write a special piece which we would publish in the following issue of the magazine, and he would read it that afternoon at a Hunter College auditorium. Several hundred of our readers would have come from far places for the celebration, and the Oakeshott lecture would make the trip even more worthwhile.

A panel of the senior editors would sit on the platform while Oakeshott spoke and be his interlocutors at a brief question-and-answer session to follow the talk.

The great day came. Michael Oakeshott walked out on the platform and was introduced by Bill to great applause. He placed his article, a rather massive document, it seemed to me, on the lectern and started the lecture. After first greeting the audience with a gentle smile, Professor Oakeshott never again looked up at them, but stolidly read on, and on. His British accent presented some difficulty, as did his speaking style, which could be described as low mumble. In addition, the acoustics in the auditorium were not particularly good. Nevertheless, after a few minutes the ear sorted out the difficulties in hearing what he was saying.

The problem that filled me, as I sat on the platform, with growing apprehension, wasn't that I didn't hear his words, it was that I didn't understand a thing he was saying. How, oh how, when that awful moment came, would I ask him a question when he might as well have been speaking Amharic. But as I glanced around at my fellow panelists—and I knew them all very very well—I could tell that they were equally baffled: Frank Meyer didn't know what the great Michael Oakeshott was talking about, and neither did Jim Burnham, Jeff Hart, Bill Rusher, or Bill Buckley. On and on he droned. And when, at long last, he was through, Bill thanked him, and won the eternal gratitude of the panel by pronouncing that since the brilliant reading had taken a little longer than planned we would, alas, be forced to forego the question-and-answer period.

Jim McFadden later told me that he overheard a woman in the audience comment. "That was Buckley's greatest hoax. That was an actor playing the philosopher." To which her companion replied, "and it was never going to end!"

You Must Be
Out of Your Mind

VERY EARLY in my *National Review* career, Bill, Maureen and, I took up skiing. We drove to Pico Peak in Massachusetts, rented skis, boots, and poles, and signed up for a lesson, after which we headed to the top of the mountain. This is not recommended. We got to the bottom some hours later, bruised and frigid and wet through and through but, against all odds, with limbs intact. That single run made aficionados of at least two of us. Bill and I have been skiing ever since and both of us spend some time in Switzerland every winter on the slopes near Gstaad.

We soon found that lots of people we knew were also skiing buffs, but to get to the ski slopes in northern Massachusetts, New Hampshire, or Vermont when you work in Manhattan is not easy. It is a four to five hour drive, if conditions are not bad, on Friday night, arriving about midnight, and another backbreaking drive back to New York on Sunday night. Some enthusiasts managed this routine every weekend during the season, but we were not strong enough or enthusiastic enough for that.

Then we heard that there were large, comfortable buses that made the Friday evening-Sunday night trek every weekend, picking up passengers at three different spots in Manhattan. The operation was run by a fellow called Buddy Bombard, a skiing and sailing buff, through an outfit which he had founded called the Chalet Club. Buddy, who is a championship-caliber skier and has crewed on America's Cup races, has devoted his life to making sportsmen happy, blissfully, gorgeously happy. On Buddy's buses to the New England slopes, refreshments were broken out shortly after departure, wine, beer, and soft drinks, cheese, crackers, and platters of sandwiches. The once onerous trip became a minor party in which you could participate if you wished, or doze the hours away if you were tired. Best of all was the return journey Sunday night, no longer that awful bleak trek back from the beautiful snowy hills to the dreary cold, wet city.

In those days—late 1950s early 1960s—when charter flights were easy to put together, the Chalet Club also offered five or six flights to Switzerland and Austria every year at laughable prices: round trip for $169, and if you were one of the first fourteen or sixteen to sign up you got to sit in first class and were the recipient of first class service.

As more and more sportsmen heard about, and joined, the Chalet Club, Buddy expanded his offerings. You could have an evening sail on a seventy-foot schooner, go for an early morning balloon ride in New Jersey, sign up for a week's scuba diving in the Caribbean, or—and this is the one that I found irresistible—float down the Colorado River through the Grand Canyon for nine days. I had once, years earlier, ridden a mule from the rim down to the bottom of the Canyon and back up, and always had it in the back of my mind to return and stay there longer. Now, here was an outfit, whose trips were always first-class, ready to make all the arrangements for a rugged but exciting adventure.

What better break from the fortnightly magazine rhythm into which my life had fallen?

And so, the victim of a hard sell, a weak will, latent Walter-Mit-tyism—and my beloved Chalet Club's offer of "SPECTACULAR COLORADO RIVER-GRAND CANYON EXPEDITIONS," I succumbed, and signed up. "A person," said one of the brochures, "could take all the cathedrals in the world, lining them up side by side along 300 miles and then lift their roofs and spires up 5,000 feet, and then, if you walked through all alone, you might experience the feeling of what the Canyon is like."

That kind of thing: how to resist? *Comfortable* pontoon rafts. *Excitement*, fifty-nine rapids. *Exercise*, hikes and climbs, Indian vil-lages to be explored, fossils to be found. *Good campsites*, "excellent pure white sandy beaches." *No bugs and no humidity*: "Canyons are friendly places to sleep in." And, yes, "There is a social hour before dinner." Reserve now before the Canyon is sold out. The government limits the number of people who can run the Canyon each year to about twelve thousand.

But this turns out not to be an easy sell. I first ask my brothers and sisters, then my dearest friends, if their dearest wish has not been to run the Colorado River through the Grand Canyon. And they respond—as one man—"You must be out of your mind." Until, at an old movie club, I mention the Grand Canyon to Lyn Westsmith, a friend who has just returned from several years in Japan, and she says: "I'd like to go, when and how much?" (A week or so later another friend, Stephanie Hart, wife of Jeff Hart, a Dartmouth professor and a colleague of mine at *National Review*, says she'd like to go too. And this time it is Jeff who exclaims: "Stephanie, you must be out of your mind.")

We make our reservations and send in our checks. The price, which includes sleeping equipment, food, and drink (beer but not hard liquor), and the six-hour bus ride from Las Vegas east to Lee's Ferry, Arizona, and the three-hour trip from the terminal point in

Lake Mead back to Vegas, is, in the early 1960s when I take the trip, under $400. Only after you pay do you get quite a different set of documents. Congratulations from Chalet president Buddy Bombard, accompanied by a "Liability Release" form, which will I be so kind as to fill out, at once, and return. It says, in effect, that I shall not hold Grand Canyon's Expeditions or the Chalet Club responsible for any bumps, bruises, fractures, insect or snake bites, falls from cliffs, broken necks, or drownings that might occur. I will be subject to "being jarred, bumped and splashed upon," that a person "could be thrown out of the boat if he does not hold on securely . . . it is also possible that a boat could overturn." In the same mail I am urged to buy the waterproof *Grand Canyon River Guide* (special river-runners edition).

Sounds exciting, doesn't it? In due course the book arrives, with a map of the river and the rapids we will be running and other edifying pictures and commentary. A Mr. Frank M. Brown "drowned while surveying a railroad that was never built." A picture of the Brown inscription is provided, carved by Peter Hansbrough, "who drowned five days later." The tragic bride and groom, Bessie and Glen Hide, "probably drowned at 232-Mile Rapid." Happy notes of that sort.

Finally—we're getting to the nitty-gritty—arrives in the mail a list of the clothes and equipment we are to bring for nine days: raingear, sunburn lotion (lots of it), big floppy hats (attachable to heads), flashlights, toilet articles, sturdy sneakers (they may shrink, bring two pairs as one will always be wet), sweatshirts, swimsuits, sunglasses, underwear, towel, toilet paper, all of which except for the camera equipment, we are blandly informed, must fit in a bag (provided by them, no fools them) 16 x 12 x 8—inches.

I look at the mound of clothes that are the minimum I could possibly conceive of surviving nine days in and there's no way, no way, no way. I've taken bags bigger than that to the golf club for a quick eighteen.

And so, still with twice as much luggage as I know will fit we fly off to Las Vegas, where the party will meet the man who will be in charge of our group, our boatman, Kenton Grua.

The bags are, as advertised, exactly 16 x 12 x 8, but each of us is also given a small red waterproof ammunition box for camera and anything else we think we may need in the course of the day—digitalis? tranquilizers?

Up at 5:00 the next morning, we climb into an air-conditioned bus and ride six hours through the desert east and north to Lee's Ferry where we meet Regan Dale, the other boatman. He has been in charge of supplying the two thirty-seven-foot rubber pontoon rafts for our party of thirty. Like Kenton Grua, Regan is young—mid-twenties—wiry, sunburned, heavily bearded, tough. The two of them look like buccaneers. They wear red and blue bandanas tied around their heads (Kenton's is blue, Regan's red), cut-off jeans, and nothing else. The boats look like silvery oblong sausages, and are beautifully designed for our purpose, which is to survive with a maximum of minimal comfort. A light metal superstructure hangs down between the inflated rubber sides, and in it are carried everything: coolers, provisions, beer and soft drinks, grills, pots and pans, cutlery, and plastic water containers; also shovels, machetes, two extra 20HP motors, tools, medicine chest, walkie-talkie radio, everything we'll need for nine days. Because once we pass the first rapid there is no turning back.

Also carried in this compartment are the Porto-Potties—we are much relieved to see them—the chemical latrines that are set up every evening inside their small, twin red tents (ladies upstream gents down). Red floorboards that will at night double as working tabletops fit in over the supplies and provide us with sitting space. The bedrolls and personal-effects bags (each now marked with our names—first-name—in Magic Marker) are strapped down around the sides of the boat. The red ammo boxes march in two neat lines down the middle of the front section, and are also strapped down, and we, the fifteen passengers of Boat #1 (soon to be known by the organized occupants of Boat #2 as the "garbage scow"), take our places fore and aft. About half of us sit up front where the ride is rougher, wetter, and colder, but gamey. The others sit in the rear. We shift around during the trip, depending on mood and chill factor. Except for Bill Miller. Bill Miller, bachelor, is a New York dentist, and it is his intention to go through the trip without ever getting wet or lifting more of a finger than is absolutely necessary. He will, before the trip is over, be referred to as "The Exalted Eagle," amuse the hell out of most (but by no means all) of us, and, at least once, be given the bum's rush into the icy waters of the Colorado, with Kenton and Regan assisting on the shoving end.

First night's camp. We are cold, tired, a bit disconsolate, and stiff. Regan has just done his best to scare us. It's very serious to go overboard, he tells us. We must wear our lifejackets buckled tight all the time. "It may save your life," he says. "You don't want to go overboard, ever. But if you do, float on your back, arms out, feet downstream. Hold your breath when you see the waves coming. Don't fight it. And when you get past the rapid try to swim ashore. We'll be coming after you." Then Kenton takes over and gives us instructions on how to pack the bedrolls and the personal-effects bags to create a vacuum that will prevent the waters from sloshing in when the waves break over the raft, as they will.

Only after the lectures can we stake out our individual camp sites, change into dry clothes, wander down toward the fire, and have our first convivial moment of the trip. It's almost dark as we sit down on a rock or wet cushion, with our warm bourbon or gin and Tang (it's hard to believe, but it tastes better than . . . well, better than no warm bourbon and Tang). We look around, start to sort out the thirty-odd people we'll be spending the next week with. They're still a jumble of faces without names, but each is holding a green plastic cup from which the Magic-Markered names have not yet been washed off, and this is a help in putting names to faces. (Your green plastic cup is your dearest possession. Without it no juice and coffee at dawn, no lemonade and Tang during the hot midday hours, no drink at night, no hot soup, no strong coffee. To snitch another's green plastic cup is frowned upon.)

Bone weary, we unroll our sleeping bags. The romantics among us pitch them out on the beach under the stars. The worry-warts camp under the overhanging ledges. The worry-warts have a good night's sleep. The romantics spend the pre-dawn hours huddling deeper and deeper into ever-dampening bedrolls, pulling the ground sheet tighter and tighter over their heads against the insinuating rain.

But it's beautiful in the morning. The sun lights up a canyon peak ahead. It's a golden yellow above the red ochre cliffs. The yellow strides down the walls in giant steps, becoming paler, more translucent, less exciting, but as it penetrates deeper into the cleft toward the river, it starts to warm us.

We're still cold. And we know it's eight days to the next hot shower. The water which was a clean and frothy green at Lee's Ferry has turned an angry red overnight. Tomorrow and from then on the Colorado will be brown, chocolate-colored, swirling and tempestuous as it sweeps thousands of tons of sand westward toward Lake Mead. The water is cold, ranging in temperature from 52 to 58 degrees.

The pace of travel changes from day to day. On that first night Ken urged us to take off our watches. Watches don't mean anything here in the Canyon, he said. All that matters is river time. There is a time for getting up, for eating, for going to bed, and the river dictates it. The boatmen never tell you what to expect. Some days we run the river lazily, break often, take two, three-hour hikes up dry gulches where traces of fossils have to be pointed out to us at first, then, as our eyes sharpen, we start discovering them on our own, and are pleased.

We explore vast caves—one, said Major John Powell, the one-armed explorer who first ran the river 103 years ago, is big enough to hold fifty thousand people. We climb to Indian cliff villages and granaries high above the river waters. There are cool, clear blue-white waterfalls that cascade down from the heights, and we bathe and wash and disport in the warm pools that form under them. The sand and grime and brown of the river is laved away to rejoin the Colorado below, and possibly splash over us again later in the day. We see a couple of rattlesnakes, one spectacular black-and-white diamonded king snake, and other wildlife of the Canyon, wild burros, coyotes, lizards and small iguanas—chuckwawas, they call them.

At the confluence of the Colorado 2 and the Little Colorado, a couple of us wade across and poke about an abandoned trapper's cabin. We see the cot, the bedding, the shelves, the stove, everything as it was left when the nameless hunter picked up his pack and walked away, a half-century or more ago. A plaque identifies it as property of the government. "Please do not disturb." You wonder what he could have trapped among these inhospitable cliffs and crannies. And yet that morning, we surprised a buck mule deer, a doe, and fawn by the side of the river. The fawn bolted away but the buck and doe just watched us drift by. We've seen hummingbirds, great blue herons, ravens that soared high over the heights above us, and groups of ducks, mergansers that, flushed out of the river by our boats, fly away, plop down in front of us, are flushed again and again, and finally fly high overhead to land in the safe undisturbed waters behind us.

Other days we push along at a rapid clip. We have distances to cover, rapids to run before nightfall.

"Down these grand, gloomy depths we glide," wrote Major Powell a hundred years earlier, "ever winding, and the river is closed in so that we can see but a few hundred yards, and what there may be below we know not, but we listen for falls and watch for rocks, or stop now and then, in the bay of a recess to admire the gigantic scenery. And ever, as we go, there is some new pinnacle or tower, some crag or peak, some distant view of the upper plateau, some strange-shaped rock or some narrow side canyon."

It's not just a single canyon. The Canyon is tiered and layered, it reaches back into the distance. Primarily red, in Marble Canyon, but with streaks and stretches and outcroppings of other shades and hues: green, gray, mauve, black, brown, and white, changing in shade and intensity as the sun hits it, or a shadow swings across it. The raft rounds a bend. There's a huge brown wall with rough chunks gouged out of the sides at regular intervals. It's a Colosseum. Gargoyles leer down at you as they do from Notre Dame. A rock, five storeys high, leans precariously over the river. A breeze, you'd think, would topple it down onto your raft. It may have been teetering for a million years and someday it may crash. Let your imagination loose—what better place for it—and you'll pick out Mayan pyramids and Arab palaces, Ziggurats, Spanish hill fortresses, caves fit for goblin kings. All about you there is a richness and beauty, a stillness broken only by the sound of the racing waters, by the rapids ahead or behind, by the waters slapping the rubber boat. It's a time for thoughts, irrelevant and profound. Your back may be stiff. You may be—you are—cold and wet: sand is everywhere, in your hair, in your sneakers, under your nails. But you are caught up by a sense of timelessness, caught up by the color and the grandeur of the great canyon and the turbulent river that carved it out.

The rapids are officially rated on an intensity scale of one to ten Anything over a five will be tough going. That's when Kenton Grua shouts: "Off the tubes everybody, it's a five [or more]." We get into the raft, take our places on the floorboards. Kenton says, quietly, but with some urgency, "Hang on. Both hands. Hang on tight." There's a scramble to put away the cameras, pull up zippers at the neck and pull down hoods. But to no avail. The icy water works its way up pant legs, down the neck, splashes into your open mouth, drenches your hair. As the boat lurches headlong into the maelstrom, it's like being inside a chocolate malted-milk shaker, but the taste is mud.

The raft ahead edges into a rapid and disappears from sight. We hear the shouts and laughter, see them emerge way below, buffeted, turned sideways. They edge forward again, sheets of brown water breaking over them as they lurch on through it.

It's Crystal. Crystal is a seven to ten—always dangerous and we're taking it late in the afternoon, too late for comfort. By now we're shivering, dripping wet. There's been no sun this afternoon, just a cold wind beating up the lower canyon that turns suddenly steam-shower warm just before you hit a rapid. It's a sign to button up. We edge into it. "Hang on, hang on real tight," Kenton urges. We heel over into the rapid. Kenton turns the tiller hard left into a wall of water twenty feet high or more. When we come bubbling and laughing out of it we see why—see the massive boulder that he has managed to avoid this time again, and others like it, ahead and on all sides. Regan in the other boat has hit one, but not head-on, a glancing blow that rocks the raft sideways. But that's what these amazing craft are built to take. And then we're both through Crystal.

Six more rapids—big ones—between us and our campsite. Even the cheery souls are a bit grim from the constant drenching. The hot midday sun never put in its appearance on this long day's trip through the mile-high Granite Canyon. We pull up to a small beach. Kenton jumps out to inspect it, bounds up a sand dune like a monkey and decides we can camp here. But it will be a tight fit, he says. No one cares. We want to get ashore and dry off. There's no room for the Porto Pottee tents, so the chemical latrines are set up between rocks, facing the falls we'll be running first thing tomorrow. The women's toilet is behind the rock with the wide white diagonal stripe. You sit grandly, looking out over the falls into the dappled purple canyon wall across while, far below, on the river bank, a couple of women are making their ablutions in the bubbling brown waters.

We climb into dry slacks, don sweatshirts and sweaters, recover the bourbon from Booze Bag #1, dig into the hors d'oeuvres (this night, as most others, a box of saltines), gather warmth from the fire, the company, and the drink, and pride at the hard day we've been through, and decide it's a pretty good world.

"That Bill Miller," says someone, and, "I'll never forget the sight . . ." The sight of Bill Miller, bare-chested, in cut-offs, his straw hat garlanded, a ten-foot yucca staff in hand, standing on a promontory awarding the right of passage to as startled a group of river runners as you'll ever see. Again it's Bill Miller, this time asking Kenton what a window in a cliff wall is called. It has no name, says Ken, so what did Bill Miller do? someone asks. He stood up on the back of the Scow, raised his yucca staff (now decorated with one of Jill's Pucci bikini tops), and announced: "I, William Miller, do hereby declare that this opening shall for all times henceforward be known as Miller's window, in Miller's Gap, of Miller's Canyon." Whereupon the gods of the River strike back. The rains fall and we make camp wetly, without the assistance of the Exalted Eagle who, having picked up Miller's Ammunition Box, Miller's Personal Luggage, Miller's Bedroll is off to find Miller's Perfect Campsite while the rest of us struggle with the camping gear. (In the middle of the night—the River gods never rest—a skunk finds Miller's 'til then Perfect Campsite.)

We're at Lava Rapids. Lava is listed in the Guinness Book of Records as the hardest navigable rapids in the world. It falls thirty-seven feet in a hundred yards; when the river is high the waters thunder down at thirty miles an hour. The River Guide rates it a ten. Kenton, preparing us for it, says, "It's going to be"—he considers, Ken likes to be exact—"like ten times harder than anything you've been through. This could be the time I flip this one over." Has he ever? we ask. "No," he says, "but Lava gets to everyone in the end." Lots of us, not frightened until now, are frightened. We're gathered on a large boulder looking down at Lava's churning waters. "If," someone asks, "if we're thrown off, where do we swim to?" To the right," says Kenton. "The land juts out there below the rapids." He points to the spot. "The boat will pick you up." (Yes, yes, yes, if you're Mark Spitz the boat might pick you up.) Then Kenton says: "Let's go." And there's no chance to pursue the discussion.

We're in it now. There's a boulder dead ahead. We skid around it, and ship water. The red ammo boxes strapped tight down the middle of the deck in a double line rise up, do a jig, crash down out of line, and we're hit on all sides. One, two, three giant buffets, water all over us, drenching, pressing down. Our hands slip on the cords and we crash into each other. Stephanie laughs happily. It's as much fun as she had hoped. She had never been scared, only worried that Lava might disappoint.

The river is quiet now, on our next to last day. No sounds of rapids ahead although we'll run a riffle or two. The canyon walls no longer stretch high and forbiddingly on either side. It is hot, hot as blazes, with no rock walls to protect us from the early September sun. We tie the boats together and eat lunch afloat to take advantage of the river breeze instead of tying up at a baked beach.

Major Powell wrote on August 29, 1869: "The river still continues swift, but we have no serious difficulty, and at twelve o'clock emerge from the Grand Canyon of the Colorado."

We've eased into Lake Mead; it's desolate, with little vegetation. Kenton points out a black line five or six feet wide that winds its way along the banks of the lake well above the water. It's a line of drift-wood, marooned there when the level of the lake fell after the dam was built. The brown-silt river we've ridden for the last eight days is becoming unhomogenized, the cargo of sand separating from the waters that have carried it. And then we are out of the brown stream and in the clear warm green waters of Mead.

A speedboat races past the silver rafts with their "Grand Canyon Expeditions" grandly emblazoned on the pontoons, and the occupants stare amazed at our general unshaven, unpressed scruffiness. The boats (even #2) are a mess. The Scow's Porto Potties lie exposed. We've been using the floorboards that normally cover them to aquaplane. Empty beer cans and orange peels have been thrown into the bottom of the boat waiting for the garbage bag to be dug out tonight. Foul-weather gear lies all over the deck, along with suntan lotion, cameras, sunglasses, wet sneakers, chapsticks. More speedboats roar past. Clean people in clean, pressed boating costumes wave to us but do not approach too closely. And we are filled with disdain for their immaculate selves and their swift, noisy, immaculate crafts.

The adventure is over. We will have a final party tonight, the awards dinner (Bill Miller, an amusing and gracious MC—the things that man observed while not being splashed), and tomorrow we will go our separate ways to be reminded of each other by the photographs we have taken, the memories we share, and a certain pride at having run the Colorado River of the Grand Canyon.

⌒ 17 ⌒

The World Turned Upside Down

I T STARTS THE MINUTE I WALK IN THE DOOR. The phone rings. It's Helen Puwalski, the receptionist. "Priscilla, I've got a problem. There's something going on at Mr. Buckley's house in Stamford, and I can't understand what Eudocia is trying to tell me. I can't reach Mr. Buckley. He's taping a couple of *Firing Lines* this morning. Would you take the call?"

Of course. So Helen puts me through, but not, as I had thought, to Eudocia, Bill's marvelously talented but distinctly odd Cuban cook. (My sister Jane's maid, Josefina, who is Eudocia's god-daughter is convinced that Eudocia is a witch, and when she receives a letter from her, takes it outside the house to open and shake out the witch's dust that may be in the envelope.)

I'm connected not to Eudocia but to a telephone repair man who tells me that he is sitting atop a telephone pole outside Bill's drive at Wallach's Point, which is the safest place he could think of from which to call for help. And the story pours out.

His work sheet that morning instructed him to go to the residence of William F. Buckley Jr. on Wallach's Point and install a second telephone line. Mr. Buckley had bought some new equipment for his office and needed a second line to accommodate it. He had duly driven to Wallach's Point, parked his truck in the rear by the kitchen, and rung the doorbell. It had been flung open by a madwoman, dressed in pink (Eudocia's pink uniform), screeching and yelling at him in Spanish and waving a shotgun in and around his face. She told him to "go, go," "leave," the only words he could understand and kept pointing the gun at him until he had left the property. She wouldn't even let him stop to pick up his truck, from which he could have called his office for instructions, so he had climbed up a telephone pole to make the call. His office had given him Mr. Buckley's business number in New York City. Now what was he to do?

I asked him for his number, told him I'd get back to him, and hung up.

"Helen," I said, "let's try ringing Bill's number in Stamford and see if Eudocia answers the phone." It takes ten or twelve rings before the phone is picked up.

"Eudocia," I say—my Spanish is pedestrian at best, but Yoya speaks no English—"*Soy la hermana del señor.*"

"*Sí, señorita, señorita Priscilla, como no.*"

I explain to her in halting Spanish that the man who was just at the door is not a brigand, a rapist, and a thief, as she seems to think, but a workman from the telephone company who has come to fix *el señor*'s phone in the *oficina*.

There are protestations. That man who came to the door did not look like an honest workman but like a brigand, a rapist, and a thief. I assure Yoya that he is none of those things and get her promise to show him where *el señor*'s office is in the old remodeled garage. After she has done that she can retreat to the house and lock herself in. But I tell her, firmly, that she is *not* to take up Mr. Buckley's gun when she goes to the door. She promises, rather hesitantly, not to do so. I call the repairman and tell him it is now safe to descend from his pole and get on with the job, and hope that I am right. You can never be sure with a witch!

The moon must have been in a crazy phase that day because when I come back from lunch and wave a hello to Helen, she rushes out into the hall and stops me.

"Priscilla," she says, "I couldn't help it. This strange woman came in asking to see you or Mr. Buckley, and before I could stop her she had gone up the steps. Kevin tells me that she is sitting in your office and refuses to move until she has seen either you or Mr. Buckley. Thank God Bill is not here."

Oh dear, I think. I'm really in no mood to deal with a crazy woman. My desk is piled high with copy I have to read before the printer's messenger arrives. But nothing's for it, so I climb the stairs and head for my office.

Miss Valpolicella (that's not her name, but it was something polysyllabic and Italianate) looks, in her black-shrouded way, with her Greta Garbo hat concealing one eye, like the mother in the (Chas.) Addams family.

"You may have noticed that your brother has been acting strangely since his return from Pasadena last week," says Miss Valpolicella, as an opener. Miss Valpolicella does not ask questions, she declares. "No," I reply, "at least not more oddly than usual," a bad attempt to inject some levity into the discussion. This is not the way to handle Miss V.

"You are familiar with cellology, *of course.*"

"Well," nervous smile, "actually I'm not."

"You don't know about cellology!" Total disbelief on Miss V.'s part. She explains. Cellology is the science of the cells. Fair enough. But the problem, and believe me, it is a big one, is that Miss Valpolicella and Bill were once in the same room in Pasadena where Bill was speaking, during which time numbers of WFB's cells toddled over to Miss V., water-bucket fashion, and installed themselves in her body while

numbers of hers transferred to his: they are all mixed up, intercon-
nected. Miss Valpolicella seeks to illustrate. "If, at this very moment,"
she says, "your brother is choking, then I too will ch. . . ." (she rises
from her chair, grasps her throat, gags). I'm convinced, convinced that
I'd better get Miss V. out on the outsize chance that Bill may amble
in. The solution is very simple, says Miss V. She and Bill must sit in
the same room for a very long time, time enough to permit their cells
to unscramble themselves. I have a wild mental image of that scene
and only then remember to press the "kook" button which rings in
the office occupied by typists Evelyne Kanter and Mike Watkins.
That signals to them that someone needs help.

A couple of minutes later Vicki Marani pokes her head in the
door. "Sorry to interrupt, Priscilla," she says, "but you're needed for
a cover conference," and I flee. Someone else, who is not a Buckley,
is sent in to get rid of Miss V.

I'm still wrapping up the day's work at a quarter of seven when
my private line rings. It's Bill.

"Hi, Pitts," he says, "what *were* you doing Wednesday night?"

I laugh. "I was having supper and going to a flick with Maggie
Comstock. What *am* I doing?"

"You're flying to Mexico with Pat and Marvin and me. Come on
up," Bill it seems is in the office, " let's have a drink, and I'll tell you
all about it."

So I amble up the stairs to the conference room. We fix ourselves
a gin and tonic, and I tell him all about my day. "It can't be true," he
says, "you're exaggerating.

"But it is true," I insist, "and I'm not exaggerating, but tell me
about Mexico."

It turns out this is the weekend of Bill and Pat's wedding anniversary, and wouldn't it be fun to celebrate it in Mexico where Bill
and Pat had spent the first months of their married life, Bill as a

covert agent for CIA. Marvin Liebman is everyone's best friend and will some years later be Bill's and my godson when he is baptized into the Catholic Church. Marvin had never been to Mexico, and I had not been back since spending a few months there in 1943 nearly twenty years earlier. It would be fun and we could also visit Bill's old nurse Pupa, now retired and living in Mexico City with her two sisters and a priest-cousin for whom they keep house.

Bill's plan was energetic and comprehensive. We were to spend Wednesday night in Mexico City, drive to Oaxaca to visit the Olmec ruins, going there via Puebla, the city with a thousand churches, on Thursday morning. Back to Mexico City Friday night, then to Cuernavaca and Taxco on Saturday, the anniversary day, with a gala dinner Bill had planned at the hotel Saturday night. Return to Mexico City Sunday for lunch with Pupa and her family, a bullfight that afternoon, a quiet supper and home Monday morning. That, at least, was the plan. The execution of it was, well, flawed.

On route to Puebla, going a lickety-split eighty miles an hour down the main highway, our Hertz suffered a blow-out. Bill managed to pull us off the road without serious damage but the garage in Puebla to which we took our problem closed for three hours at midday, as did all other garages and business establishments other than restaurants, in Puebla, so it was five in the afternoon before we headed down the road to Oaxaca which was not, as we had been told, just a couple of hours away. At about ten we pulled into a little outdoor restaurant stand for a quick taco and tamale and beer. At 2:00 AM, as we entered Oaxaca, we were rammed by a drunken Mexican in a largish and distinctly oldish truck. Minutes later the *policia* was at hand brandishing tommy guns at us. A lengthy colloquy ensued as to who was to blame. We ended up spending the rest of the night in the police station, although not behind bars. By morning, the authorities, having satisfied themselves that Bill, whose fluency in

Spanish had impressed them, was not shake-down-able, permitted us to go to the hotel for a very brief sleep before an even briefer visit to the Olmec ruins.

We flew back to Mexico City that evening for a quiet and nerve-restoring dinner, hired a car (from Mr. Avis this time), and set out for Cuernavaca and Taxco Saturday morning, back on schedule. It was while visiting the sights in Taxco, and its wonderful silver and craft shops, that Montezuma's Revenge struck Marvin and me with a vengeance. It must have been that taco and tamale on the road to Oaxaca. We rushed up the hill toward the Hotel Victoria with accelerated steps, raced up the three flights to our rooms on the top floor, and just made it to our respective bathrooms in time.

Bill's splendid anniversary dinner was eaten by himself and Pat in their bedroom suite, attended by Marvin and me in our bathrobes, raising a cup of bouillon to our lips with tremulous hands from time to time. No caviar would pass our lips that night.

Marvin and I made it through Pupa's lavish lunch the next day, but just barely. The bullfight found our stomachs still on the queasy side, so the final dinner was simple, lacking a certain *joie de vivre*. And on to bed on the twelfth floor of the shiny new Mexico Hilton for five peaceful hours before being jolted awake by an earthquake that measured better than six on the Richter scale. A piece of plaster from the ceiling falling on my bed was what woke me. The shakiness underfoot was horrid, scary. I put on my bathrobe and slippers and opened the door. People were running up and down the hall in every stage of deshabille, some whimpering, some on the verge of hysteria. The doors of both Marvin's and Bill and Pat's rooms were open. No one there. I headed for the staircase, joining the crowd of rudely awakened guests headed down the twelve flights, and out on the street, where we watched as the top of the Hilton swayed left and right. We were joined by Marvin in his bathrobe and slippers. Passing Bill's room he had noted that Pat had left the jewelry she had worn the evening before on the dresser, so he had nipped in and retrieved it before taking the elevator down to the ground floor.

"Marvin," we roared, "you didn't take the elevator!"

"Well, I certainly wasn't going to walk down twelve flights. I have my standards."

It was a couple of hours before we were permitted to return to our rooms for the balance of the night and what sleep we could get before the flight home.

I couldn't wait to tell Maureen the story. She found it hilarious and said why didn't I drop in Sunday night for supper in Scarsdale, where she and Gerry had moved after the birth of their second child. Good idea, I said, and told her I had bought two most attractive A-line dresses in Taxco, a green one for little Patricia and a pink one for Priscilla. I'd bring them along.

Maureen and Gerry had been playing tennis that Sunday afternoon. She was still slightly flushed from the exertion when she came to the door to meet me, looking like a million dollars with her tanned arms and beautiful long tan legs, in a white sharkskin dress, with a long-stemmed rose twining its away across the front of it from neckline to hem. It was simple, what our grandparents would have called fetching. She took my dresses upstairs and a moment later little brunette Patricia, five, and little blonde Priscilla, four, came waltzing in to give me a big kiss and hug, delighted with their presents.

It was a particularly lovely evening. I regaled Maureen and Gerry with the story of our Mexican misadventures. We sat out on the porch after supper with our coffee. It was a lovely cool, breezy July evening, and we chatted about this and that and what an exciting week it would be for all of us conservatives, for this was the week that our hero Barry Goldwater would be nominated for president by the Republican Party in convention assembled at the Cow Palace in San Francisco. Bill would be out there writing a daily column and giving TV commentaries. Bill Rusher, as a founder of the Goldwater for President Committee which had engineered the nomination, would be there. Jim McFadden and his troops would be there, passing out copies of *National Review* to all the delegates, Mac flushed with excitement because on this election year *National Review* would, for the first time, top the magical 100,000 subscribers figure.

The rest of us would be back at 150 East 35th street to put the convention issue to bed. The editorial troops, Jim Burnham (and his wife Marcia, who would come to New York for the occasion), Bill Rickenbacker, and Arlene Croce were to come to 60 Sutton Place South after the printer's messenger had left, where I would give them a simple supper and we would watch Goldwater's nomination on television.

That noon, as we were eating our sandwiches around the table in Bill's office, Gertrude poked her head inside the door and said there was a telephone call for me. She suggested I take it in her office, which was quieter. It was Maureen's and my maid, Georgia Cobb. Georgia told me that when she had arrived at Scarsdale around 11:30 she had found Maureen on the floor, in a faint. The baby, Billy, was in his highchair and Maureen had obviously been feeding him. The two little girls had brought diapers out and filled them with ice for "Mommy's headache." They were all over the floor. Georgia had called for an ambulance, then called Gerry at his office and told him. I wasn't particularly alarmed. Maureen occasionally missed breakfast, she was always on a diet, and might have felt faint. She had recently complained of having headaches, but had no other physical ailments. I thanked Georgia and asked her to have Gerry phone me when he got to the hospital and found out what was going on.

That evening—I had left the office about 5:00 to start preparing for the supper—mother phoned. She and Jane were now in Scarsdale to help Gerry in any way they could. Maureen, she told me, had suffered a major aneurysm, and the doctors gave her just a 50-50 chance of living through the night. Jane had managed to get through to Jim

McFadden in San Francisco who would give Bill the catastrophic news. Two of Maureen's brothers were abroad. Jim, in Australia on business, would fly back the next day, as would Reid, the youngest brother, who lived in Spain.

I called the NR office and got a jubilant Bill Rickenbacker on the phone. He was instantly sobered by my dreadful news. The party was off but I would like it if Jim and Marcia would come, since I didn't want to be alone, and Jim and I had, in the years we shared an office, become very very close friends. And so they did. We had a quiet supper and talked much of Maureen who had been a particular favorite of Jim Burnham's when she worked at NR, and turned on the television after supper. I don't remember one thing about that climactic evening on TV, although I watched it all. In the course of the evening, my older brother John dropped in, as did Aloïse's husband Ben Heath, both of whom were in New York on business. And later still Arlene Croce called and asked if I wouldn't like her to spend the night. I accepted, with thanks.

It was arranged that I would pick up Reid at JFK. Maureen had died on that hot sunny July morning after Reid's flight had left Madrid. Martha Butler, a school friend of my sister Carol's who was now production editor of *National Review*, insisted on riding out to the airport with me. "You don't want to be alone," she said stubbornly when I told her it wasn't necessary. But I was happy for the company. At the arrival terminal Martha kissed me good-bye and took a taxi back into Manhattan.

Reid came bursting through the gate. "She's all right?" he said. I tried to say, "She's dead," but the words wouldn't come out, so I just shook my head. He dropped his bags and crushed me to him, and we rocked there, tight together, for a minute or two. "There was never any hope," I finally was able to get out, "never, never any hope."

We headed for Scarsdale, where the family was congregating, in the perky sky blue Studebaker convertible I was driving that year. We would have supper there, spend the night at Bill's house in Stamford, and then drive back to Sharon for the funeral. I looked over at Reid, a mature man now in his early thirties with the fiery red crown of hair of his youth now a more sedate crimson. Maureen's death, so devastating for all of us, must be particularly crushing for him I suddenly realized. They had been buddies growing up. In our family we tended to pair off, boy-girl, boy-girl. It had been John and Allie, Jim and me, Bill and Trish, Reid and Maureen. Both Reid and Maureen had been born in France, three years apart, a picturesque pair, the impetuous, red-haired little boy and quiet blonde, little girl, in a family that was predominantly brunette. He had teased her, and spoiled her, and pulled her hair, and shared his treats with her, and she had adored him.

Maureen, whom I had just really gotten to know since arriving in New York to work at *National Review*, had, as I now thought about it, been the lynchpin at the lower end of the family, three years younger than Reid, the last of the boys, and five years older than baby Carol. Her death would be intolerable to Reid, whose favored little sister was now gone, and to Carol, to whom she had been Big Sister, and Best Friend.

Most of the rest of us were too old to be companions to Carol who was born in the winter of 1938 when the storm clouds that would burst into World War II were gathering over Europe. She joined the family almost exactly twenty years after our oldest sister Aloïse, born just seventeen days before every bell in every church in Paris pealed to announce the Armistice that would end the carnage that was World War I, *la grande guerre* as the French called it.

Now Maureen was dead. She was thirty-one years old and had five children, the oldest of whom was five. She was buried in the bleak little Catholic cemetery in Sharon after a beautifully sung Latin Mass, beside her baby sister, Mary Ann, who had died six years before

Maureen was born, having lived just one day. I don't know why we were surprised to see Mary Ann's gravestone. We had forgotten that she had ever existed, but we would never forget Maureen.

How I remember her is standing with Gerry at the front door of their house in Scarsdale, smiling and waving good-bye in that white sharkskin dress as I pulled out of the driveway en route to New York on the Sunday before she was struck down.

Things, would, in fact, never be the same again. For until this time we had seemed, as a family, golden, untarnished by time or tragedy: the ten of us, my brothers and sisters and I, had had an idyllic childhood with loving, stimulating parents. We were all practicing Catholics; nine of the ten of us were married and, with spouses, had produced forty-seven grandchildren, only one of whom had any physical or mental ailment, defective eyesight.

Our only real sorrow before Maureen's sudden death was father's demise seven years earlier. But father was seventy-seven, and we had been prepared for his death by the series of strokes he had suffered in his final years.

Now the magic was gone, gone forever. And the blows would continue to fall. Two years later, John's beautiful blonde wife, Ann, age thirty-eight was also gone, felled by premature hardening of the arteries; and the following year death struck again when our older sister Aloïse Heath died of a massive brain hemorrhage. In three years' time eighteen children in the family would be motherless, Maureen's five, Ann's three, and Aloïse's ten.

18

My Cross-Hairs Were Bent

I HAD OFTEN TALKED OF GOING ON SAFARI, but it wasn't until my brother John called up the stairs to my little office in Sharon one Friday afternoon and asked, "Pitts, would you like to go on a safari to Mozambique?" that I succumbed. I knew that John must have asked every single hunter he knew—and he knew hundreds—and been turned down before he would fall so low as to ask a sister to join him on safari. But I also knew that John had been hurting, hurting badly since the unexpected death of his young and beautiful wife, Ann, a few months back, and that he needed a major break, something that would at least punctuate the despair of his everyday life. So in a moment of brief insanity, I said yes, and ponied up the substantial deposit (nonreimbursable), which meant that on the appointed day we would find ourselves headed for Beira, Mozambique.

I had quite romantic ideas about safaris, too much Hemingway and Isak Dinesen, I suppose. Those stories that culminate in *the kill* had gotten to me: "Suddenly, there he stood etched against the horizon 300 yards away, the giant kudu we had been stalking for two days. I raised my trusty 7 mm Remington Magnum to the shoulder and brought the cross hairs to bear. I squeezed the trigger. The kudu dropped, as if pole-axed. . . ." That's how every story about big game hunting you ever read ends. But there are other dimensions to safaris they don't write about because safari stories are, in most cases, written by men. Why, I even know a hunter who once missed a giant kudu!

Come spring, I got to thinking I must do something about the safari, like figuring out what to bring. The little booklet John gave me was inadequate. It listed what men should bring, and added, laconically, "women bring same."

Women bring same, indeed! What this woman wanted to know—and what every woman will want to know—is what do you do for dinner? Quarters described as "comfortable with running hot and cold water and shower," as anyone who has believed those *tout confort* signs in France should know, can be misleading. So I ended up bringing lots of unnecessary clothes. The operative factor when getting ready for supper on safari is not the facilities, it's the fatigue.

It's 6:00 PM. You've been out in the jolting Jeep or walking in the hot sun for twelve hours. A quick shower and change and cocktails. But there's no light. For reasons known only to men, the generator will not be turned on in hours that would be convenient for me. Showers I can take in the dark. But did you ever try to reconstruct a not-too-constructed face and redo a hairdo—twelve days post-dear Mr. Alfred—with candle in one hand, on tiptoe—mirrors in safari camps are positioned for tall men—and brush, comb, powder-puff, lipstick in the other? You settle for a quick surface wash, a change of clothes from dirty khakis to clean khakis, and the longer cocktail hour.

There's also no one to change for. Safrique, the Chicago outfit that has arranged our safari, lets only one set of hunters at a time use a base camp. And do you know why? Because those great, big, grownup men and women are jealous: insanely, unreasonably, red-in-the-faced-ly jealous over things like first shots, best shots, most shots, biggest trophies.

Home camp number 1 is a cluster of small, whitewashed buildings in a clearing in the heavy bush by a small river. John and I are put
up in a small prefabricated house that can be dismantled and moved,
with two bedrooms, two bathrooms (showers), a small livingroom-
dining room, and porch. Virgilio Garcia, our white hunter, has his own
quarters next to the cookhouse. There is a house for the generator, a
water tower, a poultry yard (poultry, leopards permitting). Laundry is
done daily (including Sunday even in the tent camps). The generator
is turned off at night as soon as the dishes are done.

John, who knows about such things, had brought an extra flash-
light for me. When a brochure reads: "Bring a sweater, it can be cool
in the evening," John knows what they're talking about. He brings
his thermal underwear; I bring a sweater. When a brochure says: "It's
the dry season," John, who knows about these things, reasons it won't
rain positively all the time and comes prepared. I figure it won't rain
at all and am wet practically all the time.

It's the first evening. We and Garcia, who are now condemned
to each other's company all day, every day, for twenty-one days (lions
permitting), sound each other out.

The conversation has its difficulties. Garcia is said to speak English, but his English is heavily laced with Portuguese. Our Spanish is
a bit more understandable to him than our English, but not much.
Still, somehow, we manage. The conversation turns to other safaris
and hunters. Why, would you believe it, Garcia tells us, there are even
people who come on safari who have never shot big game before!

"Imagine," say I (as a drowning man's life passes before his eyes,
so does the tableaux of my lifelong chase of four-legged beasts pass
before mine: three cottontail rabbits). This hideous knowledge, with
the moment of truth no farther away than 5:00 AM tomorrow, had
kept me from taking out a license to shoot an elephant, lion, or a
Cape buffalo earlier that day, because (1) I had no desire to shoot an

elephant, lion, or buffalo, (2) an elephant license cost $146, and (3) cowardice. Do you know that you have to be within fifty yards of an elephant (twenty, they say, is better) to shoot him? Fifty yards, contemplating it in Sharon, Connecticut, is a comfortable distance, half a football field; in Mozambique, it shrinks to ping-pong table dimensions.

It's just after dawn. The five men of the hunting gang (trackers, skinners, driver, mechanic) drive up and say a rather shy, "Good morning." They load the freshly washed Japanese-made Jeep pickup truck with the equipment, and we climb aboard. We pull up to talk to a fellow on the side of the road. Blondie, the head tracker, comes back and reports in dialect that three elephants had passed through last night. They may still be in the area, and a large herd of buffalo. Blondie points to the tracks. "*Chisena*," he says.

"*Chisena*" (today). Garcia shows us where the buffalo have beaten down the grass as they crossed the road headed for water. "Big ones," says Garcia. "Very big bouffalo." The elephants were "*zulu*" (yesterday), but the buffalo are chisena and perhaps later this afternoon. . . .

It's the first morning. John and I are nervous and excited. And a little disappointed. We've driven for a couple of hours and we have seen nothing. A couple of warthogs—ridiculous beasts ("all forehead and no ass," comments John) that trot, tail straight in the air, with a bouncy stiff-kneed jog. But too far to shoot. The morning wears on. The Jeep jolts and bucks over uneven ground, John and I hang on and wish we were in better shape. At 11:30, mercifully, Garcia calls a lunch halt. The men clear a space for us in a grove of shade trees and put down a tarpaulin, then they build themselves a fire and take out their mealie (ground corn) which they put into boiling water to make a kind of hominy—the staple of their diet.

We've just opened a can of hot peri-peri sardines, when Blondie hisses. They've sighted a herd of hartebestes across the savannah.

When we get within 250 yards, Garcia tells John to shoot. One animal drops. John shoots again, and a second drops. It looks so easy. The men cheer. The kill means the camp will have meat tonight.

There's nothing to it—if you've spent the first forty years of your life practicing picking out blobs of brown from other blobs of brown in fields of yellow ochre grass at five or six hundred yards. So now, finally, you see what Garcia has been pointing at—it's a zebra. You raise your gun. "Take your time," whispers John. "Quickly," says Garcia. And then in exasperation. "Why you no shoot?" Quickly is impossible. The animal finally lurches into the scope. Pause for a brief lesson in anatomy. If he's turning toward you, you shoot just one inch behind the front shoulder which will get him in the heart (or is in the lung?). But if he's turned at a different angle, then . . . whispered last minute instructions about the range. (The scope was sighted in for two hundred yards, after which distance the bullet will be falling therefore—now let's see . . . if it's falling, then I must shoot higher. But Garcia's instructions are in meters. A meter is thirty-nine inches, a yard is thirty-six, so if it's 225 meters, then . . . Oh hell, the golfer in me comes to the rescue. I know what it is. It's a drive and a wedge. We're finally ready. "Safety off," hisses John. "Hurry," says Garcia. It's my first shot. At a zebra. I want a zebra. I foolishly promised my sister Jane a zebra rug. I shoot. The zebras race off.

"Why you miss?" yells Garcia, crossly, as we climb aboard and the Jeep lurches off in pursuit of the herd. "I thought I was on him," I mutter to John. But, then, how was I really to know?

I had always thought that the chase of wild beasts across flowing plains by well-armed men in fast-moving Land Rovers was—well—unsporting. As we bucket in pursuit, flinging into the air as we hit logs and ditches, lurching sideways racing around the edge of forested areas and swampy ground, slamming back into the bench with a crunch of the backbone, I go through an agonizing reappraisal of that preconception, too. Suddenly we stop. The zebras have stopped also—at a distance. Garcia picks out a big one, when Blondie points some yards away where the animal I had shot has fallen. Dead. John speaks up. "She told me she was on him," he informs Garcia. One relieved brother. One relieved sister.

As the days pass the tension increases. Will you be able to fill out your license, and get a good example of each of the animals it entitles you to kill? We move to another camp. The camp helpers, the cook, the laundryman, Mario, the steward, and a couple of yard men take off early in the morning. When they leave the road to go cross-country to tonight's campsite in the woods on the edge of a fertile grassy plain that stretches a hundred miles in each direction, they blaze a trail for us, who will be following in the other Jeep after the morning's hunt. They cut a small wedge out of both sides of the trees that mark our way so that we will be able not only to follow them in, but also, a week hence, to find our way back to the road. At dusk we come to the camp: three tents for John, Garcia, and me. A cook-tent. A lean-to has been thrown up for the men, and a tall bathhouse of straw and bamboo, tied together by bark fibers, is being built. Tomorrow we will bathe al fresco in a corrugated iron washtub in the soft African evening twilight. Everything that Safrique and ten hard-working men can do to attend to our comfort has been done.

I keep possession of my rifle at night, not, you understand, for fear of a night-marauding leopard or lion, but because I have found that a rifle propped in the corner of the tent makes a handy clothes rack; where you put your clothes at night so that you can find them in the predawn dark can be vital.

So many comforts. Mario wakes us in the morning with a cup of steaming hot café-crème. He serves supper in white trousers and a gold-buttoned jacket. In due course, we run out of fresh-baked bread and ice. But the cook picks greens from the lagoons for salad and we have fresh meat every day and delicious home-made soup spiced with peri-peri olives.

We acquit ourselves well in the plains and head for nyala country. The thing about nyalas—surely you've heard of nyalas? Never heard of a nyala? Well, neither had we two weeks before. The nyala—an antelope with unusually beautiful markings—can be shot nowhere else in the world but this particular part of Mozambique.

And shot he is by John that very evening as we approach our new camp. At dusk. At about 350 yards (drive, four iron, chip) in a disgusting display of expertise that even draws a snort of admiration from Garcia. Except for a giant kudu, John now has filled out his license and it is up to me to get my sable, get my nyala, get my giant kudu.

Chase my nyala we do, for days it seems, through savannahs and forest, on foot and on Jeep. The men grow quiet, John grows kind, Garcia is in turn silent and enraged. And I grow nervous.

It's just about dusk and only two days to go. Garcia taps for the Jeep to stop and takes up the binoculars.

"You see him?" he whispers.

Me: "No."

Garcia: (Incredulous) "You don't see him?"

Me: "No."

Garcia: "By that tree." (Irritated) "You see the tree?" (Sarcastic)

Me: "Yes"

Garcia: "You see the dark shadow?"

Me: "Yes."

Garcia: (Triumphant) "That's the nyala. You see him?"

Me: (Weakly) "I see the shadow."

Garcia: (The Portuguese equivalent of) "Jesus, María, y José."

It's not more than 350 yards away. There's not quite five minutes of light left. The nyala is a hemidemisemiquaver darker in shade than the surrounding bush—and I don't see him.

Oh, let the shadow dissolve, I pray. But it doesn't. So I shoot, and predictably miss. "Nyala day, nyala dollar," comments John by way of consolation.

We don't know that the following day—our next to last—I will shoot a huge sable antelope with such precision and skill that the gentlemen trackers who stand right behind us (Blondie, Jocopo, and Zecco) will pound me on the back and exclaim, "Good, lady, good shot"; the driver will shake my hand; Garcia will hug me and insist on many photographs.

And so we return: unmauled by leopard, unmangled by lion, ungored by buffalo, unsqueezed by python, unbitten by mamba, unflattened by elephant. What did we get out of it? Experiences and sights we will never forget, a cantankerous new friend in Garcia, and lessons learned. I'm the girl who can identify a "just a moment, please" thorn at a glance. That's the kind of thorn that when it gets imbedded in your clothes, or worse still in your flesh, hangs on. I can look at any given leg and tell a chigger from a cootie from a tick from a mosquito from a redbug from a flea bite, and what to do about it. Want to know the relative tastiness of warthog, reedbuck, and harbeste steak? I can tell you. Actually, sable is the best of all (don't try buffalo tongue unless you like tongue-tongue). And there is not another lady at the Sharon Country Club, I'm sure, who can tell a buffalo dropping from an elephant dropping at a glance, and whether it is *zulu* or *chisena*.

Was it worth it? Of course. But with one small caveat, nyala plenty dollar, nyala safari.

19

The Illustrators

WHEN NATIONAL REVIEW STARTED UP, about the last consideration that came to mind was how and with what we would break up the density of its pages. Editors in general like to fill every single inch of white space with beautiful type. But one soon learns that pages of black ink marching all in a row are discouraging to the average reader. What is needed are breaks in the solemnity of those pages in the form of what we call "read-outs"—those informative few lines at the top of an article that tell you what it is all about, subheads, to encourage you to proceed no matter how daunting the subject matter—and, best of all, illustrations. Illustrations are immensely useful. They stir the imagination, give a visual picture of what the author is writing about, and can be ordered in convenient sizes and shapes.

How we came up with our original illustrator I don't know. He was already on the scene when I joined NR and I never thought to ask. The one thing I did know by this time was that his services must come cheap, or he wouldn't have been considered.

But cheap did not mean shoddy. Our original illustrator, the only one we used for the first two or three years, was Alois Derso, a Hungarian artist of a certain age, now at the tail-end of a distinguished career that had started in the 1920s. He had style and could, with a handful of strokes, identify not only a subject, but the subject's character. He was said to carry around ten thousand portraits in his head.

Back in the Europe that emerged from the First World War, which was where Alois Derso first made his mark, newspapers relied heavily on illustrators. Every leading newspaper had a stable of illustrators who accompanied reporters on the major stories of the day. A major story of the post World War 1 world was the League of Nations, Woodrow Wilson's last best hope for humanity. And the two illustrators who lived and worked in Geneva—in the years that saw hope for a world forevermore at peace shrivel when Mussolini sent his legions into Ethiopia, and then die at Munich—and whose line drawings of the great political leaders and statesmen of the day became world famous, were Alois Derso and his partner Emery Kelen, a fellow Hungarian.

Kelen, who was a few years younger than Derso, had after World War II become a television director at the United Nations, but Derso, having chosen to continue as an artist, had fallen on hard times when he landed the job at *National Review*. He lived in a small seedy hotel in Greenwich Village. He had always been and continued to be a night owl. No matter what the emergency, we were discouraged from calling him before 3:00 PM.

After I became managing editor, Mr. Derso, as we all called him, would drop in to see me on Monday afternoons to discuss his assignments for the week. He did line portraits for the "Books, Arts and Manners" section of the magazine and pictorial scenes for the Article section. He would check in with the receptionist every time he arrived. Most regular visitors simply mounted the steps to the second floor and walked in, but Mr. Derso, a product of the old

Europe, was formal. He would then knock at the open door of my office, wait for the invitation to come in, and bow before coming to the desk and shaking hands.

He was very tall, well over six feet, with a long cadaverous melancholy face, and longish grey hair that fell over the frayed collar of his long greyish gabardine coat. He wore the coat, which just cleared his ankles, winter and summer. I never knew what he wore underneath because he kept it buttoned, and never, to my knowledge, took it off. He would have stood in front of my desk while we discussed our business had I not suggested that he take a seat on the Willmoore Kendall Memorial Couch, which was at that period in my office. He would lower himself rather awkwardly onto the couch, and rest his arms on his knees, and we'd come up with ideas for four or five drawings, which he would deliver by Thursday at the latest. They were startlingly good and stylish, and always exactly the size we had asked for.

Our conversations were usually limited to the business at hand, although he would often ask about Bill and invariably hope that my mother, whom he had met, was well and happy. I did ask him once about his early life, and his long sad face broke into a smile. As a young man, he told me, "I went to Paris, and to be in Paris as a rich young Hungarian was to be in heaven."

After leaving NR's office on 35th Street, Mr. Derso would walk up to the United Nations building. His work for NR meant that he had a UN press card, and there he would spend his afternoons, looking in on this session or that, and storing away in his head pictures of the statesmen he might be asked to draw.

We became friends, although it remained always at a Miss Buckley-Mr. Derso level. After my father's death, when Bill and I published a book on father's life, *WFB: An Appreciation*, we asked Mr. Derso to illustrate it, and he produced a series of wonderful drawings, among them extraordinary caricatures of what our father would have called "those old ruffians," Obregon, Carranza, Zapata, and Pancho Villa. He was insulted when we tried to pay him for them. Were we not friends? Was this not what a friend would do for a friend? End of discussion.

One day, at the end of our business talk, Mr. Derso paused at the door as he was going out and then came back into the office. Rather diffidently he informed me that his old League of Nations partner, Emery Kelen, had written a book about the League, *Peace in Their Time*. It contained a number of line drawings by Derso, and although he knew that the book was not significant enough to warrant a review in *National Review* perhaps, because it contained drawings familiar to *National Review* readers, Mr. Meyer (Frank Meyer, our book editor) might bend the rules sufficiently to consider running a brief review of the book. But of course he would understand if that proved to be impossible. I assured Mr. Derso that I would bring the matter to Mr. Meyer's attention that very afternoon when he called in and that I was certain that Mr. Meyer would go along.

Frank was delighted. He thought the book merited what he called a "number two" length review (eight hundred to one thousand words), and asked me to do it. It would be a pleasure, I said.

When I conveyed this happy news to Mr. Derso, he pulled himself off the Memorial Couch, raised himself to his full six-feet-three-inches, and bowed almost to the waist. "Madame," he said, "that was my secret desire."

I had told Frank that it would be a pleasure to review *Peace in Their Time*. And it was. Kelen turned out to be a gifted writer who brought his artist's eye to the printed word. The stories he picked to tell were charming, as just one example, how French Foreign Minister Aristide Briand got the last word at Mère Léger's restaurant when Gustave Stressman tried to grab the check. "I'll pay for the lunch," said Briand, "you can take care of the reparations." His word pictures of the statesmen in Geneva were masterly: "Slim and trim [Austin

Chamberlain] stood and walked square-shouldered, as if he had swallowed a coat hanger . . . his nephew [Neville] could not laugh, and if he smiled, the smile ran down the tips of his wilted mustache like the juice of a bitter melon." "Senator [Claude A.] Swanson's mustaches needed a good clipping, but his frown did not, as it was almost clipped to his face by a pince-nez lest it slide off his beaky nose." Two stout women rolling down the Quai Wilson with heavy Venetian beads looked to Kelen "like a couple of overflowing barrels of pirate treasure just fished out of a lake."

Mr. Derso was delighted with the review, and I was in turn pleased when I noticed that he carried a copy of that issue of *National Review* around stuffed in the pocket of his long grey coat for a number of weeks.

⁓

C.D. Batchelor came calling one day when NR was still at its first quarters on 37th Street. Batchelor was as tall as Mr. Derso, or maybe even taller, because whereas Derso's grey locks hung down over the collar of his coat, Batchelor's salt and pepper brush went straight up in an overgrown crew cut that added a couple of inches to his height.

C.D. Batchelor was a Pulitzer-Prize winning cartoonist for the *New York Daily News*, at that time the most conservative newspaper in the city. Like Mr. Derso, he had been around a long, long time. He once told me that the first political contribution he had ever made was the five dollars he sent to General Botha as a boy to protest the British war against the Boers in South Africa at the turn of the century. Batch, as he was called, was a conservative through and through, and had come to offer his services as a cartoonist to NR, pro bono publica. And so every Monday morning he also showed up in my office at NR, but he came in bright and early carrying a half-dozen or more roughs of cartoons, from which I would chose one which he would then draw in final form for the current issue.

Batchelor was a magnificent draftsman, but it must be admitted that after fifty years or so of drawing daily cartoons for the *News* he had pretty much run out of fresh ideas. His cartoons were on the order of a magnificent galleon under full sail heading for the rocks. The galleon might be labeled, "SS Presidency," and the shoals, "Congress." As Mr. Derso was our only illustrator for the first few years, Batch was our original cartoonist.

Batchelor, who had been married five times, used to joke that he was always a bridegroom and never a bachelor. He was a man of immense charm and a thousand amusing stories. He knew everyone in the trade going back many years and he would linger, after our business had been taken care of, and chat for a while. He soon found out that I loved newspaper stories and regaled me with them.

He had a collection of canes, and arrived every week with a new one, which he would show me and describe when and where he had acquired it. Many of them were beauties. Every once in a while he would sweep me off for a long, happy lunch to the grand Longchamps in the first floor and basement of the Empire State Building, where he was well known.

And once he and his wife, the charming Allegra, invited me to supper in their Tudor City apartment on 42nd Street. My fellow guest was the famous columnist Westbrook Pegler, who had recently been fired by his syndicate after losing a libel suit brought by a fellow columnist. Peg was down and out. He didn't know at the time that he would never have another job. He was full of good cheer and snappy rejoinders that evening as we sat over a gin and tonic on the terrace. One comment he made I will never forget. Batch had asked him if so-and-so had been a Communist.

"A Communist?" he replied. "Why she was as red as a fresh cut throat."

Peg had been a thorn in the flesh of the New Deal, and was, or if he wasn't should have been, on FDR's enemies list. One column he had written years earlier had particularly tickled me. In it, he warned other columnists off. They were not to encroach on his standing as the founder of the HEFC (Hate Eleanor First Club).

There was a blackout in the course of the evening. We waited a while to see if the lights would go back on, but they didn't, so about 10:30 when I said goodnight to the Batchelors, Peg asked where I lived and said he would walk me home. It was about twenty blocks or so.

It was a soft summer night, fairly cool and very pleasant. We were sauntering up Lexington Avenue, past Grand Central Station, when a tall red-headed young man accosted us. He introduced himself as a reporter for the *Daily News* and asked if he could interview us for a man-on-the-street story about the blackout. Peg was gracious and gave the boy several quotes that would make good reading and would, hence, please the young man's editor. The reporter thanked us politely, and asked for Peg's name and address. Peg gave them. There wasn't a flicker of recognition. The young reporter had evidently never heard of Westbrook Pegler, which was the equivalent of an early TV viewer never having heard of Walter Cronkite or Edward R. Murrow.

As we walked on Peg commented, a trifle sadly: "I could have been that young man forty years ago, tall, red-headed, in from the sticks, on my first job in the big city."

It wasn't long before NR was using other cartoonists. Some of them emerged from conservative campus journals that sprang up in the late Sixties and early Seventies, cartoonists like Steve Kelly, Tom Payne, and the great Jeff MacNelly, who got his start working for former NR summer editorial assistant Ross Mackenzie, now editor of the *Richmond News-Leader*. Most of these were eventually syndicated. But we also developed our own cartoonists, the mad and insanely talented John Kreuttner whose captions often took more space than his crazy elliptical drawings. The flower children and hippies of the late Sixties were bread and butter for Mary Gauerke. Mary dressed all in black, used a scarlet lipstick slashed across a pale face, and favored very high-heeled black pumps. She was seldom seen without a long cigarette holder from which hung a glowing cigarette. She was to the potheads and beads and sandal generation what Helen Hokinson had been to the New Yorker Long Island matron. And then there was Mal Hancock.

Mal Hancock was introduced to NR by Harry Elmlark, a liberal Jewish newspaper syndicator with a Damon Runyonesque look about him, who despite his liberalism turned out to be one of *National Review*'s major benefactors. It was Harry who first decided that Bill Buckley should have a syndicated column and proceeded to syndicate him. When Bill's secretary, the indispensable Gertrude Vogt, retired, it was Harry Elmlark who told Bill that a most able British secretary at the *Washington Star* was bored and ready for a change of pace. And that was how Frances Bronson, without whom Bill Buckley could not have survived, came to *National Review*, where everyone, starting with her boss, conspired, as she would say, to drive her bonkers, but no one ever succeeded. And finally Harry brought us (in addition to a friendship that we all valued), young Malcolm Hancock.

As a young man, Mal was playing golf with his father one day and, searching for an errant golf ball, fell down a cliff and lost the use of his legs. While undergoing rehabilitation for months he started drawing rotund little figures with expressive faces (happy, sad, melancholic, desperate, depressed, thrilled, you name it) to amuse himself, and pretty soon he was adding captions, and making jokes with them. They were highly sophisticated, and as simple as Kreuttner's cartoons were complicated. We signed Mal up at once, on Harry's insistence, and ran three or more of his cartoons in every issue of the magazine for many years. Although he was later syndicated, and his cartoons featured in the *Washington Post* and a number of major magazines, Mal continued to give NR the first chance at his new drawings. He would send me in a batch of ten or fifteen every week or so, and it was only after we had returned those we didn't want that he would market them elsewhere.

He suffered a great deal, but never complained. We never met. He was to come from Michigan where he lived to one of our NR anniversary dinners, but at the last moment he simply was not strong enough to make the trip.

But Mal and I chatted by phone every two or three weeks for twenty years or more. We would talk just about everything under the sun, but also a great deal about golf, which had been his greatest youthful enthusiasm, and is my life-long love. I once told him the disastrous story of my first entry into big time golf, in the Women's Amateur championship, and he laughed and laughed. Every now and then he would ask me to tell it to him again because he had forgotten this highlight or that. He urged me to write about it, and eventually I did but alas, it was after Mal's death, too young, of cancer.

20

Clear Fairways, Miss Buckley

T HE FRONT PAGE OF THE SPORTS SECTION of the *Philadel-phia Inquirer* carried a picture in May 1949 of three bewil-dered young women under the head: UPSET. The caption explained that if any of the three won her match in the first round of the Women's National Amateur Golf Championship at the Marion Cricket Club, it would be the upset of the tournament. I was one of the three. This was my first appearance in what was then the big league of women's golf, the crowning moment of my golfing life.

I am twenty-seven years old, five feet, two inches tall, and dressed on this day in a creased chambray dress, a relic of college days, having been told too late that shorts—the basics of my golfing wardrobe—are banned at the Amateur. My opponent—the favorite—is one of those rangy long-legged, easy striding golden Western women, wearing tailored, light-tan slacks that match her bag, which matches her shoes, which match her cap, which matches her blond locks and handsome, lightly-tanned face. Her bag proclaims that it belongs to Dot Kielty, her cap says "Dot," and the beaded belt around her (disgustingly slim) waist spells out "D-o-t-t-i-e."

We are called to the first tee; Dottie climbs over the rope, I—after measuring the height—wriggle under. "Miss Buckley on tee," roars the loudspeaker. Miss Buckley tees up, nervously, takes a practice swing, nervously, and is asked to step back, which she does, nervously. The television cameras must be positioned, and back in 1949 that takes some time. Miss Buckley obligingly swings for the camera crew as they align their instrument.

"Clear fairways, Miss Buckley," says the loudspeaker. Miss Buckley—by now a near basket case—cranks up a mighty swing, and the ball rolls—ever so slowly—over the front edge of the tee, coming to rest on the tee's downward slope still within easy range of the cameras. Miss Buckley staggers off making way for Miss Kielty who takes a no-nonsense swing and slams her ball 250 yards right down the middle. Dottie picks up her tee (smirks at the crowd) and pauses to say: "Miss Buckley, I never converse when I play tournament golf," and strolls ten feet ahead to await my second shot.

So you ask? How can I continue to love a game that inflicts such constant, almost gleeful humiliations on its votaries? The answer is: I have no choice. I can no more purge golf from my being than I could shuck amoebic dysentery, which when you get it, you have for life.

"Golf," the *Columbia Encyclopedia* informs us, is a "game of hitting a small hard ball with specially made clubs on an outdoor course sometimes called links. The object is to deposit the ball in a specified number of cups, or holes, using as few strokes as possible."

Which shows how much they know. That's a description of what you do when you play golf, but that's not golf. Golf is a till-death-do-us-part situation: a blessing and a curse, both of biblical proportions: it humbleth the proud, and bringeth the mighty low, but does not, necessarily, raise up the humble. Golf is aggravating, entrancing, humiliating, uplifting, amusing, baffling, depressing, exhilarating, frustrating, debilitating, joyous. It is the kind of game where you are always picking yourself up, dusting yourself off, and starting all over again, and again, and again. It can sunder friendships, it has sundered marriages. It is expensive, and time-consuming, but as any golfer will tell you, there is nothing quite like the exhilaration of a well-struck drive, of a crisp six-iron to the green, or of that impossible putt that careens thirty feet on a slick and treacherous green to drop into the cup. There is nothing to beat stepping up to the first tee in a friendly but competitive foursome. Golf is one of the few sports where players with widely disparate talents can enjoy playing together because handicaps do indeed level the playing field. Golf is fun.

Golf is also an open sesame to friendship. Once the word gets around that you play golf, golfers gravitate toward you. You speak the same language. Next thing you know, you are booked for a round next Saturday, and a whole new set of friends awaits.

The more seriously some golfers take the sport, the more laughs the others get. Half the fun of the game is the stories they tell sitting on the terrace overlooking the 18th green with a tall beer after the round is over. Like the woman in the eighth flight of the Carolinas Woman's Championship, at the Dunes club in Myrtle Beach some years back, who held up the entire field (temperature: 98 degrees) by her insistence that her opponent play the ball where it lay. The opponent refused to do so. The Green's Committee was summoned and ruled the opponent could replace her ball two club's length from where it lay—which was against the scaly hide of a somnolent alligator sunning itself by a pond on the right of the 10th fairway.

Or, at that same tournament, the woman who enlivened the cocktail party that evening by recounting that twenty yards from the 18th hole her small black caddy had handed her a three-wood. The older, experienced caddy, whispered, "Man, why you give that lady that club?" to which the smaller boy had replied, "Man, that lady ain't going to get on no green, nohow, with no club." "And he was perfectly right," commented the lady, by that time well into her third Tom Collins.

P. G. Wodehouse wrote dozens of stories about golf and golfers, wildly convoluted morality tales in which the intolerably stuffy practitioner of the game ends up unstuffed, stories that could, given the zaniness of golf, almost be true. One of Wodehouse's golfers, for instance, having missed a critical putt, complains that the "confounded clatter of butterflies" in the next field has destroyed his concentration. A true golfer hearing such a tale will nod sympathetically. Wodehouse would have approved of Arnold Palmer's (or was it Jack Niklaus's) reply to the fan who asked how on earth he had gotten a 13 on a certain hole. "Because I missed my putt for a 12, ma'am."

Sad to relate, golfers can be picked out in a crowd by a certain glazed look in the eyes of their spouses, family, and intimate friends. It is the glaze of boredom, the visible mark of endlessly endured hours of listening to a golf round relived, hole by endless hole, stroke by endless stroke. No, no, not again, prays the unhappy wife—a prayer that is always unheeded—he's not going to describe yet again that shot on the 16th hole of the Number 2 course in Pinehurst when. . . .

By the way, lest I forget. Dot Kielty beat me, but not until the 17th hole. I could describe the match, hole by hole, shot by shot, but I won't. Even at this remove I can see the glaze in your eye. . . .

21

The Poet

Je suis appalled at Charles de Gaulle
I do not dig *la gloire* at all.
I think the *force de frappe*'s a fraud
La Russie's hardly overawed.
I worry when he mentions "*moi*";
The overtones suggest "*le roi*."
However, though de Gaulle's *de trop*
(They say he'll move to Fontainebleau!)
I'd like to borrow his *esprit*
To stiffen les Etats-Unis.

CHARLES DE GAULLE HAS JUST ANNOUNCED that he is pulling the French military out of the North Atlantic Treaty Organization, just *comme ça*. You can almost see him snap his fingers, with one gesture wiping out years of what he considered affronts to his beloved France (not to say to himself) *de la part des sales Anglo-Saxons*.

National Review will take up the challenge in its editorial pages. But nothing we will write will be as cogent or as apt as Bill von Dreele's poem on the subject. The von Dreele poems delight our readers. They break up those heavy editorial pages, and make them laugh. They have appeared in virtually every issue of the magazine from 1964 to the present day.

But entry into NR's pages didn't come easy for young Bill von Dreele. The Second World War had interrupted his college career. He was drafted after his first year at Middlebury College and served in Europe with the 78th Infantry Division. He crossed the Roer River as a scout on a patrol in the spring of 1944 that was so hairy that he and the other four members of the patrol were rewarded with a hard-to-get forty-eight-hour pass in Paris. And, Bill smiles when he tells you this, that was how he missed what should have been the crowning moment of his war experience, the crossing of the Remagen Bridge, the only bridge over the Rhine the Germans had failed to dynamite in their retreat. The 78th Infantry discovered the bridge was intact, stormed across it, establishing a bridgehead east of the Rhine and held it long enough for the 7th Army to punch across the Rhine and bring the war into the German heartland. Young Bill spent the day of the historic capture of the bridge in Paris freezing in the Hotel du Gare du Nord, and at the equally freezing opera, but happy to be out of the front lines for however brief a time.

Bill returned to Middlebury to complete his undergraduate education and got his Masters at NYU, during which period he decided that what he didn't want to do was be a teacher. He flailed around for a while and finally went for an interview at IBM, where the personnel director told him, "What is a nice young man like you doing in New York?" but then gave him a job. And so he worked for IBM for twenty-five years on their in-house publications, loathing every minute of it.

He was an avid reader of *The Reporter* magazine in those days and noted that every issue carried a poem by Maria Mannes at the front of the book. A poet himself, he liked that. He also liked *National Review*, which he had just started reading and to which he started sending light verse in the hopes that NR would emulate *The Reporter* and start publishing light verse on a regular basis. He tells me that it took him a year before NR printed his first poem. But once inside the door, he was in great demand. Bill would wait until Sunday before starting to write the four or five verses he would deliver to NR's office every Tuesday morning before going to work at IBM. His verse was highly political, and what was even more important, highly topical, and most important of all, very funny. Some examples:

On the Establishment's feelings about LBJ

> Fulbright's wretched; Morse is mad;
> Javits says we have been had.
> Wechsler hints at "Budapest";
> Huntley-Brinkley look depressed.
> Reston's mad enough to spit;
> Lippmann's rage is exquisite.
> Oh what fun it is to say:
> All the way with LBJ!

On the Establishment's feelings about the Kennedys

> I swear if, on the Senate floor
> The shades of orators of yore
> Appeared—like, say, Diogenes'—
> The Press would push the Kennedys.

> The reason's difficult to plumb.
> (Diogenes was hardly dumb.)

But nothing Greek *begins* to please
Like quoting from the Kennedys.

Indeed, if Jacob Javits spoke
Bereft of toga, shorn of cloak;
With nothing on but BVDS—
They'd focus on the Kennedys.

On the Establishment's utter dismay at the very thought of Reagan

Like a giant organ swelling
    Over something from Gounod;
Like a saturation shelling. . . .
    Like a real nor'easter blow.
Like a Grecian peroration;
    Like a deluge from above;

Like a stripper's slow gyration
    Teasing off a leather glove.
Watch 'em shudder! Hear 'em bellow!
    As the liberals detect
Ronald Reagan is the fellow
    All us kookies may elect.

Bill von Dreele would do anything for NR. He wrote Christmas
verses, and anniversary verses, and special presidential election verses.
When Bill Buckley ran for mayor of New York in 1965 and *National
Review* published several eight-page inserts on that spirited contest
for the benefit of its New York readers, von Dreele agreed to edit the
supplement. When Bill Buckley was asked to read the Ogden Nash
verse for Saint-Saens *Carnival of the Animals*, he found the verses
tedious and asked Bill von Dreele to compose another version, which
Bill von D. dutifully did in the allotted two days' time.

At one point, *National Review* tried to hire von Dreele, but Bill von Dreele is nothing if not cautious. He took a day or two to think it over, compared IBM's retirement benefits to NR's uncertain continued lifespan, and sorrowfully declined.

In the mid-1970s an appalling fate befell our hero: IBM moved its headquarters from Manhattan to the sticks, to White Plains, New York—*White Plains*. It was a move away from those dozens of charming small restaurants at which Bill von Dreele and his buddies were wont to while away an hour or two each day before returning to their tedious tasks. In White Plains, unless he called a taxi for a ten or fifteen minute drive to a reasonably possible restaurant, Bill and his cronies were reduced to eating lunch in the company cafeteria. It was practically the final blow, the worst thing that had happened to von Dreele since he missed his moment of possible glory at the Remagen Bridge. This was probably what firmed up von Dreele's decision to retire the very minute he had put in the twenty-five years that would earn him a handsome IBM retirement.

Retirement day was glorious. When Bill von Dreele emerged from his apartment on West 84th Street, in what had very recently been one of the worst streets in all Manhattan, there was a large white stretch limousine parked in front. A liveried chauffeur jumped out, tipped his hat, and informed Bill that the limo had been hired by some of his friends to take him to White Plains for his final day on the job. The limo was there at noon to whisk the retirement celebrants off to a posh White Plains restaurant, the poshest available, where a dry martini or two were savored. And after work, his desk cleaned out, Bill von Dreele was driven in state back to New York. At the front door of the apartment, the chauffeur swept open the door, swept his cap off, and said: "Happy Retirement, Mr. von Dreele."

22

Feeling Our Oats

I T's 1970. *National Review* has been around for fifteen years, and we are feeling our oats. What began as a tiny journal of conservative opinion with bleak prospects and a balance sheet that would remain in the red for a good twenty years was now the center of a burgeoning conservative movement. NR had built up such a stable of devoted readers that when Bill wrote the subscribers every spring outlining the perilous financial picture of the magazine, and asking for contributions to keep it alive, they opened their hearts and their wallets and sent in enough to take care of that year's deficit.

NR was now more than just a magazine. In the Goldwater campaign in 1964, those clean-shaven young men and neatly dressed young women who formed his honor guard and cheering section wherever he campaigned were, so many of them, probably most of them, Yaffers, as the Young Americans for Freedom were called. And YAF, which had been founded in our parents' home in Sharon, Connecticut, in 1960, was now a powerful counterweight to the New Left on most American campuses, and the first editor of its national magazine, the *New Guard*, was an NR alumnus, David Franke.

In New York, in the 1960s, two young lawyers, brothers-in-law they were, Daniel J. Mahoney and Kieran O'Doherty, had founded the state's Conservative Party to pull Republican politicians to the right as the Liberal Party pulled Democratic politicians to the left. And among the founding fathers of the Conservative Party were two *National Review* senior editors, Frank S. Meyer and William F. Rickenbacker, a twentieth-century equivalent of the Renaissance man.

In 1965, in a spirit of gay abandon, Bill Buckley had agreed to run for mayor of New York on the Conservative Party ticket against everyone's pet liberal Republican, John S. Lindsay, and Bill had recruited his older brother Jim, an international oil executive, as his campaign manager. The totally inexperienced would-be mayor, and his totally politically inexperienced brother put on a campaign of such spirited razzle-dazzle that Bill ended up with an impressive 14 percent of the vote, and John Lindsay's presidential ambitions took such a drubbing that he was practically never heard from after leaving City Hall.

But here the Law of Unintended Consequences kicked in, and when the Conservative Party was looking for a candidate in 1968 to run against liberal Republican Senator Jacob Javits, it turned to the (until three years earlier) politically unknown second Buckley, Jim. He agreed, like his brother three years earlier, to be a sacrificial lamb, and was duly defeated by Javits as everyone had known he would be. But Jim's campaign had put him on the political map and earned him friends and supporters, drawn by his honesty, diffidence, and, in such contrast to Bill, his unflamboyant style.

But 1970 was another matter. President Nixon had appointed a conservative congressman, Charles Goodell, to replace Robert Kennedy in the Senate after Kennedy's assassination, and Goodell, upon being sworn in as the junior senator from New York had made a sharp left turn politically, such a sharp turn that the Conservative Party felt it could not support him for reelection. Would Jim Buckley, now a veteran of two New York campaigns, consider running again, this time in a three-way race, as the Conservative candidate against Goodell, Republican, and Rep. Richard Ottinger, Democrat? Only, said Jim, if there was a chance this time of winning. He was wonderfully good-natured, but not good-natured enough to play the role of sacrificial lamb yet again.

And this was why we, at *National Review*, were full of beans. Because on election day, which came just a week or so before our fifteenth anniversary party, Jim squeaked through to win on the Conservative line. We had us a senator. So we decided that our party this time round would be different—informal, and boisterous, an informality that was reflected in the invitations, which ran as follows: "To remark the Fifteenth Anniversary of *National Review* Magazine, Nika Standen Hazelton and the Sponsors request the pleasure of [name] at a [turn the page] PERFECTLY SMASHINGLY ABSOLUTELY WILD KNOCKDOWN DRAG-OUT NO HOLDS BARRED GREAT BIG NOISY UNINHIBITED BRAWL OF A P*A*R*T*Y*."

It was held in Central Park at the Tavern-on-the-Green, music by Wild Bill Davison and his Dixieland band, and by The Repairs, a rock band led by Fairfield U's Peter McCann. Mexican food.

Five hundred people turned out. And the roars of laughter could be heard all the way from Central Park to the sedate offices of the *New York Times,* when Bill Buckley introduced his brother Jim, the world's most mild-mannered and courteous man, by reading Robert Morris's lugubrious column in *Newsday,* on November 5, the morning after Jim's election:

> It crept in during the night. It was hanging over the city when we awoke yesterday, gray and imponderable, like the fog. Morning became afternoon and still it would not go away, the shame, the burden, the thorny crown of collective guilt. We sat in darkened apartments, Dostoyevskyan, vaguely aware of grey light filtering in

through the windows, unable to stir outside, unwilling to face our neighbors, eyes cast down, unseeing. New York! New York had come to this . . . On one dark night New York removed Allard Lowenstein from the House, and placed James Buckley in the Senate. That's enough dirty work for a decade . . . It is difficult to be a gracious loser when you are branded before the nation, as all New Yorkers are today, with the letter C for Conservative on your forehead.

When Jim got up, to the roars and laughter of the crowd, he greeted the revelers as "fellow night-riders of the right," using the term that had figured in a *New York Times* editorial a week earlier denouncing Jim's candidacy.

"The shame of New York" and "night-rider of the Right" went on, after his term in the Senate, to serve as undersecretary of state under Alexander Haig, as president of Radio Free Europe/Radio Liberty, and was named by Ronald Reagan to the federal court of appeals for the District of Columbia, where ten or twelve years later he was rated Number One among the justices of that court by *Washingtonian* magazine. He continues to have the letter C molded on his forehead, and in his heart.

23

Narrow Boats

J IM'S ELECTION WAS INDUBITABLY SPLENDID for the Conservative Party of New York, which could now boast of having placed a big-C Conservative in the United States Senate. It was great for the Senate to have a freshman senator with such integrity and intelligence. It even shed a little reflective glory on *National Review*. But it wasn't such unalloyed good news for Jim's friends in New York and Connecticut, starting with me.

Jim and I had shared an apartment in New York for over a dozen years. On Fridays, I worked in the little office he and my brother John had established in an old carriage house at Great Elm, and we socialized a lot. But that happy informal companionship was now a thing of the past, since Jim and Ann had removed to Washington.

We were discussing this one night with George and Jodie Stone, who usually came to dinner at my sister Jane's on Thursday nights when I drove out from New York. The Stones had been Jim's friends initially, but by this time they were surrogate members of the Buckley family. Jim and George had been at Yale together, and very shortly after the end of World War II, George and his very young bride Jodie had moved to Lakeville, Connecticut. George taught mathematics at Hotchkiss, and would eventually head the Hotchkiss math department, and Jodie worked in the administration. They were an impressive couple, George topping six feet, five inches, and Jodie well over six feet tall.

It was hideous outside this particular night, typical of the cold, raw, stormy early March northern Connecticut weather. Though the fire was blazing in Jane's monstrously large fireplace, the outlook was generally bleak and spirits at a low winter ebb. That was when Jodie first mentioned narrow boats in England. It seemed to her, she said, that if we wanted to see more of Jim and Ann this summer than we had last summer, we had better do something to orchestrate it. And the something she suggested was that we charter a narrow boat for a week on a canal in England or Wales.

"Have you ever thought of a narrow boat trip?" she asked. "Should we?" Followed by a quick, "What do you mean by narrow boat?" Followed by, "What's it like?" "What's involved?" and the invariable, "How much?" All of which Jodie, being Jodie, efficiency being her middle name, told us, whipping out brochures, price lists, scheduled departures, alternate routes, travelers' insurance forms, and the exchange rate for the pound as of close of business Friday last.

And so the seed was planted, and an excited telephone pitch made to Ann and Jim who signed on, on the spot, providing we could find a suitable date when the Senate was not in session. Which was why we found ourselves in Llangollen, Wales, to see for ourselves one of the wonders of the canal world, the Pontcysyllte span.

Nearly two hundred years ago the great English engineer Thomas Telford undertook what seemed an insuperable problem. How to carry a canal from Horse Falls north of Llangollen in the Welsh hills across a deep gorge in the valley of the River Dee to join up with a system of canals that would bring ninety thousand gallons of mountain water to the city of Chester and its surrounding Shropshire countryside. This was the period of great canal building in England. It took Telford ten years, but in 1805 while the trumpets trumpeted and the drummers drummed, the Pontcysyllte span was ready. High, narrow arches of stone soar 120 feet up from the valley floor to support a masonry cradle. In it rests a cast-iron trough through which the barges would sail, and welded to it a wide towpath for the horses and mules that pulled them.

Today we will cross the aqueduct on the narrow boats, *Castle* and *Rose*. *Castle* and *Rose*, which cruise in tandem, are each fifty feet long, six feet, two inches wide. The locks on the Llangollen Canal are seven feet wide.

It is the big moment. Our forward patrol (Helen, who serves as mate) makes sure the way is clear. The first boat to enter the aqueduct has the right of way. The passengers, my sister and brother, Jim and Jane, Jim's wife, Ann, George and Jodie Stone, and I, sit atop *Rose*, our feet dangling over the side. Captain Kirk edges onto the aqueduct. There's no balustrade on our side, only on the other, the towpath side, so we are looking down 130 feet to the valley floor, a heady (if not totally enjoyable) sensation. As one man, we edge back a little. Way down there, a young man is practicing golf shots, but we are too high, too far away to comment on his form. Upriver the waters speckle white as the river dashes across the rocks between the lush, narrow banks. We glide along smoothly, marveling at Telford's genius. It's unreal, hard to explain.

A hundred years ago, Sir Walter Scott gazed up at Pontcysyllte and called it the greatest work of art he had ever seen. C.T. Rolfe writes in *The Inland Waters of England* (don't leave for a barge trip without it) that Telford's "soaring bridge is to other aqueducts as a Gothic cathedral is to a Norman church." A man walking along the towpath brings us back to earth. "Are you enjoying your peanut butter?" he asks. "Yes," we reply, laughing. Brother Jim's request for peanut butter at breakfast has evidently caused a flutter in the small world that is the canal.

It is because of the Pontcysyllte aqueduct that we picked this particular trip. The narrow boats run in pairs. *Rose*, the butty-boat that has no engine and is pulled by the *Castle*, had the guest accommodations, six tiny cabins, four singles and two doubles, plus a toilet and a shower. (The six of us had taken all twelve berths for the week at a cost of just under $400 each.) *Castle* had the crew's quarters, plus a toilet, a tight little saloon and a dining room with two tables, each seating three people. Jodie and I ended up with the double cabins. We also got everyone's empty suitcases on our extra bunk. When I stood in front of the washbasin I could reach anything in the room without moving my feet. And I am short.

The day starts with the knock on the door that heralds a smiling Katherine, the cook and stewardess, with our early morning coffee or tea. This will hold us until breakfast: cold cereal and fruit, juice, hot toast, and great plates of ham, eggs, and stewed tomatoes. Our week's trip will take us along the Llangollen and Shropshire Union canals from Llangollen to Chester, sixty to seventy miles by water.

Kirk casts off and we glide out of town and into a leafy everglade, all sounds muted, the leaves so heavy overhead we'll have to use our flashes to snap pictures. The trees thin out. We are sailing along a mountain hillside, well above the valley floor, with sheer limestone cliffs to our left. Sheep graze down to the canal's edge. In the old days, mules and horses pulled heavy barges laden with Welsh slate and coal along this waterway. At a lock we step ashore and walk ahead for a mile or two. It's late afternoon when we put up at Marston's lock, not far from Mad Jack's pub, and George, our iceman, tucks the small white ice bucket we found in the saloon under his arm and heads for Mad Jack's. He returns in evident ill humor. Mad Jack's will not open until 6:30, forcing a postponement of our cocktail hour. Mad Jack's is George's retreat from Moscow, his only defeat in Operation Ice Procurement in this year of our Lord 1971. As a math professor and the owner of a primitive calculator he is our bookkeeper. His other major duty is to make sure we have enough ice every evening to cool our preprandial drinks.

It's just before 7:00, the sun is streaming in my cabin widow when I wake up the next morning. A cock is crowing, a mule brays. The last sound before going to sleep was an owl's hoot. Kirk brings in the eggs he's just bought from a farmer. They're big and small, white and brown, and speckled just as they used to be when they came from the nest, not the box.

At one farm, a sheepdog keeps anxious watch, dogging the strays back into line. We stop at White Mere for lunch—an enchanting lake, left behind when the last Ice Age retreated ten thousand years ago. It has no surface entrance or exit waters. It's calm, remote. We watch ducks and grebes at play. Jim, our ornithologist, tells us that it is believed that a grebe's eyesight is so sharp that it can see a gun firing and move out of the way of the shot. Jim, our lawyer, adds that he can't confirm the accuracy of that statement.

Now the country changes dramatically. We are traversing the Whitwell Moss, a boggy area of grey, brown and black peat and swamp. There is so little bottom to it that to build this stretch of canal they had first to fill it in, then dig the channel through the fill. The canal runs straight for miles, under old stone bridges and an occasional lift bridge. Once, Katherine, at the tiller, warns Jodie that the three books she left piled on top of the barge, where we sit and read and sun in the mornings, may be swept off by a low bridge. Kirk races ahead, pulls a chain at a lift-bridge to get it moving, then puts his weight on the balance beam, and the roadway lifts slowly to permit us to pass. (Be sure to lower the bridge and leave it the way you found it! every canal book exhorts you.)

From time to time we walk along the towpath, lending a hand with the opening and closing of the gates. At Grindley Brook Lock—a three-chambered staircase lock, where the bottom gate of one lock serves as the top gate of the next—we help Helen pull the butty-boat from chamber to chamber to chamber. We will have dropped over forty feet when we are through.

En route to Nantwich, which will be our penultimate stop, we traverse a countryside thick with pine forests and clusters of oaks. A beefy-faced fellow on a pleasure boat draws along as we are sunning on the roof and comments, "Oh, I say there. She's a beauty. She's just lovely," looking at the bright blue, yellow, and black one-hundred-foot length of our combined barges, the helms striped horizontally in bright red, blue, green, yellow, and white, their brass tillers shining. The petunias make a brave show among the fresh mint in the flower boxes topside. We agree, with embarrassed pride, as though *Rose* and *Castle* were ours, as indeed, for this week, they are. This week we are the *QEII*, *Normandie*, *United States*, and *France* of the Llangollen and Shropshire Union canals, the only two-boat hotel barges plying these waters.

Nantwich is off the main route, but so of course is this entire trip. That's its charm. It's a wonderful, relatively untouched town whose people are very proud of its picture postcard half-timbered houses, tilting drunkenly to left, to right, and over the street. In the square in front of the church a red and white sign apologizes for the inconvenience caused by the city's "re-pedestrianization" program, which will turn old Nantwich into a pedestrian mall.

We board the narrow boats for our last stretch of canal. Later this afternoon we pull up alongside the walls of Chester and moor under King Charles's Tower, so named because it was from its window that Charles I saw his Cavaliers break for the last time before Oliver Cromwell's Roundheads. They were never to make another stand:

from King Charles's Tower to the scaffold was now but a matter of time. We walk the walls of the city that night, stop at a pub for a final beer, and in the morning say goodbye to the good companions of the last six days, Kirk, Katherine, and Helen.

Would we do it again? Absolutely. But in reverse next time, starting from Chester and the Shropshire lowlands and spending the rest of the week ascending into the Welsh hills, which are of a singular beauty, with the crossing of Pontcysyllte, the final, soaring highlight.

24

Jane Comes Aboard

M Y SISTER MAUREEN retired from *National Review* shortly after the birth of her first child, Patricia Egan O'Reilly. One of her tasks had been to answer all incoming editorial mail and this, which originally had taken an hour or so a week, was becoming a major burden. Bill was now syndicated, three times a week, in about 350 newspapers around the nation and was heard at least once a week on his public broadcasting TV show, *Firing Line*. What he had to say, particularly in those early days, was contentious in the extreme, and NR was now hit by an avalanche of responses to his views, not only as editor of the magazine, but also as a conservative speaker on the college circuit, and as a spokesman for the growing conservative movement in America.

Looking around for a replacement for Maureen, Bill's roving eye fell on my sister Jane, who had moved back to the States from Calgary, Alberta, where her husband Bill Smith had been in the oil business. The Smiths, Jane, Bill, and the six children, were now living in a lovely old brick house on Sharon Mountain, about two miles from Great Elm. Surely Jane would like something to occupy her mind, Bill reasoned, and put in the call. Bill can be irresistible and, in fact, Jane thought it would be fun to do. It was arranged that she would get a packet of mail once a week. Most of the letters could be answered by form postcards, with a brief handwritten note on each to personalize the response, but many called for an informed opinion on world matters, and good judgment. The volume, particularly when *National Review* engaged in internecine battles, as when it took issue with the John Birch Society, could be voluminous. But Jane, who is marvelously efficient—Bill Rusher approved of her—handled the job with firmness and tact. Given that she was a sister, it was also easy for her whenever faced with a matter of delicacy, or if uncertain of NR's position, to pick up the phone and ask Frances Bronson, or Bill, or me about it.

By the mid- to late 1960s Jane's marriage to Bill Smith was foundering for various reasons, including his growing irrational need for domination over the children, which frightened her. She decided she must remove them from his unhealthy influence. The situation reached its climax when a devastating fire, starting in the attic, destroyed their home, Stoneleigh, and Jane and Bill and the children took shelter in an old stable at Great Elm, renamed the Barn, that Father had remodeled as a guest house for his children and grandchildren. In considering what to do next, Jane came to the realization that after seventeen years of marriage, she didn't want to set up a new household that included Bill Smith. The fire proved to be the catalyst to her decision to leave Bill and get a divorce.

It was a dismal fall and winter for the Smiths. The children, who ranged in age from the sixteen-year-old twins, Kim and Ron, to six-year-old big little Susan, were torn between their devotion to their mother and their loyalty to their father. They had lost the only home they had really known, and now they would be a family divided.

I got in the habit, when I drove out of New York on Thursday nights, of stopping at Jane's for supper. In fact, after mother moved south for the winter I had most of my weekend meals with Jane and the children.

It was on a grey and chilly night in January, after supper at the Barn, that Ben Heath, our sister Aloïse's husband, called. Aloïse had had a terrible headache at supper, he told me. He had rushed her to the hospital, and as they headed up the steps her left leg had started to drag. By the time they got her on a bed she had fallen into a coma.

I offered to drive to West Hartford, and Ben said he would be most grateful if I came. So I packed a small bag and rushed off. Ben met me at the door. We drove to the hospital. The news could not have been worse. There had been massive ruptures in the blood vessels in her brain. A surgeon came to the little room where we waited with Father Noonan, the silver-haired parish priest at St. Timothy's where the Heaths attended Mass. He was a close friend of Aloïse's. The surgeon told Ben that the damage was extensive. He could operate and see what he could do to repair it, but the operation might be useless, too late to salvage the situation.

"If you operate," Ben asked, "and the operation is successful, what will it mean?" The surgeon thought it over for a minute. Mrs. Heath, he said, might regain 50 or maybe 60 percent of her functions. What can that mean, I thought? A wheel chair? blindness? paralysis? speech impediments? I couldn't envision an Aloïse working at 50 or 60 per cent of capacity. We all waited—waited for Ben's decision. Finally, he asked, "Doctor, if it were your wife, would you operate?" "I would," the surgeon replied, and Ben authorized the operation.

We sat, the three of us, the husband, the sister, the parish priest, in the little room for an hour or more, talking occasionally, but mostly in silence. Then the surgeon returned. His failure was evident in his posture. The brain, he told us, had, in effect, been washed away: Aloïse could not hear, see, talk, think, feel. The only thing that kept her alive was her heart, still strong at age forty-eight. It would be a long ten days before it eventually gave out.

"I want to see her," I said, suddenly. The doctor, at the door, paused and came back into the room. "Don't," he said, "Miss Buckley, don't go see her." He told me that the body lying on that bed with tubes running between it and pulsing machines, was nothing but a body. She, the Aloïse we all knew and loved, had departed. She would not know I had visited her and I would be left with that last awful memory.

His admonition brought back how long it had taken to recapture the image of my father, the vibrant man sitting in the big chair at the foot of the table, his light blue eyes slightly magnified by the thick lenses in his pince-nez, entertaining a table full of children with wonderful yarns of his adventures and misadventures as a young man in revolutionary Mexico. That, the true picture of father, had been obscured by the later, also vivid memory of the cripple in a wheelchair, his right arm inert, speaking more slowly and with some difficulty, the father of the last couple of years of his life, after the strokes. The surgeon, I knew, was right, and I was grateful that tired as he was he had taken the time to intervene.

Father Noonan accompanied Ben and me to the dark parking lot, shook our hands and told Ben he would be by 29 Colony Road in the morning. We drove home to a house filled to the rafters with children, an empty shell, absent its animating spirit.

I spent the balance of the weekend at 29 Colony Road, amidst a pack of disconsolate, heartbroken children—Aloïse and Ben had ten, ranging in age from twenty to six—doing what I could to console the unconsolable. I volunteered, with the help of Jimmy Heath, the oldest, to clear Aloïse's clothes and belongings out of the master bedroom and ended up taking home a number of things that Ben thought I could use, including an unopened acrylic painting set that Allie had acquired over Christmas.

It was a dismal, miserable, ten days, a dismal winter altogether but made less hard for me than for Jane because I had my job and all the preoccupations involved in putting out a magazine every other week. Still, it was hard.

But life goes on, and sometime that winter Jane and I opened up the acrylic paint set. We went to a small art supply store in the neighborhood and bought, for one dollar each, a series of how-to-paint books: how to paint landscapes, seascapes, barns, clouds, trees, animals, still lifes, and so on. We papered the floor of a small extra bedroom with newspapers, set up our table easels on two chairs, sat on the folding seats that had come with the set, and started painting. We found it totally engrossing. When painting you can't think of anything else, anything other than your frustration at not being able to achieve on that white canvas the effect that is so clear in the back of your mind. Painting was a lifesaver, a much needed new fascination. We couldn't wait to get out our easels every weekend.

With spring came a lightening of the spirits. Jane bought a comfortable old house about a mile down south Main Street near the country club, a house we had lived in earlier when a fire at Great Elm in the late 1930s had forced mother and father to rent emergency quarters. The Smith children were all back at school, involved in school activities and sports, and becoming accustomed to their new life, and excited about their new home at Carrier Close.

There was a guest house on the grounds, and Jane turned one of its rooms—a big, light, airy room—into a proper studio. Bill, who was also an amateur painter, sent us a large case in which to store our paints. We bought regular easels, a couple of high stools, and acquired painting smocks. Our canvases got bigger, and soon we were inviting friends, who also painted, to join us of an evening in the studio. Jane managed to paint a portrait of the family Persian cat that actually looked like the family Persian cat, and I did seascapes from photographs I had taken on sailing trips with Bill and Pat. Later that summer we joined a small local art club and for twenty-five years, our group, the Sharon Artists, put on a show in late August at the Sharon Country Club. We sold a few paintings, some even to people we didn't know.

Untutored as we were, painting added a new dimension to our lives. Driving in and out from New York, I realized that I was watching changes in the scenery with a different, more interested eye, musing on how one could transcribe this or that effect, the yellowing of the willows as spring approached, or the roseate look of the hillsides in early May. It was all new, all engaging.

The following spring at the fortnightly cover conference at NR, which was attended by Bill, Jimmy O'Bryan, the art director, Jim McFadden (wearing his promotional hat), and I, we couldn't come up with any idea that pleased us. James Jackson Kilpatrick was writing the lead article that would be about the New Hampshire primary, but the article was still to be written and we had very little idea of what its thrust would be. Bill tried some of his red pen squiggles on a sheet of manila paper, but nothing seemed to jell.

Finally, he turned to me. "You're an artist, Pitts," he said. "Why don't you paint us a cover?" This I knew to be a challenge.

Growing up in a large family we were constantly challenging each other to do this or that: Dare you dive from the roof of the bathhouse into the pool. Dare you jump into the hay from that high beam in the barn. Dare you swim the length of the pool underwater. Dare you tell father we're going to the movies tonight. Dare you crawl into the cave. By our code, as children, all challenges had to be accepted.

"Sure," I said to Bill, and turning to a stunned Jimmy O'Bryan, "Would Monday morning be soon enough?"

Over the weekend, in a panic, I tried several ideas, none of which seemed to work. Finally I painted a reasonable resemblance of Al Jenkins' rundown Notions & Sundries general store, a battered but still classy structure on Sharon's Main Street, put a flagpole in front of it, added a grey winter sky and patches of browning snow on the ground. The effect was small town New England and shabby. Jimmy O'Bryan—that delicious man whose weekend had surely been as panicked as mine at the thought of what I might produce—then contributed some red-white-and-blue campaign bunting across the front of the building and, presto! we had us a cover. (I did not add painting of magazine covers to my biographical notes in *Who's Who*.)

25

The Noel Coward of Sports

I'VE BEEN WONDERING about something special for Jane's fiftieth birthday, and once again Buddy Bombard's Chalet Club comes to the rescue. His latest brochure announces the inauguration of hot-air balloon flights once a week, in scenic New Jersey, winds and weather permitting. Although Jane skis and was a beautiful rider and swimmer in her day, she is not what we would call a jock, so I raise the subject tentatively. She's entranced. What a splendid idea. She can't think of anything she'd rather do to mark the start of her second half century, and so it is that we spend a night in a godforsaken motel in less-than-scenic New Jersey and foregather shortly after 5:00 the following morning for our first balloon ride.

We are entranced, becoming instant balloonomanics. And so enthusiastic about our first flight that that fall, when Buddy has closed out his balloon trips for the season, we entice Rick, the pilot on our maiden voyage, to come to Sharon for a week. We have rounded up eight friends to help finance the venture. We will draw lots to determine the order in which we board for a possible two flights each day, one shortly after dawn, and the second shortly before sunset when winds in general are at their lightest. Rick arrives with his very own balloon which is, let us face it, not as classy as Buddy's. Where Rick's falls short is in the basket department. He hasn't been able to afford the customary sturdy wicker basket in which he and his two passengers stand. This makes the landings relatively painless inasmuch as these baskets can—should the contingency arise, and believe me it does—be pulled over stone walls and through barb-wire fences with very little damage (to the basket) and to its passengers. Rick's basket is an altogether gamier affair, four steel poles driven into the platform on which the passengers stand, surrounded by several layers of sturdy tarpaulin. But in the excitement of the moment none of us notes this departure from usual hot-air ballooning form.

It turns out to be a bracing week. Jane, and the famous retired racing driver, John Fitch, a Le Mans veteran, land in a sandpit thirty-six miles down wind from Sharon, having been airborne just a little over an hour, as the result of a miscalculation of the strength of the prevailing winds. John, who knows about things like stresses, is terrified. Jane, whose grasp of physics is minimal, thinks it a lark. Two days later in a late afternoon ride, Rick and I collide with a branch of a towering elm which, however, turns out to be moribund and crashes to the ground, permitting us to plow through it safely. And on the final day, with fortunately a muscular twenty-five-year-old aboard, Rick runs out of propane and the balloon is shredded as it descends, from one limb to the next of a towering oak on the banks of the Housatonic River before coming to a halt ten feet above the ground. It was a somewhat more adventurous week than we had counted on, but it did nothing whatsoever to dull Jane's and my enthusiasm for our newest sport.

And so, on another decimally important birthday, Jane and I headed for Europe where our old friend Buddy Bombard, having folded the Chalet Club some years earlier, was now the commodore of a fleet of beautiful light-blue hot-air balloons large enough to carry the pilot and six passengers. Buddy's Fabulous Hot-Air Balloon Adventures, as they are advertised in elegant brochures, are just that: both Fabulous and Adventures. They can be savored in France, in the Loire country where the famous chateaux reside, or in Burgundy, which the equally famous wines call home. Around Sienna in the Tuscan hills of Italy, in the Swiss Alps in the Gstaad area in winter, among Turkey's fabled ruins in the summer months, and in the beautiful Austrian Tyrol. Since this summer Jane and I had been invited to visit our brother Jim and his wife Ann in Munich where he was now president of Radio Free Europe, we settled on a three-day balloon trip in Austria, just a short drive from Munich.

At 7:20, when Buddy's call awakens us, it is light enough to see that the waters of the Fuschlsee, which fronts on our bungalow, are dark but still, not choppy as they were yesterday morning, the first of our three days on "Buddy Bombard's Great Balloon Adventures" in the Austrian Tyrol. It had been too gusty yesterday to fly, but Buddy hopes we can get in two flights today to make up for lost time.

The winds continue friendly, which is to say very light, when we set out in the chase van from the Hotel Schloss Fuschli, where the accommodations, food, and service are on a par with the lakeside setting. But the high meadows are still draped in mist, so we drive to a valley four or five miles away for take-off. Out from the sturdy navy canvas bag comes the balloon, which will carry Buddy Bombard and his six guests into the sky. While several of us hold wide the mouth of the balloon, two large gas-powered fans pump it full of warm air. It ripples and heaves and shakes itself free from the ground, stirs into life. The sturdy basket we will ride in is tilted up so that Buddy can direct jets of flaming propane gas into the balloon. As the air inside heats up, the balloon rises slowly, gracefully, humorously. Buddy's balloons are light blue, and ornamented with tulips and daffodils, butterflies and grasshoppers.

Ready for take-off. The chase crew—tall, blonde Lana from Denmark; tall, dark-bearded Angus from Scotland—step back from the basket. Buddy rings a cowbell. A grandmother standing nearby with a baby in a perambulator waves up at us. George, one of our fellow passengers, yodels—a quite respectable yodel ("I've been practicing all year," he says)—and he moos. Cows in a field already far below us respond. And we're on our way. Valleys all around us: long swooping swatches of green, dark green where the cut hay lies drying, bright green where it is uncut. Other fields are freshly plowed and earthy brown. It is still misty.

We pass a copse of trees. Two deer dart out and hightail it for cover across an open field; a third bursts out of a patch of vines and races off trailing green tendrils from its antlers. A dozen horses look up, take fright, and gallop away across a long field, manes streaming, tails high, flanks glistening as the sun breaks through the mist and now, for the joy of it, they turn and neigh and canter back.

Behind us a mountain meadow spills down from the wooded hills in the special radiance that late summer lends to green meadow and field. It is down this slope, Buddy tells us, that Julie Andrews ran, singing, "The hills are alive with the sound of music," in the opening sequence of the film. As we cross a small wood, Buddy lets the basket sink slowly, skillfully, into a tiny clearing, and we gather pine boughs from the surrounding trees. Up again, across another stretch of forest that conceals from all sides except above a tiny cottage, for all the world like the witch's gingerbread house in Hansel and Gretel.

We pass over a neat cluster of farm houses, the balconies spilling over with white, red, and purple hanging geraniums. There are flowers everywhere. In Austria, this last week in September, summer still holds court; the Virginia creeper shows only the tiniest hint of scarlet. A young mother pops out a dormer window, baby in arms, and waves to us. Everyone waves to everyone else. Jane finds herself waving vigorously at a cat's tail that is to-ing and fro-ing, so startling the cat that it streaks across the yard for the shelter of an open barn door, anything to get away from that screeching monstrosity in the air, our beautiful cerulean balloon, and possibly from that crazy lady.

We float over a tiny white-spired church on a hillside, and the wind deserts us. We lie becalmed above the church. Buddy swooshes the burners, taking us up eight hundred, a thousand feet, in search of wind. But today's wind is chancy, coquettish, elusive. Ten minutes later we find a breeze at about a hundred feet, but it is blowing in a new direction, away from the Alpine lake and the village we have been heading for; we drift now toward Salzburg. But that is ballooning. The only control the pilot has is up and down; direction is wind-dependent, and the wind at one level may be going in a different direction from the wind at a higher or lower altitude. The experienced pilot watches for signs of these changes—the smoke from a chimney, for instant, that shifts directions at a certain height.

Buddy points to a ridge ahead: "If we can get to that ridge," he says, "we can see Salzburg. I hope we can make it. It is a spectacular view."

We 're moving briskly now and cross low over a tiny village. Kindergartners spill out into the front yard of their school. They shout and wave and laugh, that wonderful high-pitched squeal of delight of the super-excited small child. Buddy rings the cowbell. Jane blows her whistle. George yodels. We swoop ever lower over the school, and the children sweep through it and out the other side into the play yard. But the wind won't let us tarry, so it's a fast wave to the village postman on his bicycle, to the town constable in front of the town hall, and off toward Salzburg we sail.

We pass over the ridge, see the town, assure Buddy that it is indeed a spectacular view with its spires, and castles, and gardens green. And we prepare to land. The chase crew is in place, driving slowly along a road parallel to our course, ready to catch the rope that Buddy will throw out, and pull us in.

"A great flight," says Buddy enthusiastically. But as we start to put down in the field he had picked out twenty minutes earlier, the wind shifts. The field now lies an unattainable thirty feet to our left and in very short order we find ourselves heading down the main railroad tracks into Salzburg. Never again will any of us see that gorgeous city from a such a vantage: the sprawling Hohensalzburg fortress on the peak, overshadowding the bronze domes, onion towers, and baroque façades of cathedrals, churches, and market squares, the Salzburg river dividing the old city from the new. It's all a bit misty, to be sure, but stunning.

For the second time today, the quirky wind deserts us. We have caught a glimpse of Salzburg town and, try as we may, we cannot leave it. Up and down we go, like a yo-yo, seeking the capricious breeze—any breeze—that will blow us in any direction. It is not there at two thousand feet, not at a thousand, not at a hundred. And while we have a fair supply of propane to burn to keep the balloon afloat, it is a dissipating resource. We are on our own. Angus and Lena, in the chase van, are tangled in traffic somewhere below.

With the propane supply now perilously low, Buddy spots a tiny green oasis near the Mirabell Gardens on the right bank of the river. We are drifing ever so slowly towards it.

"We're going down," he says, and we position ourselves for landing as we have been taught with our backs to the padded center section of the basket, our knees bent, holding the looped-rope handles in front of us tightly. We ease down through the top of a tree, caress the side of a small apartment building, then swing away from it over some telephone lines, toward the improvised landing site. A rope is thrown out. As we watch appalled, it hits a woman in the head, knocking her to the pavement. Two passersby rush to her assistance but a third, responding to shouted instructions from Buddy and George, whose German now comes in most handy, grabs hold of the rope and starts to pull us in. The air inside the sheath of the balloon is cooling and we are losing altitude. Buddy throws out a second rope which another man catches and with the help of our impromptu ground crew we touch down, ever so gently, safely, to cheers from tourists leaning over the balustrades of the Mirabell Gardens. The Mirabell Gardens lie to our right, to the left is a tall angular modern structure, the Sheraton Hotel.

The manager of the Sheraton and his wife are at this moment having a late morning cup of coffee in their penthouse apartment.

"Dear, do you see what I see?" asks the wife. "That's one of Buddy's balloons, and I don't think it should be below us but it is."

Arrives at the scene a few minutes later, (1) the local constabulary, which would like an accounting from Buddy of how come we landed in Salzburg—had he filed a flight plan?—and (2) a grey-flannel-suited angel of mercy, the manager of the Sheraton. He finds six chilled balloonists, all mighty glad to be on the ground and needing tender loving care, which he proceeds to provide. After a few words with Buddy our new friend, the manager, gathers us up, whisks us into the hotel, guides us to a quiet corner in the bar, directs us to the facilities, and upon our emerging therefrom, prescribes warming and potent libations for us.

When we are cleaned up in body and refreshed in spirit, he summons two taxis and sends us on our way to a delicious lunch at the Castle Gallanegg which, wonderful as it is, pales in comparison with the graciousness of Elizabeth, our hostess.

The manager is also kind enough to phone Elizabeth and ask her to assure us that the woman who had been targeted by Buddy's rope was more frightened than hurt by her misadventure. "She will be all right, and you are not to worry about her," Elizabeth tells us. (I have a sudden, wonderful mental image of the scene when our victim gets home. Her husband asks: "Gretchen, what happened to your head, how did you get that bruise?" "A rope fell out of the sky and hit me on the head," she replies. "Gretchen, dear, ropes don't fall out of the sky, not in Salzburg," with Teutonic assurance. But the last laugh will be hers when the next morning's Salzburg gazette arrives with Buddy's balloon splashed all over the front page.)

⁀

This morning's call is at 7:30 AM for an 8:30 flight.

Buddy has assured us that balloonists after a hazardous flight must, like horsemen after a bad spill, get right back up, on the horse in the one case, and into the air on the other, ours. So he has decreed that our sextet will fly again today, although that was not on the schedule.

"The winds are just right," Buddy greets us as we arrive at the launch site and our hearts dance a light fandango in anticipation. It's up up and away over the glorious Tyrolean hills and meadows and, as if to make up for yesterday's misadventure, today's journey culminates with a flight over the Fushlsee, its waters so black this morning when we got up, and now, at midday, that cool green-blue so typical of glacier-fed Alpine lakes. We see too, from the sky, how that modern and comfortable Hotel Schloss Fuschli—on a promontory to our right—fits within the sturdy walls of a fortress that was already five hundreds years old when Columbus sailed the ocean blue. Nothing, nothing we conclude can be as much fun as this.

As we drift to a perfect landing Buddy rings his cowbell, Jane blows her whistle, and George gives out with one last triumphant yodel.

26

Bill as Editor

T WO VERY FINE BIOGRAPHIES were published in 2002, nearly half a century after the founding of *National Review* about two of its major editors, James Burnham and Frank S. Meyer (*James Burnham, and the Struggle for the World* by Daniel Kelly, and *Principles and Heresies, Frank S. Meyer And the Shaping of the American Conservative Movement* by Kevin J. Smant). Both biographies outline the major ideological conflicts between Burnham and Meyer as well as others within the inner circle of the magazine, and make the point that without Bill Buckley's diplomatic and firm though quiet direction these conflicts most certainly would have derailed the enterprise. Meyer was in constant disagreement also with Russell Kirk who wrote the "From the Academy" column for twenty-five years, and from time to time Burnham's political pragmatism drove Bill Rusher and Bill Rickenbacker up the wall. But the disputes never reached their explosive potential in large part because of Bill's sure handling of his brilliant but highly disputatious colleagues.

This analysis of Bill's importance to the magazine as a peace-maker is correct, but it leaves out a major dimension in the success of *National Review,* and that is Bill Buckley's skills as an editor. Consider his problems. The liberal intelligentsia had pronounced conservatism dead, as dead as the Edsel. Lionel Trilling had provided a rather off-hand obituary of conservatism in the early 1950s: "In the United States at this time liberalism is not only the dominant but even the sole intellectual tradition," an obituary in such Olympian manner that the name of the deceased was not mentioned, so irrelevant did it seem.

On top of this, the magazine was always short of cash. Bill had raised less money than was needed to start it up and consequently could pay little for the articles and reviews he would publish. In addition, there was a major deterrent to attracting first-class pieces, inasmuch as many who might have liked to contribute to this bouncy conservative upstart feared to do so, lest they find themselves in that intellectual limbo that James Burnham described with such precision in 1953 after he had been forced to resign from the *Partisan Review:* "In our land also there is an *official* history, or what amounts almost to that. Historians who deviate too far from its norms are not exiled or shot, but they seldom taste the grants of the great Foundations, nor do they sit in the endowed Chairs of the major universities. To them the State Department does not easily open its doors or files. Their road to a publisher is rocky, and in the leading book sections, though physically still immune, they will be spiritually drawn and quartered."

The Establishment's first reaction to *National Review* was to ignore it. With any luck it would founder because, after all, its philosophy was preposterous. But NR refused to go away. It was becoming an active annoyance; thus six months or so after its arrival on the scene in November 1955, the liberals rolled out their big guns, a triple salvo intended to blast the interloper out of the water.

Boom! went John Fischer, editor of *Harpers,* in a lengthy and ponderous critique. Boom! Boom!! followed Dwight Macdonald, all condescension, in *Commentary*. Boom! Boom!! Boom!!! went Murray Kempton, bringing the eighteen-pounders to bear in what was intended as the *coup de grace*. In many thousands of words they all came to the same conclusion: A conservative journal was needed, but *National Review* was not it. Or, as Bill summed it up in his reply in the August 1, 1956, issue of NR:

> All three of the journals [*Harpers, Commentary, The Progressive*] seem to resent the mere existence of *National Review*—not, understand, because they are intolerant of dissent (there-is-nothing-they-would-welcome-more-than-genuine-dissent); but because it pains them to be bored by it, and when they are not being bored by it, they are being affronted by its vulgarity, appalled by its insouciance, or dismayed by its ignorance. Nothing, absolutely nothing, is more urgently needed than a real conservative magazine; but, alas, ours is not such a thing, and they must, accordingly, continue to scan the heavens for it.

Murray Kempton, whose writing Bill admired and who would become a good friend, was particularly vicious. "The New American Right," he wrote, "is most conspicuous these days for its advanced state of wither." That being the case, Bill commented in his rebuttal, "How can one reasonably expect a magazine, written and edited by mortals, to arrest something far gone in putrefaction, and bring it back to life?"

There we were again, DOA, dead on arrival.

All of which proved infinitely satisfying twenty years or so later, when the same Murray Kempton wrote Bill to suggest that he would "like to do a piece a month somewhere that is just rumination. . . . Candidly, yours is the only editorial mind and NR's curiously the only temper with which I could conceive of myself as fitting. Would it be possible?" It was, and the column called by Kempton "Thoughts

Astray" appeared three or four times before Kempton apparently lost interest in it.

What was most important to Bill in editing *National Review* was that the writing be distinguished. It seemed to him more important that a writer write beautiful prose than that the writer be a movement conservative. Indeed some of the people we published never were conservatives. Young John Leonard certainly was not, and is not. Some started out as conservative, or perhaps as nonpolitical, and ended up as flaming liberals, Garry Wills, Joan Didion and her husband John Gregory Dunne, among them. What they had in common was that all of them were prose stylists. And *National Review* profited from their skills, at least for a while.

In his search for good writers Bill was much aided by Frank Meyer and Senior Editor Jeffrey Hart. Frank, sitting in his mountain eyrie in Woodstock, New York, would reach out by phone to anyone he noticed or someone recommended to him as an interesting writer.

Frank slept in the daytime and worked at night, while Elsie lived more normal hours. This resulted from Frank's fear that he might be eliminated after he broke with the Communist Party in which he had been an important functionary. During his Party years, as Jeff Hart once told me, he had recruited converts to Communism. Now he was still proselytizing but it was under a different banner. He recruited young conservatives both as potential writers for *National Review* and as cadres for the conservative movement. He would engage the youngster—they were usually youngsters—in long telephone conversations and before you knew it he, or they, would have suggested they try their hand at a "Brief"—a 150- to 250-word—book review. If it worked out, it was so much to the good; if it didn't, little had been lost. It was through Frank that Joan Didion, Renata Adler, Richard Corliss, the movie reviewer, Christopher Simonds, Joe Sobran, Chilton Williamson, who would succeed George Will as book editor, and

Arlene Croce, who would go on to become the *New Yorker*'s ballet critic for many years, and many others made their first appearances in NR's pages. A running joke at NR was Willmoore Kendall's quip that an emergency phone call between Frank Meyer and Brent Bozell was a call that interrupted their usual call. Frank Meyer was AT&T's best customer.

Jeff Hart, one of Frank's reviewers, would end up playing a pivotal role at *National Review* while continuing as a professor of English at Dartmouth College. His transition from occasional reviewer to senior editor was swift. He started coming in from Dartmouth every other week to help write the editorial section, and very soon proved essential to the smooth running of the operation. When both Bill and Jim Burnham were out, it was Jeff Hart who ran the editorial section.

Jeff—who is stocky and red-haired with bright blue eyes, and a hearty, almost abrupt laugh—arrived punctually from Hanover every other Tuesday, no matter how fearful the weather, and New Hampshire winters are known to be fierce. He would drive wherever he must, to get on a train or plane that would bring him to New York in time for the editorial conference Tuesday morning. He is a man of deep learning and of wide interests, and he could be counted on to write an informed, and when the subject warranted, lyrical, editorial on anything from football to Maria Callas. He is wonderfully unassuming, easy to get along with, the perfect colleague, and a stalwart support in moments of crisis.

As the outstanding conservative on the increasingly liberal Dartmouth faculty in the late 1960s and 1970s, Hart attracted a bunch of bright young men and women, first by his celebrated lectures and seminars, and next by his philosophy and personal warmth and interest in them. A bunch of them eventually put out a conservative publication, the *Dartmouth Review*, whose hijinks sometimes landed them on the front page of the *New York Times*, which was, needless to say, appalled at their conduct. (What Dartmouth needed, the *Times* once implied in an editorial reproving the young Dartmouth editors, was a good conservative paper, but the *Dartmouth Review* was not it. We had heard this before.)

It was Jeff who introduced *National Review* readers to D. Keith Mano, whose brilliant novels he found entrancing. Keith started writing major book reviews for NR and then launched a column, "The Gimlet Eye," that our readers either loved or hated. There was a touch of genius about it that couldn't be emulated or duplicated. And when Mano had to drop the column some years later because of illness, NR didn't even try to replace it. As Bill had once noted, no one should try to write like Murray Kempton who wasn't Murray Kempton, and no one should try his hand at a Mano column who wasn't Mano.

Jeff also brought to the magazine's attention young Dinesh D'Souza, one of the *Dartmouth Review* editors who wrote a number of pieces for NR before going on to publish *Illiberal Education* and other works the liberals simply hated. It was at Jeff's suggestion that NR hired as editorial assistants Peter Robinson, who went on to become a Reagan White House speechwriter and author, and Paul Gigot.

Paul worked as an editorial assistant at *National Review* for two years after his graduation from Dartmouth, before winning a Luce journalistic fellowship for study and work in the Far East. It was on that assignment that he was picked up by the *Wall Street Journal*, which after a number of years sent him to Washington where his weekly Friday column brought him to the attention of the *McNeil–Lehrer News Hour*. For some years Paul Gigot was the weekly sparring partner of Mark Shields on that show. In 2001, Gigot succeeded Bob Bartley as editor of the *Journal*'s editorial page.

Just before leaving *National Review*, Paul Gigot invited me to lunch at a local bistro. He was in those days a big, rather awkward young man. It was midwinter and I, like every other woman in New York that winter, was wearing a bulky down coat. (Tom Wolfe commented that New York women that year walked about looking like hand grenades.) The Back Porch restaurant had a large clothes rack by the door that was jam-packed with bulky winter coats when Paul and I walked in. Paul took my coat, and his, to hang up, and they proved to be two coats too many. The clothes rack toppled over, knocking me to the floor, where I disappeared under a mound of bulky coats. It took some few minutes for the restaurant staff to get us back on our feet. Paul was aghast at what he had done, until I joined the cascading roars of laughter of the Back Porch's other delighted clients: it had been a sight to behold.

The next time I saw Paul was two years later, when I was in Hong Kong as a member of the U.S Advisory Commission on Public Diplomacy, and we were given a tour of Hong Kong's harbor on the consul general's yacht. Paul Gigot, then working for the *Far Eastern Economic Review*, had been invited by the consulate staff to join the group. We fell into each other's arms, delighted to meet an old friend so far from home.

Another of the young conservative writers, David Brooks, former senior editor of the *Weekly Standard* and author of *Bobos in Paradise*, who succeeded Gigot on the *News Hour* and has a regular column on the *New York Times* op-ed page, put in a stint at NR at the recommendation of Milton and Rose Friedman. David had worked with the Friedmans on their thirteen-week TV series. When the noted (but not then noted) economist Alan Reynolds started sending in unsolicited articles to *National Review*, he was running a J.C. Penny's store in California. While on the West Coast on a speaking tour, Bill called Alan, met him, and hired him then and there.

George Will was working as a legislative assistant for Senator Gordon Allott of Colorado when he submitted the first of several articles to *National Review*. They were outstanding, sharp, to the point, exceedingly well written. When Frank Meyer died in 1972, Bill called Will, who was temporarily unemployed, Senator Allott having lost his last election, and proposed that he take over Meyer's job as book editor and serve also as *National Review*'s Washington correspondent. Bill figured that if Will did both jobs we could pay him a living wage. The timing was great as far as most of us were concerned, but terrible so far as Bill Rusher was concerned. Will started his column at the height of the Watergate scandal, and could quote you the content and scandalous meaning of each and every one of the damning White House tapes. He took a tough approach toward Nixon, which put him in instant conflict with Rusher, who remained a Nixon loyalist—or, to be more precise, who thought that Nixon was being railroaded by the usual liberal suspects—until almost the very end of that sad saga.

It was a difficult time for NR in general, since 50 percent of its readers loved Nixon and agreed with Rusher that he was the victim of a liberal lynch mob, while the other 50 percent had never really liked him and hoped he would go away, the sooner the better. George carried out both assignments for us for three or four years, but we couldn't hope to keep him. He was too good, too attractive to others with deeper pockets. We lost George Will when *Newsweek* made him an offer for more money than we could afford, to write the last-page editorial that runs in each issue. One of the conditions of his employment by *Newsweek* and the syndicated *Washington Post* column that soon followed was that he remove his name from the NR masthead. That he did, but he remained, and remains, a good friend and principled supporter of the magazine.

Another NR discovery, Rick Brookhiser staged a counter Moratorium to the major anti-Vietnam Moratorium in Washington at his local high school in Rochester, New York, and wrote a piece about it for NR when he was fifteen. At sixteen, he sent in an article arguing that the reason Nixon had engaged in detente with Red China was that he, Nixon, was a romantic. We published that one too, hired young Brookhiser as a summer editorial assistant his junior year at Yale, and told him he had a job at *National Review* upon graduation.

He came, and he conquered, and when a year or so later he told Bill that he thought he should go on to law school, there was panic in the ranks which was resolved by promoting Rick to a senior editorship—at age twenty-three. He still works regularly for NR, continues as a mainstay of the editorial section, writes a column for the *New York Observer*, and has carved a place for himself as a historian of the Revolutionary War period with popular biographies of Washington, Hamilton, the Adamses (John, et. al, not Sam), and Gouverneur Morris.

The list could go on and on. Looking back on it, this was a disparate group, they came tall and short, male and female, skinny and fat, blonde, brunette and red-haired, most of them very young, united in one thing: every one of them could write.

Finally, what Bill had was the courage of his editorial convictions, and a spark that makes all the difference in the highly competitive magazine world. He did, on one occasion when he thought it important, devote an entire issue of the magazine to Michael Novak's rebuttal of the Catholic bishops' namby-pamby policy paper on a just war. His decision to write his own set of Pentagon Papers to counter the Daniel Ellsberg version that the *New York Times* and the *Washington Post* had splashed across their front pages took courage and panache. The idea came to him, as he told an enraged press, *ex nihilo*.

When Ben Bagdikian, editor of the *Washington Post*, professed shock, horror, and a serious lack of professionalism in NR's Pentagon Papers, Bill Buckley responded amiably. "Dear Mr. Bagdikian: Inasmuch as you published over 2,000 words from the [NR] papers, would you be agreeable to paying us the usual reprint fee? I would suggest $150."

There was a touch of Peck's bad boy in certain of its responses to world events. Two weeks after Lyndon Johnson assumed the presidency, *National Review*'s editorial section opened with this paragraph: "The editors of *National Review* regretfully announce that their patience with President Lyndon B. Johnson is exhausted." *Time* magazine called this "the impetuosity of the week."

The week that Ronald Reagan was elected president, NR's editorial section solemnly proclaimed: "With the election of Ronald Reagan, *National Review* assumes a new importance in American life. We become, as it were, an establishment organ, and we feel it only appropriate to alter our demeanor accordingly. This is therefore the last issue in which we shall indulge in levity. Connoisseurs of humor will have to get their yuks elsewhere. We have a nation to run." (This was the kind of paragraph that Maureen had advised the editors many years earlier to identify with a large black "J" for joke: some of our readers straggled a few steps behind the editors in the humor department.)

There were plenty of yuks a couple of years later when the editors sat around the big conference table after going to press one evening and tried to figure out what headlines would make the Susan Sontags and Ramsey Clarks of the day totally, deliriously, happy. This morphed into a bogus NR cover piece—a take off on the *Times*'s front page set in the nearest type we could find to the *Times*'s headline and body type proclaiming such liberal dream stories as: "Pope Abandons Infallibility"; "Hiss Typewriter Forger Confesses"; "Panthers Seize Selma."; "Franco Assassinated"; "Fires last night swept portions of Beverly Hills, completely destroying the homes of John Wayne, Jimmy Stewart, Raymond Burr, Efran Zimbalist Jr, and Morrie Ryskind"; "J. Edgar Hoover Exits in Wake of Scandal (having been caught in a men's room propositioning)". This last, incidentally, caused William F. Buckley Jr to be moved in a single step from the "FBI friend" to the "FBIs enemy" list.

27

Notes & Asides

WHEN NATIONAL REVIEW STARTED UP, every senior editor wrote a column that appeared either weekly or fortnightly. Bill Buckley's was "The Ivory Tower," and it dealt with the undergraduate college life. He was just twenty-nine and having gone to college after serving in World War II, was still relatively close to that scene. But that was no longer so a few years later when he abandoned "The Ivory Tower" and started a new column, which he called "Notes & Asides," and which was like no other column in the magazine. What it was was an ongoing dialogue between the editor and his readers with no subject out of bounds or too outré to be considered. This gave the readers a look not only at the inner workings of NR but also a feeling that they—by their comments and suggestions—were making a contribution to the enterprise. It was more than just fun and games, but fun and games were what gave it its pizzazz.

For instance, very shortly after Jim Buckley was elected to the Senate, Bill Buckley appeared on the *Rowan & Martin's Laugh-In* show on television. Everyone, but everyone, tuned in on Sunday nights including a lawyer (who shall be nameless, we are not sadists) in Buffalo, New York. He went screaming from his TV set to his typewriter, and wrote, as was recorded in "Notes & Asides" two weeks later:

[Letter from nameless lawyer]

Hon.? James Buckley
Senate Office Building
Washington D.C.

Sir:

Now that my nausea has subsided after accidentally observing your appearance on *Laugh-In* last evening, I, as one of your constituents and former admirers, am constrained to comment.

Your silly grin as the inane and vulgar questions were asked and your equally inane replies were less than worthy of a Senator of the United States.

The fact that you appeared on that program at all was an insult to the decent people whom you represent.

The disgusting episode in which you freely participated and apparently enjoyed—as an accomplice in lending your position to a disgraceful program—is an affront to the dignity of the Senate, to your family, to your church, and to your constituency. I trust that your acting the clown insured the support of the addicts of the program who undoubtedly enjoy its indecencies. I trust, too, that they are in the minority.

I am,

[Jim's reply]

Sir:

I have forwarded your letter to my brother, the columnist—William F. Buckley Jr. It was he, not I, who appeared on *Laugh-In*.

I can't help but be curious as to why you consented to watch a program of which you so strongly disapprove.

Sincerely,
James L. Buckley

Dear Mr _____:

It is typical of my brother to attempt to deceive his constituents. It was, of course, he, not I, who appeared on *Laugh-In*, just as you suspected. On the other hand, you need not worry about it. His greatest deception is as yet undiscovered. It was I, not he, who was elected to the Senate. So you see, you have nothing to worry about. You are represented in the Senate by a responsible, truthful man.

Yours,
William F. Buckley Jr.

"Notes & Asides" was a laugh-in all on its own. In one issue it might contain outrage such as the above or perhaps an even shorter and spicier attack: "Dear Mr. Buckley: Your syntax is horrible. Roy Kelly, Mattoon, Ill." To which Bill replied: "Dear Mr. Kelly. If you had my syntax you'd be rich. WFB." Or perhaps a bit of whimsy that had struck Svend Peterson, who composed the "Trans-O-Gram" that ran in the back of the book for many years, as he perused the daily news. "Dear Mr. Buckley: I see that the Senator from South Dakota made a speech in a church. Do you suppose we could get HHH [Hubert H. Humphrey] and [Jacob] Javits to debate in a temple? That would be a case of a pedagogue and a demagogue having a dialogue in a synagogue."

Or he might use it to set the record straight in a letter to *San Francisco Chronicle* columnist Herb Caen that most of NR's subscribers would never see unless they lived in San Francisco and Herb Caen was man enough to make public. Caen had written: "It was to

[Peter Maas's lovely sad-eyed wife] Audrey that Bill Buckley said: 'What is the secret behind those sad eyes?', departing hastily when Audrey replied, 'It is the sadness of a socialist looking at a fascist Republican.'"

Bill's reply: "a) I have never laid eyes on Mrs. Maas, so far as I know, b) I have never said to anyone, 'What is behind those sad eyes,' and c) if Mrs. Maas or anyone else had proffered such an explanation to me, her trouble would not be sad eyes, but black and blue eyes."

Given Bill's interest in the English language "Notes & Asides" also served as a running commentary on language, grammar, linguistic velleities of all sorts, for many years. A discussion of the pros and cons of the serial comma might give way to pyrotechnics over palindromes. One discussion between Hugh Kenner and WFB on a nicety of phrase brought in a cogent and witty comment from a Miss Linda Bridges which Bill duly printed. In the event, it turned out that the learned Miss Bridges was a nineteen-year-old sophomore at the University of Southern California. A few letters later, and she was hired as NR's editorial assistant the summer of her junior year, and on her performance that summer promised a fulltime job as soon as she graduated.

Linda arrived at 150 East 35th Street in 1970 neatly attired, a small round person with huge horn-rim glasses, her brown hair worn in a severe bun, the picture of a modern day bluestocking until someone said something funny and she broke into a beaming smile that started at one ear and carried on to the other, and emitted a laugh more raucous than delicate, destroying in an instant every effort to appear sober, serious, and scholarly. She was, she is, a joy, in all ways but one. But then, no one is perfect. In the interest of total honesty it must be reported that Miss Bridges was a high flyer in what became almost an Olympic sport at NR, our Messiest, Dirtiest Office Division.

The Gold Medalist in this division was indisputably Joe Sobran, who once missed a telephone call because eight rings later he was still having trouble locating his phone under mounds of paper, six packs, radios, lives of Dr. Johnson, suitcases, magazines, empty envelopes, and important lost manuscripts that formed a five-foot-high ziggurat on his desk. His caller rang off, concluding that Joe was not home. Contenders for the Silver Medal were Chris Simonds, who served for a while as "Arts & Manners" editor, and later as assistant managing editor, and Linda.

But Chris ultimately edged Linda out on what was really a technicality. Both their offices were pigpens. Both were papered by abandoned newspapers, magazines, and dead coffee cartons on the floor. But while Chris's desk was a table with a limited surface area to be profaned, Linda's was an old-fashioned rolltop desk with a dozen or more cubbyholes that spouted geysers of paper: papers—of all kinds and shapes and colors—topped by a shelf of shabby dictionaries, thesauruses, and other reference books. Here was a significant parting of the ways. Whereas there was no point in asking either Joe or Chris to produce a mislaid manuscript, a letter, or an important clipping, this was not so with Linda. "Linda, have you seen," or, "do you have"—whatever it was you needed—evoked a gratifying response. Linda would blink once, crinkle her forehead in thought, reach up to the myriad cubbyholes above her head and, as if waving a magic wand, pluck out the paper you desired. While her office was Messy, she, Linda, was not, which meant she only got the bronze.

Linda would follow me as managing editor and, when NR started a small publishing operation some years later, she and Bill Rickenbacker collaborated on a charming small book, *The Art of Rhetoric*.

In 1970, when an inflamed young conservative, Tom McSloy, wrote Bill a long letter criticizing NR for being out of touch with younger conservatives, Bill was so struck by it that he published the entire thing in his (for this issue) expanded "Notes & Asides" column.

It made for lively reading: "I'm damn tired of [your] little innuendoes about the things young people like, and of the fact that every pomposity uttered by some SDS moron is duly punctured, while you let all sorts of foolishness pass if it happens to be directed at young people, or by some totem conservative. . . . You certainly haven't thumped on the Nixon Administration with the gusto of old. The bureaucracy is still enormous and parasitic, the debt mounting, taxes oppressive, inflation spiraling. . . . I really do like NR, but you can be terribly stuffy at times, really."

Bill had each of the senior editors write a public reply to young Mr. McSloy's criticisms and the reaction from NR's readers was tremendous. Realizing that there was indeed a void in NR's coverage of cultural events, Bill asked Chris Simonds, who was a Beatles and Rolling Stones fan like McSloy, to write a regular column, which he called "For Now," addressing the concerns of younger conservatives.

Young, blond, and at that point roly-poly, Christopher Simonds joined the staff in 1967 after writing a number of brilliant book reviews for Frank Meyer. He was amazingly versatile, a bright and arresting writer, and competent in all sorts of fields. He soon took charge of a number of ancillary operations, including what became a burgeoning business for NR, the sale of custom-made political buttons commenting on everything from the immanentizing of the eschaton to support for Moise Tshombe.

In this capacity, Chris sent a memo to Bill as reported in "Notes & Asides":

TO THE EDITOR:
FROM: The Minister of Buttons

Our anti-Moratorium buttons are the biggest hit yet (bigger even than the National Committee to Horsewhip Drew Pearson). Having sold out the initial six thousand I have had to reorder both buttons. Our Shipping Department has mailed out 4,757 buttons so far, and the orders continue to pour in. One thing. Some button-buyers cause trouble by 1) writing messy, undecipherable names and addresses; 2) not bothering to write them but assuming that we'll copy them off the check or the outside envelope; 3) forgetting to enclose payment. These omissions make life very difficult for the Shipping Department, who has consented to marry me, so of course, I want to keep her happy and healthy. It's only natural, right?

Chris and the Shipping Department, the lovely blonde Miss Pat Carr, were married soon after, immediately produced two daughters, decided New York was no place to bring up children, and retired to Connecticut to teach at a pre-prep school, thus depriving NR of one of the most talented, innovative young writers ever to come down the pike, in Chris, and one of the world's best copy editors, in Pat, a sad double whammy, for NR if not for the young Simondses.

At times, Bill might use N&A to rein in misplaced enthusiasm on the part of the ever frisky Jim McFadden.

Memo to: Promotion Department

My beloved colleagues: It is embarrassing enough to read accounts of my published works in the promotion pages of the magazine of which I am the editor.

I have for years been aware of the necessarily hyperbolic nature of promotional prose, and have with exemplary docility permitted my works to be likened to the great masterpieces of the Western world.

I am not in the least opposed to quoting samples of my wit and wisdom in said advertisements,

HOWEVER,

When, as in page 1453 of last week's issue, you gave as an example of that wisdom a fifty-word passage of prose which not only did I not write, but I BURLESQUED in my book; words spoken not by me but by RAMSEY CLARK, all I can say is,

NATIONAL REVIEW has been infiltrated. WFB.

Or N&A might prove useful in letting our readers in on some of the tensions that rend the inner circle of editors from time to time, as indicated in an item that appeared in a summer issue in 1968, just prior to the Republican Convention in Miami.

"Thought you'd like to see a gently mutinous memorandum by one of the editors addressed to his colleagues, and written after receiving one memorandum too many from the publisher, carefully explaining what is going to happen in Miami. . . .

From: William F. Rickenbacker
To: William A. Rusher's memos dated 7-15-62, 9-9-64, 12-29-66, 3-30-68, 5-3-68, 5-31-68

I owe it to you to make my position irrefragably clear. If Rockefeller fails on the first ballot, Romney squares with Percy, and O'Doherty and Rusher remain above the conflict, then McKinley is a shoo-in. If, however, Stassen and Dewey announce for Nixon before the third ballot, Clif White swears off martinis, Mahoney and Alessandroni arrive at an understanding with Nixon, and Rockefeller undercuts Reagan's early strength by divorcing Happy and remarrying the former Miss Clark, then, it seems entirely possible that Claude Kirk of Florida and Charles Percy of Illinois will be the immediate (though by no means final) beneficiaries. There remains the possibility of a premature combination between Rockefeller, Reagan, Nixon, Stassen, Romney, Scranton, Lindsay, Javits and Spinoza, to thwart the rapidly expanding presidential ambitions of Buz Lukens. In this event I would look for a brokered convention.

28

Foreign Accents

ERIK VON KUEHNELT-LEDDIHN had a column in the very first issue of *National Review* and would still be writing for the magazine a quarter of a century later. The column, "From the Continent," was a misnomer, since Erik seldom confined his musings to any one continent or any one period of time. Erik knew everything. Period. And he did his very best to tell you everything every time he put pen to paper.

Erik would blow into town twice a year, stopping in New York for a day or two before undertaking a whirlwind speaking tour, mostly of college campuses. He was every bit the Austrian aristocrat, super tall—six-foot-two or three or maybe four—with receding brown hair, a droopy mustache, penetrating eyes, bushy eyebrows, a surprising rather high-pitched voice that immediately seized the high ground and dominated every conversation. There was no stopping Erik when he got going in his most fluent, but highly accented, English. But once you learned to sit back and simply permit his words to flow over you like the incoming tide, conversations with him, while distinctly one-sided, were both pleasant and instructive.

He dressed, to my knowledge, only in shades of brown, and you could not tell from one year to the next if what he was wearing was old or new. But the presumption was that it was old because Erik was a saving man. He lived an entire lifetime on the edge of penury. When Bill, meeting him at a train station in Switzerland one time, asked him what on earth he was doing in a third-class coach, Erik replied that he was on it only because there was no fourth-class coach available.

Erik had been hired to cover European developments for us, but his interests were all-encompassing. While we saw him only a few days a year he considered himself a charter member of the inner NR family, and that's how we looked upon him. One might get exasperated with Erik, but there was no way not to like him. He was in many ways like a big wooffly St. Bernard..

"From the Continent" appeared every other issue. It ran in one version or another in a number of publications all over the world, one even in far-off Australia. What Erik did in practice was to send a copy of the same column to each of his client publications. There was no overlap in readership, so this presented no problem. The columns arrived, single-spaced, on the thinnest, flimsiest of transparent paper, typed tightly from top to bottom (by Mrs. Erik), with side margins an eighth of an inch or less, all this to save on postage, you understand. They usually ran about fifteen hundred words. In the month between columns we would receive four or five of these missives which would have to be cut down to about nine hundred words to fit into one *National Review* page. There was no way to edit the original copy, the flimsy paper wouldn't take it, so someone would have to read all the columns, decide which one would be best for NR, and then get a secretary to type it out triple-spaced for whatever unfortunate young soul was assigned to the editing task.

Erik's columns were a wonderful training tool in the gentle art of editing. We would explain to the young writer that Erik had his crotchets. He hated, positively loathed, democracy, so they were free to search out any anti-democratic diatribe—there would be at least one in every article—and excise it. He loved monarchy, so they were free to search out all pro-monarchist sentiments and excise them as well. We would tell them rather sternly that references to the Field of Gold—or any other historic event on which Erik might expatiate at length—even if relevant to exchanges between, say, Charles de Gaulle and Anthony Eden, could go if they took up an inordinate amount of space. The German habit of putting verbs at the end of the sentence was not such a good idea when writing English. Above all, we would say, forget the passive voice, which Erik loves. Try as hard as you can to use the active verb. And we would leave them to fight their way through copy that was always fascinating, extremely informative, soundly based in history, but that needed to be sculpted into usable news commentary before it could appear. A well-edited K-L was a joy to behold and strikingly different both in content and understanding from too often banal foreign reporting. "From the Continent" was popular with NR's more perceptive readers.

Erik was wonderfully understanding about the mayhem committed on his copy. He seldom complained about the editing and the few times that he did, he was totally justified in his criticisms. But he was less understanding about *National Review*'s inexplicable failure to recognize his prowess as an oil painter. Somewhat late in life Erik discovered oil painting. He specialized in portraits. Admittedly, the subjects of his portraits were recognizable but the portraits themselves were—dreadful will have to do for want of a better word. He would plead for us to include them in his articles. But we couldn't, we just couldn't, not even for our beloved Erik, may the dear soul rest in peace.

Nika Standen Hazelton was an altogether different proposition.

Nika was brought up in Italy. Her mother was Italian, her father German. In looks she was totally German, but there was a great deal of Italian in her temperament. She was a large Brunhilde of a woman with heavy blonde braids she wore wound on the top of her head. She was forceful. She was positive. She was, when she chose to be, as immovable as a boulder.

She came into our lives when a desperate advertising manager persuaded the editors to give up a single page every issue to coverage of food, drink, and travel in order to help him sell space to upscale advertisers in the food, drink, and travel industries. So it was decided at an "Agony", which is what we called the quarterly conferences of the publisher and senior editors that were held regularly three times a year, to establish a new column that we would call "Delectations." It would be devoted in alternate issues to travel, food, and wine.

By a stroke of rare good luck Bill was able to sign Alec Waugh, Evelyn Waugh's brother, a well-known and graceful novelist and travel writer, to handle the travel assignment. Bill tried to get James Beard to write the food and drink column, but Beard was overcommitted. However, he strongly recommended Nika Standen Hazelton as one of the best and most versatile writers in the cooking field.

It was arranged that Nika and I would have lunch to discuss the project at Nicola Paone's restaurant on East 34th Street, between 2nd and 3rd Avenues, *National Review*'s absolutely all-time favorite restaurant.

When I arrived a very few minutes late, Nika was already in deep conversation with Nicola Paone, both jabbering and gesticulating in Italian. Nika was a large woman, garbed as always in a flowing tent of a dress, and on this day using one arm crutch because of the terrible arthritis that was already crippling her and would make her final years excruciatingly painful.

Nika started by telling me all the things she *wouldn't* do for *National Review*. She wouldn't praise any restaurant or brand of liquor or vintage of wine in order to help us sell advertising. She wouldn't write on any subject she hadn't chosen herself to write about. No one must tamper with her column. She must be totally free in every way. When I had agreed to all of this, she asked how often the column would appear. Yes, even with her present commitments she could manage a monthly deadline. How much did we propose to pay? Nika was all business. When I told her one hundred dollars, she practically fainted away. She wouldn't consider working for such a price. Even to offer it was all but insulting.

It was a bad beginning. But as the meal progressed and Nika indicated her professional approval of Paone's cuisine, and her enjoyment of the Chianti he was serving as table wine at the moment, she warmed up. Actually, she said, she would enjoy having a different forum in *National Review*. Mostly she wrote cookbooks and articles in gourmet magazines and would like the opportunity to address readers who had different interests. By the time Mr. Paone had brought out his superb, light zavaglione, Nika had mellowed considerably. "Do you think, Miss Buckley," she said, "that you could possibly pay me $150 per column?" By this time I was considerably mellowed myself, and most anxious to get to know this formidable and intriguing creature better. There was something wonderfully attractive about Nika Hazelton despite her initial gruffness.

I thought it could be arranged, I told her, and she promised to have her first column in a week from that Friday.

"If there's anything you don't like about it," she said, unexpectedly, "just give me a call and let me know."

As Humphrey Bogart said to Claude Rains, it was the beginning of a wonderful friendship.

Nika's columns made for fascinating reading. She would explain, for instance, why an American who had studied at the Cordon Bleu in Paris could return to the States, cook the very same meal the way she had been taught, and come up with something that would be tasty, but different from the meal cooked in Paris. This was because, Nika said, the flour she used, the butter she used, the meat and vegetables she used when bought in France were themselves different from those produced in America. The cows, and chickens, and beef were raised on different feed, and the beef butchered differently. The soil and the European sun meant that the French *haricot vert* had a different flavor from the American string bean, hence the difference in both flavor and texture. On New Year's she might write a column on hangover remedies, or turn in an article or two on the extraordinary icons she and Harold, her husband, had discovered in some orthodox churches on a recent trip to Bulgaria.

She was also wonderfully accommodating. When we first went to computer typesetting, we had a problem with recipes. The computer would produce one-half cup, as ½-cup, and one quarter cup, as ¼-cup, but no matter what Evelyne Kanter and Mike Watkins, our typists turned computer typesetters, tried, one-third cup in a recipe emerged as 1/3-cup.

"What shall we do?" Linda asked.

I said I'd call Nika and put our dilemma to her.

"I don't suppose," I suggested, "that you could triple the recipe?"

Nika laughed. "Not unless *National Review* readers are so affluent that they regularly cook for twenty-four."

"I'll call you back," she said, and hung up.

She was back ten minutes later with a new recipe to substitute for the earlier one, this one with no 1/3-cups!

She might devote a column to how long one should stay when invited to dinner. Didactic as always, she recommended three hours, no more: thirty to forty minutes for cocktails, a leisurely hour and a half for the three-course meal, which should be unrushed to permit good conversation, an additional thirty to forty minutes for after-dinner coffee in the living room, *never* at the dinner table, and cordials. A cardinal must for the hostess was that she have available half a bottle of wine for each guest.

Nika's dinner parties were not grand but always good. She would invite four to six friends at least once a week, since she was religious about testing every recipe in every cookbook she wrote, and she wrote dozens of them. And she would mix her guests up in the hopes of inducing interesting conversations.

She and Harold had a large, airy, roomy apartment in an old building on 103rd Street and Riverside Drive overlooking the Hudson and the New Jersey Palisades. It was painted white, and it seemed to me that the tall windows were always open, the entering breezes unrestrained by curtains. The apartment would have seemed colorless had not every possible inch of wall space been filled with floor-to-ceiling shelves bursting with books. Harold's upright piano stood against the wall to the right of the dining room, and Nika usually sat between the windows under a portrait of a stern Italian ancestress. The food was good, but simple. Nika was not a flossy cook. The wine copious, the conversations stimulating, the whole warmed by Nika's ready laugh and tart remarks, and Harold's smile.

Nika, then married to "the dreadful Tony," had arrived in New York with their infant son shortly before the outbreak of World War II. She soon landed a job as a researcher for *Fortune* where, for a while, she worked in tandem with John Chamberlain, the author, book critic, and one of NR's original editors. John and I were great friends. And he told me over a lunch at Paone's one day of taking Nika along for an interview with Boss Kelly of Chicago. I was appalled, he told me, when Nika suddenly asked Boss Kelly where he had gotten his money, would he please account for it? John laughed. "I expected Al Capone to come in the door tommy gun at the ready to punish such impertinence, but Boss Kelly just laughed, shrugged away the question and went on with the interview." That was Nika.

In due course Nika and "the dreadful Tony" Standen were divorced, and she married Harold Hazelton. Harold was as small and slim as Nika was large and stout. But as you realized very soon, he was his own man and knew just how to handle the imperious woman he had married. Harold's ambition had been to be a concert pianist, but one day walking down the hall outside the practice rooms in the conservatory where he was studying in Chicago, he heard a fifteen-year-old playing a Beethoven piano concerto. It was a virtuoso performance and stunned Harold into the realization that no matter how hard he worked he would never play as well and with such understanding and feeling as that boy. He gave up music and, when he graduated from college, went into advertising, which he was good at, and loathed. After he retired, he developed an interest in genealogy and was now, in his late seventies, running the New York Genealogical Society, and enjoying every minute of it.

Often when I went to dinner at the Hazeltons I would pause in the hall outside the door to listen to Harold play as he awaited the arrival of the evening's guests. He was a masterful performer. He and I became great friends, and I was immensely flattered on the occasion of his eightieth birthday, when Nika asked him what he would like, he said, "Dinner with you and Priscilla at the Four Seasons."

It was a great night. The manager of the Four Seasons sent a limousine to pick Harold and Nika up and to take them home after dinner. The following year I invited them back for another Four Seasons extravaganza. And there it ended. By Harold's eighty-second birthday, Nika was pretty much bedridden with arthritis.

Instead we celebrated the birthday in the bedroom of the Hazelton apartment, Harold and I eating off small tables pulled up by the side of the bed. But trust Nika. It was still a grand party. She had suborned a local Chinese restaurant into sending a waiter over for the evening to serve us a Peking duck with all the fixings. It was all lubricated with a vintage champagne which led me to recount, in all its glory, an epical duck hunting expedition with my brother Reid and his wife Tasa.

29

A Santee-Cooper Christmas

M Y BROTHER REID IS MUCH EXCITED. He has the perfect
present for me and he can't wait 'til Christmas to tell
me about it. "Priscilla," he phones, "I'm taking you duck
hunting on the Santee-Cooper for your Christmas present. It is
wonderful, beautiful, and you have never seen such duck shooting
in all your life. Just ask Tasa." Reid's talent for hyperbole is, even for
a Buckley, well developed, so I take the last with a grain of salt. He
also lets drop that the Santee-Cooper, an hour and a half ride from
his home in Camden, South Carolina, means we will have to leave
"a mite early."

As the days roll by, that "mite early" throbs dully like an aching
tooth. It won't go away. Reid, as a matter of course, rises at an un-
godly hour, and a ninety-minute drive with Reid can be a long ninety
minutes. Not that he's not a lovely man, but Reid's conveyances—
only generically are they cars—are by Travelall out of Land Rover,
camouflage-green hunting vehicles with busted springs, screeching,
ill-oiled frames, layered inside with sodden brown paper bags, dogs,

boys, guns, gun cases, tormented bits of clothing, and rolling empty Coke and beer bottles.

The scene: A few days later in an old plantation house where I'm having supper with my old Camden friends, Whit and Alice Boykin. They ask what I'm up to this vacation, and I tell them that Reid is taking me hunting on the Santee-Cooper.

"SANTEE-COOPER?" Sheer. Stark. Disbelief. "Priscilla, don't go! Nothing," says Alice, Alice the intrepid sportswoman, "would make me go shooting on the Santee at this time of year." "I must," I say. "It's Reid's Christmas present."

"When?" they ask.

"Tomorrow."

"TOMORROW!" They excuse themselves to reappear ten minutes later with enough arctic gear to equip a polar expedition: a down-filled zip-up-the-front camouflage flight suit Alice has worn goose hunting on Maryland's eastern shore, gloves, scarves, long underwear, down vests, greatcoats, waders—and two half pints of Rock'n'Rye delivered as I depart, with their condolences.

Reid and Tasa pick me up at 3:30 AM as agreed. The drive is as long as one knew it would be, and more uncomfortable. The heater isn't working, neither is one windshield wiper. We pull into a ramshackle marina and out of the pitch comes a country fellow.

"Mawning Mr. Buckley, should be a great day for the ducks." He spares us the usual spirited recounting of the five thousand he saw on the flyway just last night. We pile the equipment into a long flatboat: four guns, fifty plastic decoys, lunch hamper, shotgun shells, waders, extra clothes, camouflage webbing, four still warm bodies. Reid's Boykin spaniel, a dog of exquisite judgment, will have no part of this expedition and retires to the relative warmth of the pickup. The Boykin's name is Chicken.

Harry, the guide, starts up the motor, which being an outboard comes to life reluctantly. We head into the middle of the lake, then

Harry takes it full out. Slap, slap, slap, goes the prow as it hits the water. Tasa and I lie in the bottom of the boat seeking some protection from the wind. We spot campfires here and there on shore and agree that not even Reid would suggest camping out the night before a shoot. Harry's powerful spotlight cuts a pitiful swathe in the blackness of the night. How he can find his way by it is a mystery to me: whether we will arrive safely wherever it is we are going, I have no doubts whatever about. We won't.

Sometime back we had veered left into a cypress swamp, still going at a spanking clip. In better days I once visited the extraordinary Cypress Gardens near Charleston, and our guide, poling us around in a shallow boat, was careful to steer clear of the exposed cypress knees through which the trees breathe. My question is: How does Harry know we won't hit a cypress knee right now? And why wouldn't it tear a hole in the bottom of the boat, sending us to the bottom of the Santee-Cooper, our bones to mingle with those of other misguided hunters of duck? My waders I have yet to don, but in my long underwear, flannel shirt, sweater, flight suit, scarf, gloves, woollen cap, all-weather jacket I could pass for the Michelin Tire Man: I have about the mobility of an Egyptian mummy. The rest are worse off: they're wearing their waders.

The cold creeps in, mildly uncomfortable at first, progresses through Shivers & Shakes to Teeth Chatter, and finally, to Numb. It was 19 degrees Farenheit at 5:00 AM, and it would be 26 degrees at noon.

We slow down. From time to time Harry points out a small orange ribbon tied to a branch just about eye-level: his blaze to guide him to this morning's hunt. We're moving ever so slowly, circling it seems. Harry mutters to himself. He asks Reid the time. Running a little late we are.

Harry is lost.

We cautiously explore the channel. It's a cul-de-sac. It takes all four of us, pulling and shoving to back the boat out. We twist and turn slowly, then Harry spots an orange ribbon and we're on our way again. It's getting late, and we still have to get to our blind and put out the decoys. There's a perceptible lightening in the east. We unwind the lines and lead weights from around the decoys with cold stiff fingers and hand them to Harry, who tosses them out in clusters around the anchored boat.

Harry thinks the ladies better shoot right from the boat. It's rained, rained a lot, and the water's pretty high. The ladies, he's observed, are pretty short. The ladies nod vigorous agreement.

"You can get out, Mr. Buckley."

Mr. Buckley, ever impetuous, leaps overboard and goes down, down into the Santee, past his ankles, his calves, his knees, his hips. The water slops in over the top of his waders to settle squishilly and chillingly around his toes. Reid bravely wades out to his stand while Harry affixes black rods upright in slots on the four corners of the boat, slides in crossbars, and hitches the camouflage netting on to this frame so that Tasa and I now crouch in a floating blind, hidden, it is earnestly hoped, from the sharp eyes of the soon to be circling ducks.

The blackness has receded from the sky, making way for a grey ribbon along the horizon. You begin to pick out the silhouette of trees and bushes against the lighter backdrop. It's time to load up. Frozen fingers edge shells into chambers. Mine won't slip in, and it's not the cold fingers. Something's wrong with my gun, a two-shot Browning 12-gauge automatic, long since discontinued for just such misbehavior.

"My gun's hung up," I whisper to Harry with admirable restraint.

He fiddles with it, is baffled, and carries it over to Reid, slosh, slosh, slosh. Reid fiddles. Slosh, slosh, slosh, and Harry is back.

"Mr. Buckley says it will have to go to the shop. Here's his gun." Reid's five-eleven is closer to my five-two than Harry's six-two, so I now have Reid's gun, and Reid has commandeered Harry's. Harry sloshes off a final time to take up his post. We hear ducks now, circling overhead, their wings whistling. Reid is right. It's a perfectly beautiful scene, unforgettable. Harry starts to call them in. They circle, look us over, and flare off. Something's spooking them. Harry comes over, checks the blind, warns us not to look up until we're ready to shoot. We know, we know, we've been here before.

From other parts of the swamp we hear cascades of shots, guns barking there in the distance to our left, coming closer as other hunters pick up the flight, but never reaching us. Those ducks that do fly overhead are out of reach. Reid chances a high shot or two, but he doesn't have the range. Lord, but he must be cold. The firing starts to die away.

In ten minutes or so it will be over. Reid is right. At dawn, the Santee-Cooper is arresting in an eerie, lost, abandoned sort of way. The light is soft, heavy with siennas and umbers: it's a Turner sky transplanted to a wild new world. The waters are black and still. Harry calls again. He is a master of the duck call, and swooping low through the trees behind us comes a flight, too far from Reid, but right over our blind. Tasa handles the birds that skitter off to the left with her usual competence. I take a mallard to the right, and it splashes in the water.

From the edge of the swamp, through shivering teeth, comes a call from Reid. "Merry Christmas, Pitts," he says and we all—soaking wet, cold, ninety minutes from a heated room and a hot cup of coffee—commence to laugh. It's been a wonderful present.

⌒ 30 ⌒

The Friend

I T WAS BACK IN 1956, very shortly after my return from Paris to join the *National Review* staff, and already it was party time. Cynthia Castroviejo was giving a three-month-old birthday party in her New York townhouse. I was a bit nervous when I read the cards and saw I would be sitting next to James Burnham, whose *Managerial Revolution* I had studied not so many years before at Smith College.

He was tall, with a professorial appearance, a well-tailored grey suit, hair thinning and going grey, thick-lensed glasses, a shy smile, a courtly manner. He asked me courteously what I had been doing in Paris, and it wasn't an exercise—Jim was insatiably curious. He really wanted to know what was entailed in working the desk at United Press. I rattled on, much relaxed, and before I knew it we were talking about geese, geese as household pets. Burnham, the philosopher, was engrossed by the behavior of the abandoned gosling he and his wife, Marcia, had found and rescued the previous spring. The goose, having been brought up with the Burnham's dogs in their Kent, Connecticut, home, thought he too was a dog and would periodically startle a roomful of guests by taking a flying leap onto Jim's lap. It was a wonderful, warm, offbeat, laughing evening, too short by far. The start of a friendship.

In due course I became managing editor and, in the resulting reshuffle, Jim and I ended up sharing an office. "I think," he said, after the first week's try-out, "that I could be content here."

Jim spent two days a week in New York and it came to be understood after a while that we would eat together unless either of us had another commitment. I always paid my share except on those occasions—a birthday, a return from a trip, even an editorial coup—when one of us would treat the other. When Jim's wife, Marcia, was in New York, which she was quite a lot back then, our dinners *à deux* were more often than not *à trois*.

Somewhere in my files I have a memento of one of those evenings that records our easy camaraderie. I can't now remember what the controversy was about. All the note says is: "Dear Priscilla. My husband is always right. Love. Marcia."

Jim was proud of Marcia and took her opinions and, most particularly, her intuitions seriously. They loved to travel. And letters would float in from exotic places, usually enclosing a column—which would arrive with clockwork precision whether mailed from Kent, or from Katmandu—with long, leisurely comments, many of them wonderfully Jim-like. From a chartered yacht in the Dodecanese islands: "The tourists have really spread over Europe in waves, just about like those which started from the northern parts in 3000 BC The most recent waves are engulfing Spain and Portugal, have hit here, and now I guess it's on to Turkey. We're just in time."

We talked about everything, and as the years passed we kept little of a personal nature from each other. Jim's mind was extraordinary, logical, and penetrating. Never was there a man so little misled by surface rhetoric. Jim looked not at what a man said, but at why he thought it necessary to say it. What were the underlying causes? The tactical considerations? The power vectors? This did not ingratiate him with his political opponents; it also deflated many a rhetorical flourish at editorial conferences, discomfiting a number of his colleagues. This cool exterior of Jim's led many to believe that he was cold. There was nothing cold in the Jim Burnham I knew.

His warmth: Once, when I confessed to him my worry over mother's prospective double cataract operation, he reminisced a little about his own mother. She had been perfectly well, he said, until she had a trifling operation in her early eighties—a nothing operation—but she was never really the same again. He had noticed about older people that often it was one small thing that triggered the beginning of the end. It was Jim's way of warning me, without saying it, that perhaps mother would emerge from the upcoming ordeal changed, and in truth she never did recover her old élan.

His sense of mischief: Time after time at our editorial conferences ("Agonies"), he would suggest that perhaps our book section, then edited by Frank Meyer, could do with shorter reviews, four-hundred-word reviews such as *The Economist* ran. This would, predictably, send Frank right through the ceiling. The other editors would wait in joyful anticipation for this moment, sure that this time Frank would let it pass. But like Charlie Brown, Frank never failed to rise to the bait. "*Tu es méchant*," I told Jim one morning after a partcularly spirited explosion from Frank. He smiled. "I know," he said.

His kindness: He would take in hand a young editor who was having a hard time writing an NR editorial paragraph and patiently explain where he had gone wrong without ever hurting his pride. At one point he decreed that editorial paragraphs in the *National Review Bulletin* should run no longer than ten lines (about a hundred words), and within six weeks the young editorial staffers were writing terse, pointed short editorials, and were much pleased with themselves. The youngsters in the office had a very special feeling for Jim Burnham, a respect and a love they accorded to no other editor in my experience.

His insight: Often I would find myself calling him when an office situation had arisen that worried me. He would listen carefully, ask penetrating questions, and, oftener than was good for my self-esteem, analyze what had gone wrong and suggest a course of action that would never have occurred to me. Frequently I accepted his recommendation, but when I didn't he was never offended. It was not Jim's way. I remember how startled I was when I recounted the misbehavior of a since-departed colleague, and he replied: "But, Priscilla, you must understand he is not a first-rate human being." Of course, that explained it.

In late January 1978, Marcia, a solemn Marcia, called from Kent, said there was something Jim wanted to tell me, and put Jim on. The news was terrible. On their flight back from Columbia, South Carolina, where Jim had joined George Will and Bill Buckley *v.* Ronald Reagan, Roger Fontaine, and Patrick Buchanan in a famous *Firing Line* debate on the Panama Canal, Jim found he couldn't see. An examination disclosed that he suffered from macular degeneration: he would in the not-too-distant future be blind. I was appalled, and I stuttered the usual palliatives and perhapses: perhaps he should get a second opinion, perhaps there was some cure. Perhaps. . . But true to one of is own beliefs—that if there's no alternative, there's no problem—Jim shot down my hopes. He would simply have to make the best of it, but of course it would mean the end of his writing for NR. It was arranged that I would drop in for supper in Kent Thursday night en route home to Sharon.

I expected Jim to look different, somehow, but of course he didn't. He came out of the little study—the informal living room where he worked and where he and Marcia spent much of their time—to greet me as I drove up, and to silence the dogs. Our hug that evening was less perfunctory than usual. He made me a drink, poked the fire, brought over the nuts and cheese, and called up the steep irregular box stairs to tell Marcia I had arrived. He was anxious to tell me not about his illness and his despair, but about the steps he had taken to cope with them. He had ordered Eleanor Clark's book, written when she was going blind from the same disease. He much admired her as a writer and digressed for a moment or two to tell me more about her. He had contacted the Library of Congress and ordered the free player and list of recordings available to the blind. He found it quite wonderful that he would be able to switch back and forth to what he was interested in in the tapes of contemporary journals—including NR—that he had ordered. It was a cozy, pleasant evening among friends. Jim Burnham was in this as in all else a realist.

It was the precursor of nine sad years. A stroke late that same year—when he was seventy-three—left him physically unimpaired but without short-term memory. Without the tools, the building blocks of facts, the brilliant searching mind was short-circuited. Marcia bore up magnificently under the burden of Jim's incapacity. They still came to New York for an occasional editorial dinner, but it was never really the same. Then Marcia—the pillar—died suddenly, unexpectedly, aged seventy.

A year later, Jim was stricken with the cancers that would kill him. I would drop over once or twice a week, and, so long as he could, he would stand up to greet me and smile. "Hello, Priscilla," he would say, and then, as if surprised. "You are looking remarkably well." I would thank him but could not reciprocate in kind, for on every visit he was frailer, more withdrawn. So in the silence we would smile at each other and thus communicate our love.

It was a great joy to many of Jim's friends that in those final days he was reconciled to the church he had rejected as a graduate student at Oxford. (Marcia's husband was not always right.) The funeral Mass was at the Sacred Heart Church in Kent. Through the Purgatory of his final decade he was spared one thing: the macular degeneration that threatened him with blindness was, mysteriously, arrested. The doctors recorded the fact but could not explain it. I pray and find comfort in the thought that it was a sign of God's all-encompassing mercy and grace.

Moscow, Here We Come

AS WE APPROACH OUR TWENTIETH ANNIVERSARY in November of 1975 Bill is bitten, suddenly, by a very particular travel bug. For weeks he has been reading Intourist ads offering a quite tantalizing eight-day trip to the Soviet Union, four days in Moscow, three in St. Petersburg, luxury accommodations, all expenses paid including air fare, for just under $800. It sounds too good to be true, and he has visions not of sugar plums dancing in his head but of *National Review*'s editors parading through Red Square as guests of Intourist. What would the Soviets make of that? *National Review* has been in the forefront of the anti-Communist, anti-Soviet-aggression battle for twenty years. The idea is too delicious, and what Bill finds delicious in prospect only too often becomes so in fact. So—looking for something to top the grand party NR had given at the Tavern on the Green, on its fifteenth birthday—he invited the senior staff to join him on a pre-Christmas visit to what will, five years later, be labeled "the evil empire" it was.

The first inkling NR readers get of the trip appears in an anguished note in "Notes & Asides," January 23, 1976: WILLIAMOVICH

PRISCILLANOVNA IVANOVNA VOTSISSDRAWAOWE MIT
MUSCHOVICHES? VOTS TO HAPPEN CREDIBILITOVICH
NATIONAL REVIEWOVICH? CHECKOVICH BUGSOVICH
ROOMSOVICH YOU BETCHUM BETTER KOMMEN SIE
HOMEOVICH QUICKOVICH. /s/ REIDOVICH [BUCKLEY]."

To Bill's astonishment not all of NR's key people share his enthusiasm. Jim Burnham refuses because Marcia rightly fears for his
safety, particularly since Jim was a CIA consultant in setting up both
the anti-Communist Congress for Cultural Freedom, and *Kultura*,
the dissident Polish journal published in Paris. Jeff Hart couldn't go.
He had four children and a wife who put a higher priority on Christmas preparations than on gallivanting abroad, particularly without
them. Assistant Publisher Jim McFadden wouldn't go because Jim
won't board a plane. Bill Rusher won't go because he hates the Soviet
Union. The business end is represented by Ed Capano and his wife,
Margy. Ed is Jim McFadden's second in command, and he will end
up as *National Review*'s publisher.

But most of the editorial staff sign on. My sister Jane and I will
share a room as will Copy Editor Vicki Marani and Production Editor
Barbara Devlin. Kevin and Jo Lynch, Joe Sobran, and Linda Bridges
round out the editorial staffers in the group. Then there are members of the various departments: Advertising Director Rob Sennott,
Robin Wu, and Henry Fasciani of the Library, Helen Puwalski, the
receptionist who is indisputably the head of her department even if
it is a department of one. A couple of columnists, Nika (and Harold)
Hazelton, and Keith Mano (and his wife). Then there are special
friends: ex-Executive Editor Dan Oliver and Louise—Dan will be a
great help as a graduate of the Russian language school in Monterrey,
California; John Leonard, our long ago editorial assistant, and Sue,
his wife-to-be; Jim Manzi, Bill's research assistant on his most recent
book, and Marvin Liebman, everybody's best friend. And to make
sure everything goes right, the unflappable Frances Bronson.

And let's not forget Bill's wife, Pat, queen of the tuck box. Pat comes prepared for any contingency. A superb cook and hostess, she suspects that the food will be "inedible"—her favorite word for other people's cooking—and comes prepared, among other things, with mountains of peanut butter, without which none of my brothers can live.

My sister Jane is, like Pat, not only a good provider but a good anticipator. Very important to Jane after a hard day's touristing is a refreshing, ice cold vodka on the rocks in the evening, and this she came prepared for. Out of Jane's carry-on bag that first night at the Hotel Moskva come: one ice tray, a supply of water-purefying tablets, a number of baggies and elastic bands, a ball of twine, two plastic glasses, and a plastic bottle. Every morning before departing the hotel, she fills the icetray with water which she has purified the evening before in the plastic bottle, places the icetray in one of the baggies, secures it with elastic bands, ties the string around it, and places it cautiously outside the window which I close ever so gently so that the contraption hangs face up. This, after all, was mid-December in Russia, and when we return exhausted of an evening there would be our ice cubes ready to cool the contents of the small bottle of vodka which could be readily acquired at any dollar store. (This was our secret weapon, Jane's and mine.)

There were, of course, the usual glitches, one of them particularly of the Soviet harassment type. On the Tuesday before our scheduled departure, the Intourist office in New York phoned *National Review* to announce that it had not received visas for Dan Oliver and two other of the would-be travelers, and that if they hadn't arrived by Friday those three could not make the trip. They picked the wrong target to play games with. Bill told Frances to call them back and tell them that we were a group of twenty-six, and unless all twenty-six received visas, none of us would go. It was all or nothing, as the police had discovered in Oaxaca when they tried to shake Bill down after our car had been hit by a drunken Mexican driver. On Thursday, Intourist called back to say the missing visas had arrived, and it was all systems go.

Customs at the Moscow airport were as long and as cumbersome as we had expected, and compounded by the absence of two or three suitcases which, we were assured, would arrive on the next flight ("with any luck at all," we said under our breaths, but we were wrong). Then, terribly weary from the long flight in the Spartan accommodations offered by Aeroflot, the Soviet airline, we boarded a bus along with a number of Baptists from Florida who had been on the plane with us for the ride into the city. It was cold and dark, with spitting bursts of icy rain and snow. The windows of the bus were filthy, but still we could make out the long rows of ugly apartment buildings that lined the highway and noted the absence of cars on the road and of lamps in the windows. Most of the apartments seemed to be lighted by bulbs at the end of electrical cords hanging from the ceilings. It was a dismal sight, but I suppose so commonplace that Lyra, the bright and attractive Intourist guide who would be with us during our entire Moscow visit, made no attempt to explain away the general bleakness. Nor did she reply when Bill, as we entered central Moscow, asked her in a spirit of mischief if she could point out for us the world famous Lubyanka prison. That little nonexchange did brighten our spirits and soon enough we were at the Moskva, which was brightly lit and comfortably appointed.

We were rushed in to the dining room, which was about to close and assured that our bags would be in our rooms after the meal. The food was, as Pat had suspected, practically but not entirely inedible. The soup, a borsch, was delicious, and the dark bread chewy and tasty, but for the life of us, no one could figure out what kind of meat we were being served with the rock-hard wizened carrots that seemed the only vegetable available to Muscovites at that season. No-name meat and carrots were the regular entrées on the Intourist menu in both Moscow and Leningrad. The ice cream was good, so good that Helen Puwalski ate only ice cream thereafter, morning, noon, and night.

Next morning, refreshed and anxious to see the Russia we had read so much about, but that none of us had experienced, we were bundled into a smaller bus that held only the NR party (and its, we were sure, KGB driver), and taken to the Armory, with its fantastic and fascinating treasures. But first, at the door, we were required to (1) check our coats, and (2) put large felt slippers over our boots lest we injure the parquet floors of which at this point there was no evidence. This was routine, applicable at every museum we visited: coats off, slippers on. It was particularly hard for Nika Hazelton with her bad hips and knees, but she was good-natured about the inconvenience, sorry only that her awkwardness in putting on the slippers sometimes held us up.

The exhibits at the Armory were eclectic, a running story of Russian history, ranging from a saddle cover made from the skins of 20,000 canaries sent to a czar in the middle ages by a Persian king, to a handful of Fabergé eggs; from the cunningly designed throne with a cabinet behind it in which the older sister of a boy czar who sat on the throne could whisper advice to him, to the huge and beautifully furnished sled that Catherine the Great used to travel the seven hundred miles from Moscow to St. Petersburg in dead of winter. It was drawn by twelve, or maybe it was sixteen horses.

Helen Puwalski, our Polish receptionist whose legs were chronically swollen and painful, agreed that what she had seen at the Armory was spectacular, and simultaneously announced that that was the last museum she intended to visit on this trip. Helen's Russian adventure consisted largely of eating ice cream. She saw nothing that could not be seen from the window of a bus or train. She would board the bus every morning with the rest of us, but when we attained our destination would remain seated until our return, except for one afternoon when driving back from a visit to an old monastery we paused to watch some children sledding. They were laughing and shouting, throwing snowballs, having a whale of a time. They sat upright on their sleds as children do in Europe, and whirled down a precipitous slope with shrill giggles—and not a little apprehension—to come to a bouncy stop in a snowy meadow below. We urged Jim Manzi to join them, but he said with a grin that it was too scary. Every now and then, one of them would hit a rough spot and take a tumble, getting up, brushing off the snow, laughing, and plunging down the hill to recapture the runaway sled. It was great fun.

We were enthralled by their sheer joyousness. Even Helen climbed out of the bus to watch. These playing children with their smiling happy faces were in such stark contrast to the parents and grandparents we had watched trudging the streets of Moscow in their drab brown, grey, or black winter coats, not speaking to one another, their faces expressionless, proceeding from this point to that on what was apparently the dreary business of life. Once, they had been laughing children like these, once upon a time before the rigidities and hopelessness of life in the Soviet Union had ground them down.

Lyra was an entrancing guide. Her English was excellent, with just the slightest trace of an accent to add to its attractiveness. She was young, slim, and stylish, and she swung with the punches and Bill's teasing (in sharp contrast to Ludmilla, our Leningrad guide, who insisted on giving us the doctrinaire answer to every inquiry). On our second day in Moscow, as we drove back into the city after a visit to a nearby "nonfunctional" church, Lyra approached Bill and said, in a low voice, "Mr. Buckley, that building you asked about when we came in from the airport. It's to the right." The Lubyanka. Nothing in its bland surface to indicate its tortured, bloody history.

To everyone's amusement but his, young Jim Manzi was swept right off his feet by Lyra. Jim is short, and sprightly, with a huge slightly hooked nose and a shy smile. None of us knew him very well because most of his research for Bill's book had been done out of the office, but it took only a day or two for Jim to become a general favorite. He was smitten, oh how he was smitten, by Lyra, and he came up with a dozen schemes for getting her out of the Soviet Union, even though Lyra showed not the slightest desire to leave her homeland. She couldn't be happy, Jim told us forcefully, no matter how carefree her manner. How could one be happy in the Soviet Union? But we were in Moscow only four days, not long enough to execute a spectacular break-out for Lyra, like it or not, so nothing came of all of Jim's plans. Jim wrote Lyra a couple of times after returning to the States, but never heard back, obviously a prudent move on her part.

Red Square and the cluster of domed churches around St. Basil's were impressive, breathtaking. On one side of the square was Gum, the huge Soviet department store. At the center, across from Gum's, was Lenin's tomb with the honor guard of soldiers at rigid attention at the portal. Behind Lenin's monument were buried many of the leaders of the Bolshevik Revolution, those who had survived Stalin's bloody purges. Stalin's tomb was there, but diminished in size following Nikita Khrushchev's revelations of his crimes.

In daytime, the center of Red Square was crowded with people standing in line to visit Lenin's tomb. We got into line and were instructed to pair off. Guards saw to it that coats were buttoned from top to bottom and that our hands were in our pockets. We were warned not to speak and to be respectful. I was paired with Keith Mano. We entered the elaborate tomb and went slowly down the stairs toward the crypt. Soldiers with tommy guns stood at rigid attention at each level. The light was dim. As Keith and I moved toward the glass coffin and the waxy effigy within it, Keith muttered more loudly than made me comfortable: "I have seen the anti-Christ."

Fortunately for us, the guard was not bilingual.

On our last night in Moscow, we attended a performance of *Rigoletto* at the opera house on the far side of Red Square from our hotel. We checked our coats at the door, as usual, but were spared the felt slippers. The opera started late. The intermissions were long. And it was sung in Russian, which was discombobulating to our ears. After the second intermission most of our party left, but Linda and I stayed to the end, which included the joyous moment when the Duke sang *donna e mobile* (in Russian), and an American tourist in the row behind us whispered to his wife, "Dear, that's the toreador song."

It was almost midnight when the curtain came down. Linda and I found that the Intourist bus had left. There were no taxis so we had no recourse but to walk home. It wasn't much of a hike. A light snow was falling, and it was chilly but not bitterly so. Red Square, teeming with life in the daytime, was deserted by all but the two of us and the guards in front of Lenin's mausoleum. The clock struck twelve as we crossed the square toward St. Basil's, whose profile seemed insubstantial and wavy, blurred by the softly falling snow. A door swung open and an honor guard goose-stepped its way into the square to relieve the rigid, frigid, sentinels. We stood there for a moment, taking it all in, the temple that housed Keith Mano's anti-Christ and the beautiful old domed (nonfunctional) churches, dimly lit at the far end of the square. It was a moment to savor, to remember.

The rule, someone's rule, was that on any eight-day Intourist trip one night had to be spent in a city other than Moscow or Leningrad. It befell our lot to spend a night in the rather disheveled barracks of an old hotel in the city of Kalinin. Kalinin was named for that famous medieval merchant-explorer that I bet you never heard about even though our Kalinin guide insisted that he was far better known, to say nothing of a better explorer, than Marco Polo. The statue of the merchant-explorer, a rather pudgy fellow, stood on a pedestal on the banks of the river that ran through Kalinin. It was just about the only thing worth seeing in town, possibly because it wasn't yet another figure of Lenin.

At breakfast the following morning, which was served cafeteria-style, I headed for a spare place at a table with Robin Wu and Henry Fasciani. Henry asked if I didn't want some orange juice. I did, I said, but I hadn't seen any when I went through the line.

"I'll get you a glass," he said. A moment later he was back, a twinkle in his eye: "Priscilla, would you like it with, or without, vodka. The price is the same."

We boarded a train in Kalinin for the final three- or four-hour trip to Leningrad. And sat, in that train, all the way to Leningrad, backwards. Could it be that Soviet railroads had no turntables? Or no seats with backs that could be swung back and forth given the direction you were headed? Could it possibly be that in the Soviet Union the custom was to ride from Moscow to Leningrad backward, and from Leningrad to Moscow forward? There was no Lyra or even a Ludmilla to explain the phenomenon to us. The only Russians in the car were two stolid KGB types who climbed aboard just as the train left the station. At the front of the car, there were four seats facing each other. Harold and Nika had taken two of them because of the extra leg room.

The two husky fellows in overcoats and fur hats took the two seats facing Nika and Harold, from which they could keep their eye on the rest of us. Nika was knitting a sweater for a grandchild and hoped to finish by Christmas. But the seats were rather slippery and her ball of yarn kept falling to the floor, to be picked up patiently and handed back to her by one of the KGB men. She would thank him each time, and each time he would unbend a little more, and finally, he smiled. Before the trip was over, he was holding the yarn for her, and doing his best to make her comfortable, won over as everyone always was by her warmth and charm.

Leningrad was a gracious city, airy and beautiful. The ravages of the long siege it had undergone during the war had been obliterated. With its golden domes, lovely open squares, and freshly painted buildings it seemed light years away from Moscow. This was the city of Peter the Great's imagining, with many wonders and fair sights.

Chief among them the Hermitage, with among other things its impressive collection of French impressionist paintings that had been hidden away from the world for many years, until, in fact, just recently. There was a long line waiting to get in, but we favored Intourist guests were guided right to the door. Once inside there was the cloakroom-felt slipper scene. We sat on low benches, Nika getting down to one with trouble. But when she bent over to put on the slippers one of the babushkas who were overseeing the operation, rushed up to her and started waving her arms vigorously and almost shouting. Linda—she was the only one in the party aside from Dan Oliver who spoke Russian—rushed over to interpret. She told Nika that the attendant was saying that there was no need for Nika to don the slippers. She could visit the museum just as she was, in her serviceable walking flats. Nika nodded her thanks and asked Linda to tell the old woman how kind she was. Then Nika stood up, with some help, and reached into her cavernous purse, fumbling around for an appropriate gift. What she pulled out of the grab bag was most surprising: a fancy lipstick with a black-gold-and-red case. This she presented to the babushka with a word of thanks. The old woman's eyes brightened. She smiled. She was delighted with the gift. She leaned over and embraced Nika, two sturdy, bulky old women full of affection, and yes, for all of their bulk, of grace.

During most of the trip Joe Sobran had been unhappy. Much as he enjoyed the extraordinary sights we had seen, he couldn't divorce them from the horror that he perceived to be the dreary daily round of life under the repressive Soviet regime. He seemed to me to wear an expression of wariness, almost of sorrow. Joe had bought a black fur hat early on, which matched his somber black winter overcoat. He pulled it low over his brow. He seemed to skulk on the outside of every crowd. It was here in the Hermitage that one of the Florida Baptists, who had arrived at the hotel in Leningrad from another city the night before, nudged me, and said, in a whisper: "See that fellow, there?" he pointed to Joe. "We figure he's the KGB guy." I did not disillusion him. I couldn't wait to tell Joe.

Returning on the bus that evening we asked Ludmilla about Catholic Masses. She did not take the question kindly. Of course, she would have no idea of the hour of a Catholic Mass or whether there was one in Leningrad. Of course, there would be no question of an Intourist bus taking us to such a place. But then, unbending a bit—Ludmilla, for all her doctrinaire Sovietism—liked to oblige, she suggested we ask the desk clerk.

Dan and Linda, although neither of them was Catholic, were delegated to find out how those of us who were Catholic could go about attending Mass the next morning. At supper they reported that it was easy. The desk clerk had been most obliging. Mass was at 11:00 AM, and he would order four taxis for 10:30 the following morning.

However, next morning when Dan checked the desk after breakfast he was told that no taxis had been ordered. The obliging desk clerk of the day before had solved his problem by doing nothing. Dan ordered up the taxis and rushed upstairs to alert us. We should go right down and be at the door when (if?) the taxis arrived because they wouldn't wait if the passengers were not at hand.

Two taxis straggled in at about 10:15 and five or six of us took off. The rest followed a few minutes later.

The church, a fairly run-down brick building, was in what was obviously a working class area, with the usual grim blockhouse Soviet apartment buildings flanking it. They, like the church, were run-down.

It was obvious that the ukases of Vatican Council II had not penetrated this part of the Soviet Union. The bearded, middle-aged priest had his back firmly to the congregation. The Mass was in the old, familiar Latin. We rejoiced to respond "*et cum spiritu tuo*," instead of the bland and graceless "and also with you." The church was not full, but it was certainly not empty. The parishioners, for the most part, were older women, their heads covered with hats or black shawls. The priest probably wasn't conscious that there were foreigners in the congregation because when the Mass was over, and the final *Deo gratias* pronounced, he retired to the sacristy, and not back down the main aisle of the church to greet the parishioners at the door.

The taxis were there when we got out, having been liberally tipped (with cigarettes) on the outward trip. It was only noon, but it was a bitterly cold, grey day as we drove back to the hotel. The Neva, as we crossed a bridge to the Nevsky Prospeckt, was turbulent, its blue-green waters choppy and angry, with ice floes here and there. It could have been on a day such as this that the Bolsheviks stormed the Winter Palace, bringing to an end a Romanov dynasty whose most prominent early leader was Ivan the Terrible, and the last, Nicholas the Mild.

On our last night in Leningrad we feasted. Marvin had discovered the whereabouts of a posh private restaurant and managed to reserve most of it for our party. We started with caviar and vodka, and washed down the rest of a splendid meal like none we had experienced in the past week—Pat pronounced it "edible"—with a somewhat sweet but nonetheless delectable Soviet champagne. En route home in the Intourist bus, Marvin, who seldom drank but had on this occasion, seized Ludmilla's microphone and gave us his version of the historic sights we were passing. Oh laughter, oh joy! We couldn't imagine how the driver, if he was, as we thought, the KGB plant, would report this one to his bosses.

We were roused very early the next morning for the ride to the airport. Ludmilla, who had done her level best in three days to make Soviet admirers of us all, said good-bye politely, but without warmth. She did not wave as the bus pulled out, which hurt a little. We hadn't meant to offend her with our jokes and putdowns, but we had, and we were sorry. She was only doing her job and we had, thoughtlessly, made it harder than it should have been.

The airport scene was a disaster. It was so arranged that the entire 120 or 130 of us passengers had to push and shove our bags across a vast hall to passport control. Then push them back where we had started for customs. Then shove them along to the ticket counters where the big bags were checked, and at this point removed by porters. Then we were ushered into the departure lounge, which was furnished with three or four chairs but had no tables, no kiosks, no shops, no restaurant, no coffee shop. We managed to get two chairs, one for Nika and one for Helen, but the rest of us sat on our handbags or on the floor for six or seven hours. There was an ice storm, and Leningrad airport's de-icing equipment was antiquated.

At about 5:00 PM, we rode small buses out to the plane, negotiating icy spots on the tarmac between the bus and the steps. The same group of Baptists who had started out with us from New York eight days before were once again part of our group.

When the plane lifted off there was a spontaneous cheer from the passengers, but our troubles weren't over. For the next hour or so the husky flight attendants went up and down the aisles striving to sell us souvenirs. We were not in the mood for lacquer boxes or dolls or shawls. They might have persuaded us to buy some caviar—it was eight or nine hours since we had last eaten—but they had nothing to spread the caviar on.

Finally, they came down the aisles with tall glasses, a shot of vodka topped off by, believe it or not, 7-UP. The two Baptists sitting behind Jane and me had a great deal of trouble trying to make the attendants understand that they wanted the 7-UP but not the vodka. Then came supper, a tray dominated by an unappetizing-looking half a chicken, some of them with a feather or two still unplucked.

The man behind us asked his friend: "Brother, what do you think this is?"

To which his friend replied: "Brother, this is a Soviet chicken, and it has led one hell of a life."

The plane was cold, the seats uncomfortable, and the lavatories, like the churches in Sovietland, nonfunctional.

We had to put down in Shannon airport to refuel for the trans-Atlantic hop. We poured off that plane with whoops of joy. One half of us heading for the clean, light airy white-tiled rest rooms with their running hot and cold water. The other half to the bars where we ordered up restorative Irish coffees. At the half time, the passengers exchanged positions. Jane found time to buy a blanket which she wound around herself for the trip home. As I said earlier, Jane is both a good provider and a good anticipator.

Our farewells when we reached JFK were speedy and almost perfunctory. Our minds were churning with everything that had to be done before Christmas. And Christmas was just one week away.

Early in January I got a package in the mail. It was from Jim Manzi, a nicely framed photograph he had taken of me standing in front of the gates of Catherine the Great's palace outside Leningrad. There was a nice note, thanking us—particularly Bill and me—for including him in the trip.

A few years later, but not all that many years later, we were sitting around the big table in the conference room at NR, and someone flipping through an issue of *Fortune* magazine listing the most successful CEOs in America, gave a whoop. There, along with the Bill Gateses and Lee Iacoccas was Jim Manzi, CEO of Lotus, the enormously successful computer software company. Could it be our Jim Manzi? The nose in the tiny photograph was unmistakeable. It was our Jim Manzi.

We got back in touch and, very shortly after Jim sold Lotus to IBM for big dollars, he served as co-host of our fortieth anniversary party, an elegant dinner boat-ride around New York harbor.

⌾ 34 ⌾

Coming of Age

I T IS BROUGHT TO MY ATTENTION FORCEFULLY that I have reached
the august age of three score and ten, when the morning's mail
brought in my first, both unsolicited and unanticipated, Social
Security check. It came as a complete surprise. At sixty-five, I continued to be happily involved with *National Review* as a senior editor,
having relinquished the more arduous job as managing editor first
to Rick Brookhiser and subsequently to Linda Bridges. It had not
occurred to me to retire. My new, post-managing editor schedule was
a dream. I spent three and a half days a week in New York, researching and writing my "For the Record" column, contributing to the
editorial section, putting together the fortnightly two-page cartoon
spread which we called "Help!!!", and monitoring incoming freelance
light verse that in those days we used as fillers. The rest of the time
I spent in Sharon or traveling.

   This, the mid- and late 1980s, was a transitional period at *National Review*, a phasing in of the new guard that would take over
from the original crew: Frank Meyer and Jim Burnham had died,
and Bill Rickenbacker, remarried and now living in Vermont, no

longer came in regularly to write editorials. Jeff Hart, soon to retire
from Dartmouth, continued and continues to make the journey to
New York every second week. He very often ran the editorial section
in the absence of Bill or the new, presiding editorial presence, John
O'Sullivan, lately of Margaret Thatcher's kitchen cabinet, a charming,
talented British conservative who had for a time edited The Heritage
Foundation's *Policy Review* and Robert Murdoch's conservative *New
York Post*. John O'Sullivan had taken over as editor-in-chief from Bill
after NR's thirty-fifth anniversary at the end of 1990, the year before
I turned seventy.

On the business side, the WAR department had made way first for
Wick Allison, a brilliant Texan, editor and founder of *D*, the super-
successful Dallas magazine, and subsequently after Wick's departure
for greener pastures, for Jim McFadden's longtime number two man,
Ed Capano. What McFadden didn't know about increasing circulation and raising money, Ed Capano did, and it was largely due to his
efforts that for the first time in history *National Review* has actually
turned an occasional profit.

I knew exactly what I would do with the eight hundred plus dollars that had so unexpectedly fallen into my lap. I was the owner of
a vintage, somewhat dilapidated, but smashingly stylish 1973 green
Mustang convertible. I had bought it when Detroit announced back
in the early 1970s that it would no longer produce convertibles,
Ralph Nader spank if they did, since they were considered unsafe at
any speed. Because I thought it would be my last convertible, I had
put it up every winter so that the salt and sand would not do their
destructive work. Now, I drove it down for a consultation with Roger
Elwood at Sharon Auto Body, and it was determined that my first
two Social Security checks would pay for a smashing new paint job
and a new gleaming white, rather than dingy beige, convertible top.
My Mustang, at eighteen, had come of age, and would emerge from

Roger's ministrations repristinated. If I had to be seventy, I would be the chic-est seventy-year-old on the block, at least vehicularly. My reward was instant. Three weeks later a racing driver from the nearby Lime Rock track whistled in admiration when he spotted my sparkling Sherwood Forest green Mustang, and asked, "Lady, is that your rig?" causing such palpitations of the heart as I hadn't experienced since a construction worker last whistled at me forty years earlier.

But still, seventy is seventy, and it occurred to me that maybe this would be an appropriate time to retire, particularly since Bill had stepped down a few months earlier. So it was, once again, party time. The biggest and best party, in my opinion, of the lot. No, I can't say that.

The best had been *National Review*'s thirtieth anniversary party, which President Ronald Reagan attended. We were particularly pleased that the president could make it, since he was just back from his first summit meeting with Mikhail Gorbachev in Geneva and we had feared that the press of business would force him to cancel out. But the Gipper was game.

It was 1985, the year I was retiring as managing editor, and Bill had decided to seat me at the right hand of the president in the grand ballroom of the Plaza Hotel where the gala was held. I confess I faced this singular honor with some trepidation. If other anniversary dinners were any guide, this would be a three-hour affair. How did one converse with the president of the United States, and one I greatly admired, for three hours?

All the guests were seated when the band played "Hail to the Chief" and over the loudspeaker, it was announced, "The President of the United States and Mrs. Reagan." I was at a table with, among others, Clare Boothe Luce, and CIA Director Bill Casey. The president approached our table, gave Clare Luce a warm embrace, and me a kiss, and shook hands with all the men. He pulled out his chair, sat down and said: "Priscilla. Would you like to know what I said to Gorbachev?"

Good-bye palpitations.

What a splendid evening it had been, culminating in President Reagan's glowing tribute to Bill and the movement Bill had founded with the infant *National Review* thirty years earlier when he was twenty-nine years old.

"You and I remember a time of the forest primeval," Reagan told a rapt audience:

> A time when nightmare and danger reigned. Only the knights of darkness prevailed. When conservatism seemed without a champion in the crucial battle of style and content, and then suddenly riding up through the lists came our clipboard-bearing Galahad, ready to take on any challenger in the critical battle of point and counterpoint, with grace and humor and passion to raise a standard to which patriots and lovers of freedom could repair.
>
> So Bill one last word to you. We thank you for your friendship. You are of course a great man, and we thank you also for *National Review*, for setting loose so much good in the world. . . .

And then a typically Reagan fillip, "and Bill, thanks too for all the fun."

That was a great evening, but this one would be all mine. Only someone who has worked with Bill knows the time, energy, and imagination that go into any party he puts on, and for my combined seventieth-birthday-retirement party he pulled out all the stops.

It was held at the Union League Club on Park and 37th Street, the scene of many another gala that Bill had orchestrated and I had attended, in honor, among others, of Jim McFadden, NR's renowned movie critic John Simon, and Monsignor Eugene Clark. Two fixtures at most conservative gatherings in New York in those days were Bill Rusher, as master of ceremonies, and Gene Clark, giving the invocation. And of course both of them were here tonight in the beautiful pine-paneled room in which the party was held. The tables were sparkling: starched white tablecloths, gleaming silver and crystal, fall flower centerpieces, and balloons bobbing here and there, proclaiming "PITTS—70."

Most of my dearest friend were there. My oldest friend, Carol Hill Lamb. We had met as nervous fifteen-year-olds at the Nightingale-Bamford School in New York in the 1930s, gone on to Smith College, and there roomed together. Bobby Ober Hansen and Lee Jones Schoenburg, we had been copy girls together and then rewritemen on the United Press Radio desk in New York right after college in the early and mid-1940s. Nick King, my best friend from the splendid three years I had spent working for UP in Paris. Nick had worked for NR off and on, and we had become official colleagues again when I served on the Advisory Commission for Public Diplomacy, the oversight commission of the United States Information Agency during the Reagan administration, and Nick had run the USIA's Foreign Press Office in New York.

Gertrude Vogt, Bill's first secretary, who was in her early nineties, flew in from California for the celebration, the last trip east she would ever make. She and Frances Bronson had many notes to compare, stories about Bill to tell each other. So many old friends. John Chamberlain was there, and his Ernestine; Ham Wright, my favorite golfing partner of half a century, and many others, including Ernest van den Haag, with whom my relationship had been thorny at times. When Ernest had offended me once years earlier—the *casus belli* was whether footnotes were appropriate in a news magazine—I had asked Jimmy O'Bryan to pencil in a Fu Manchu mustache on Ernest's photograph in the contents page of the issue we hand delivered to Ernest whenever he had an article in NR. Ernest is vain, and I hoped he would think the tampered photo was in every copy of the magazine. He took the caper with surprising good grace. "I surrender, dear," he said when he called, and things were copacetic between us from there on in.

Most of my family was there, all of my siblings but Reid, who was giving a seminar that week at the public speaking school he runs, and couldn't get away. My sister Jane and a few of her handsome sons and daughters, with whom I had spent so much time. Priscilla O'Reilly, the baby I had delivered on the bathroom floor, now a rangy, blonde spitfire of thirty, and most of her brothers and sisters. My brother Jim and most of his boys, Peter, Jay, and David, with whom I had golfed and skied, but young Bill Buckley, my hunting companion, couldn't make it. Jim Heath, my sister Aloïse's oldest boy and my first godchild was there. He and I had tramped many a weary mile after quail through the broom straw, branches, and pine groves of South Carolina, and after the wily grouse in the steep and rocky Berkshire hills.

The speeches were short (Bill insists on brevity, which is why people like to attend his parties), funny, occasionally sentimental, and unbelievably flattering. Carol Hill talked about our very young days; Jim McFadden, my first buddy at *National Review*, about early contretemps and adventures; everyone's best friend Marvin Liebman about poker games, sailing mishaps, and religion. (When Marvin was received into the Catholic Church one Easter's eve, Bill and I served as his godparents, and Monsignor Clark, who had instructed him, performed the baptism.) Nick King talked about our days in Paris covering the French Indochina war at a remove of eight thousand miles from the combat zone, and Rick Brookhiser and Linda Bridges, the two most successful graduates of Miss Buckley's Finishing School for Young Ladies and Gentlemen of Conservative Persuasion, reminisced about that. Gerry O'Reilly, Maureen's husband, there with all of his children and the lovely Seton who had brought them up as

Maureen would have liked, had a tall tale or two to tell. The evening wound up with a few words by my brothers Jim and Bill, and, of course, my rebuttal.

And, did I tell you that the Whiffenpoofs were there singing the songs of our long past youth as only those gentleman songsters can? They sang during the cocktail hour, they sang at dinner, they sang after dinner. I walked out, blissfully happy and mightily touched with their final number, "Good-bye, Tootsie, Good-bye . . .", 'a-ringing in my ears.

Not a bad way to go.

Index

PRISCILLA L. BUCKLEY spent forty-three years as an editor at *National Review*, twenty-seven of them as managing editor. She retired as a senior editor in 1999.

She graduated from Smith College in 1943 and spent six years working for United Press in New York and Paris, which included a clandestine stint at the sports desk. Her articles have appeared in the *New York Times Book Review*, *Harper's*, *Cosmopolitan*, and *Shooting Sportsman*, as well as the *American Spectator*, the *Human Life Review*, and *National Review*. She is the author or editor of four books, including *The Joys of National Review* and *String of Pearls*, an account of her years at United Press.

She lives in Sharon, Connecticut, where she spends her time painting, golfing, and shooting birds. Her other hobbies include skiing, ballooning, and midwifery.

This book was designed and set into type
by Mitchell S. Muncy,
with a cover design by Stephen J. Ott,
and printed and bound
by Bang Printing,
Brainerd, Minnesota.

The cover photograph is courtesy of *National Review*.

The text face is Caslon,
designed by Carol Twombly,
based on faces cut by William Caslon, London, in the 1730s
and issued in digital form by Adobe Systems,
Mountain View, California, in 1989.

The paper is acid-free and is of archival quality.

41